After the Rights Revolution

After the Rights Revolution

Reconceiving the Regulatory State

Cass R. Sunstein

Harvard University Press
Cambridge, Massachusetts
London, England

First Harvard University Press paperback edition, 1993

Library of Congress Cataloging-in-Publication Data

Sunstein, Cass R.
After the rights revolution: reconceiving the regulatory state / Cass R. Sunstein.
p. cm.
Includes bibliographical references.
ISBN 0-674-00908-8 (alk. paper) (cloth)
ISBN 0-674-00909-6 (pbk.)
1. Social legislation—United States. 2. Industrial laws and legislation—United States.
3. Administrative law—United States.
I. Title.
KF3300.S86   1990   89-78254
344.73—dc20   CIP
[347.304]

Preface

By the "rights revolution" I mean the creation, by Congress and the President, of a set of legal rights departing in significant ways from those recognized at the time of the framing of the American Constitution. The catalogue is a long one, but the most prominent examples include rights to clean air and water; safe consumer products and workplaces; a social safety net including adequate food, medical care, and shelter; and freedom from public and private discrimination on the basis of race, sex, disability, and age. The rights revolution was presaged by the New Deal and by President Roosevelt's explicit proposal of a Second Bill of Rights in 1944; it culminated, at least thus far, in the extraordinary explosion of statutory rights in the 1960s and 1970s.

The recognition of such rights has produced a wide array of federal regulatory programs, and it has dramatically affected the substance and structure of modern government. In some respects the rights revolution has been an important success. Something like the modern fabric of statutory programs is indispensable in contemporary industrialized democracies (or so I will be arguing). But in important ways the rights revolution has failed to achieve its own purposes—in the process jeopardizing important constitutional values, responding to the power of self-interested private groups, ignoring the possible nullification of well-intended programs by the marketplace, producing unnecessary inefficiencies, and downplaying the great difficulties of treating the management of social risks as conventional "rights." My principal goal in this book is to suggest reforms and principles that would promote the purposes of statutory programs and of constitutional government, while avoiding these problems.

I am grateful to many generous colleagues and friends for their help with this book. Akhil Amar, Michael Aronson, Douglas Baird, Jack Beerman, Frank Buckley, Frank Easterbrook, Richard Epstein, William Eskridge, Richard Fallon, Philip Frickey, Stephen Gilles, Don Herzog, Stephen Holmes, Donald Horowitz, Benjamin Kaplan, Larry Kramer, John Langbein, Howard Latin, Larry Lessig, Margaret Levi, Jon Macey, Geoffrey Miller, Martha Minow, Susan Rose-Ackerman, Lisa Ruddick, Frederick Schauer, Ian Shapiro, Martin Shapiro, David Strauss, Lloyd Weinreb, Robin West, James Boyd White, and John Wiley offered valuable comments on all or parts of the manuscript. Richard Stewart has been a continuing source of facts and ideas, and a generous reader and critic as well. Two extraordinary deans and friends, Gerhard Casper and Geoffrey Stone, who helped nurture the wonderful academic environment of the University of Chicago Law School, provided advice and encouragement throughout.

I am also grateful to my students in the law school and political science department at Chicago; they have been patient listeners and critics, helping to improve many of the arguments in the book. James Gimpel, Gahmk S. Markarian, Marc Porosoff, D. Gordon Smith, and Catherine O'Neill provided research assistance and useful comments. Marlene Vellinga typed and retyped countless drafts with extraordinary speed, energy, and good cheer.

An earlier and somewhat more technical version of portions of chapters 4 and 5 (as well as a few other passages) was published as "Interpreting Statutes in the Regulatory State," 103 *Harv. L. Rev.* 415 (1989); I am grateful to Daniel Bromberg for many helpful suggestions on the earlier version. I am also thankful to participants in stimulating workshops at the University of California at Los Angeles, Harvard University, and the universities of Michigan, Princeton, Tulane, and Virginia.

I owe a particular debt to three friends and colleagues whose support, generosity, criticism, and occasional skepticism have been indispensable to the project. Jon Elster provided a great deal of help with chapters 1 and 2 and with earlier efforts to grapple with some of the problems discussed there; his suggestions and his own writings on related subjects informed and shaped many of the arguments here.

He also gave generous advice on the manuscript as a whole. Bruce Ackerman read the manuscript several times and offered a wide range of helpful suggestions about the New Deal, statutory construction, private ordering, neutrality, and other subjects; and it was he who first suggested that a set of somewhat unruly ideas might be made into this book.

It will come as absolutely no surprise to Richard Posner's colleagues, at Chicago and elsewhere, for me to report that he read and commented helpfully on embarrassingly many drafts. His writings and conversation also helped inspire many of the book's principal concerns and claims, even—especially—those that fundamentally disagree with his views. I am extremely grateful for his help.

Contents

Introduction   *1*
Regulation and Interpretation
The Anachronistic Legal Culture

1. Why Regulation?   *11*
A Historical Overview • Public and Private Ordering

2. The Functions of Regulatory Statutes   *47*
Market Failures • Public-Interested Redistribution
Collective Desires and Aspirations
Diverse Experiences and Preference Formation
Social Subordination • Endogenous Preferences
Irreversibility, Future Generations, Animals, and Nature
Interest-Group Transfers and "Rent-Seeking"
The Problem of Categorization

3. How Regulation Fails   *74*
Failures in the Original Statute • Implementation Failure
Linking Statutory Function to Statutory Failure
Paradoxes of the Regulatory State—and Reform

4. Courts, Interpretation, and Norms   *111*
Flawed Approaches to Statutory Interpretation
Interpretive Principles • An Alternative Method

5. Interpretive Principles for the Regulatory State   *160*
The Principles • Priority and Harmonization
Fissures in the Interpretive Community
The Postcanonical Legal Universe

6. Applications, the New Deal, and Statutory Construction   *193*
    Particulars • The New Deal and Statutory Construction

Conclusion   *227*
    The Constitution of the Regulatory State—and Its Reform
    Interpreting the Regulatory State

Appendix A. Interpretive Principles   *235*
Appendix B. Selected Regulations in Terms
of Cost Per Life Saved   *239*
Appendix C. The Growth of Administrative Government   *242*
Notes   *245*
Index   *275*

This Republic had its beginning, and grew to its present strength, under the protection of certain inalienable political rights—among them the right of free speech, free press, free worship, trial by jury, freedom from unreasonable searches and seizures. They were our rights to life and liberty.

As our nation has grown in size and stature, however—as our industrial economy expanded—these political rights proved inadequate to assure us equality in the pursuit of happiness . . . We have accepted, so to speak, a second Bill of Rights under which a new basis of security and prosperity can be established for all—regardless of station, race, or creed.

The right to a useful and remunerative job in the industries or shops or farms or mines of the Nation;

The right to earn enough to provide adequate food and clothing and recreation;

The right of every farmer to raise and sell his products at a return which will give him and his family a decent living;

The right of every businessman, large and small, to trade in an atmosphere of freedom from unfair competition and domination by monopolies at home or abroad;

The right of every family to a decent home;

The right to adequate medical care and the opportunity to achieve and enjoy good health;

The right to adequate protection from the economic fears of old age, sickness, accident, and unemployment;

The right to a good education . . .

I ask Congress to explore the means for implementing this economic bill of rights—for it is definitely the responsibility of the Congress to do so.

—*Franklin Delano Roosevelt, January 1944*

Technique without morals is a menace; but morals without technique is a mess.

—*Karl Llewellyn*

Introduction

This book explores the rise of social and economic regulation and its consequences for American law and government. Modern regulation has profoundly affected constitutional democracy, by renovating the original commitments to checks and balances, federalism, and individual rights. The nature and scope of this transformation, which culminated in the rights revolution of the 1960s and 1970s, have not generally been appreciated. Notwithstanding the tensions between the original regime and modern bureaucratic government, I believe that it is possible to reform and interpret regulatory measures in a way that is fundamentally faithful to constitutional commitments and promotes, in a dramatically changed environment, the central goals of the constitutional system—freedom and welfare.

The book has three more particular goals. The first is to defend government regulation against influential attacks, recently found, for example, in the Reagan and Thatcher administrations and often based on free-market economics and pre-New Deal principles of private right. Although my coverage is quite broad, I focus in particular on regulation concerning the environment, occupational safety and health, broadcasting, and discrimination. I argue that regulatory initiatives in these areas are far superior to an approach that relies solely on private markets and private ordering. The modern system of governmental controls—allowing freedom of contract and private property in general, but rejecting them in targeted areas—has far more coherence and integrity than is generally supposed. Moreover, that system responds to ideas about democracy, freedom, and welfare that deserve widespread support.

My second goal is to give an account of the history of government regulation in America and its actual performance over the last generation. It is a gross misstatement, even if a fashionable one, to suggest that social and economic regulation has generally proved unsuccessful. Many areas, ranging from protection of the environment to safety on the highways to the prevention of racial discrimination, enjoyed large gains. But regulatory regimes have frequently failed, and it is possible to explain the failures. An identification of the patterns of failure leads directly to reforms that will make success more likely in the future.

My third goal is to propose a theory of interpretation that courts (and administrative agencies) might use to promote constitutional goals and at the same time to improve the operation of regulatory programs. I propose a series of interpretive principles, grounded in an understanding of the constitutional backdrop and of regulatory functions and failures, that interpreters might invoke in order to improve the performance of modern government. My ultimate goal is to provide a sympathetic assessment of the diverse functions of government regulation and to describe how regulation sometimes succeeds and sometimes fails. I will seek to develop, from these points, a set of reforms and principles with which to synthesize the modern regulatory state with the basic commitments of the American constitutional system.

Regulation and Interpretation

In the last sixty years, the government has enacted a large number of regulatory initiatives. These initiatives span a wide range of areas: occupational safety and health, consumer products, nuclear power and energy in general, the environment, fraud and deception, endangered species, toxic substances, communications and broadcasting, and discrimination on the basis of race, sex, age, and disability.

Initiatives of this sort have often come under sharp attack, largely from critics of collectivism of any sort who seek fundamental change in the form of a return to the "free market." In responding to such attacks I emphasize three principal points. *First,* regulation often counteracts the problems involved in satisfying private desires when large numbers of individuals are interacting with one another. These problems—sometimes described as difficulties of coordination and collective action—can often be best solved through governmental action. Regulation might, for example, prevent the sort of air or water pollution that is in the case of each polluter relatively trivial, but in the aggregate disastrous; or it might ensure the coordination of automobile traffic, airline transportation, or broadcasting. In such cases regulation facilitates private choice by allowing preferences to be satisfied in a context in which free markets produce chaos or irrationality. Regulation does not override private choice at all; constraints turn out to be enabling. Problems of collective action and coordination are surprisingly common. In view of those problems, regulation that is frequently derided as "paternalistic" is necessary in many settings.

Second, regulation sometimes protects collective goals and aspirations, embodied in laws that reject the choices of private consumers in favor of public values or considered judgments. The protection of high-quality broadcasting, environmental quality, or antidiscrimination principles illustrates the possibility that citizens might enact, in law, aspirational measures that conflict with their own behavior in private markets. The protection of such aspirations is a vindication of democracy. It should not be regarded as an objectionable interference with freedom.

Third, regulation sometimes responds to the fact that private preferences and beliefs are not fixed, but instead adapt to limitations in available opportunities and information, and to existing circumstances. Regulation of risks in workplaces, food and drugs, and consumer products overcomes the absence of information on the part of employees and consumers. Regulation of discrimination responds to the problem of preferences and beliefs that have adapted to an unjust status quo.

All of these points help to account for governmental initiatives. They can fit quite comfortably with a system that provides a presumptive right to freedom of contract and private ordering—while at the same time providing reasons to reject private ordering in identifiable areas. Indeed, these points suggest that in some contexts the problem is one of too little rather than too much regulation. President Franklin Delano Roosevelt's New Deal, President Lyndon Johnson's Great Society, the rise of national environmental controls and antidiscrimination statutes, and many less dramatic movements occurring at other points in the twentieth century reflected a belief that regulatory enactments might simultaneously promote economic productivity and help the disadvantaged. Optimism about regulatory controls and about solution of social problems through creation of legal rights has been shaken in recent years—partly for good reasons that point in the direction of necessary reforms, but partly, I shall argue, as a result of a too casual understanding of the functions and performance of regulatory regimes.

There are, in short, multiple defects in private markets, defects that will be poorly understood if economic principles, or pre-New Deal beliefs in "private autonomy," provide the sole criteria for evaluation. Other criteria, drawn from law, social psychology, and political theory provide the basis for a more sympathetic understanding of the functions of modern social and economic legislation. But to say this is emphatically not to say that the initiatives of the 1930s, 1960s, and 1970s have always been sensibly directed, or to deny that such legislation has had serious defects. I hope also to show that the relevant criteria point not only to a theoretical defense of modern regulation, but also toward significant changes. In particular, it is necessary to bring to bear, on the rights revolution, an understanding of the constitutional backdrop, of market forces, and of the frequent failures of regulatory initiatives.

This sort of understanding should play a large role in legal interpretation as well. In so proposing, I will reject some widely held ideas about the nature of interpretation in the law. In construing statutes, courts (and regulatory agencies) are frequently thought to be charged with the duty of faithfully carrying out the will of the legislature. While this view has an important element of truth, the task of interpretation, I suggest, inevitably requires courts (and others) to develop and rely on background principles that cannot be tied to any legislative enactment. Because reliance on such principles is inevitable, their use by judges is no cause for embarrassment, but on the contrary a potentially valuable part of the fabric of modern public law.

This claim has more general implications for the question of interpretation in the law (and perhaps elsewhere). In the modern era the interpretation of statutes ranks among the most important tasks entrusted to courts and regulatory agencies. The process of statutory interpretation frequently requires courts not only to apply a judgment by others but also to draw on background principles from the legal culture more generally. Courts sometimes make these principles explicit, but the governing norms are often unarticulated and latent, and frequently they are extremely controversial. For example, some of the relevant principles are held over from nineteenth-century conceptions of the relationship between the citizen and the state, conceptions that are inconsistent with the values underlying the modern regulatory state. Judicial (and administrative) approaches to regulation have also been misdirected as a result of a naive understanding of the probabilistic character of regulatory harms and the complex systemic effects of regulatory intervention.

When people disagree over the meaning of a statute, what is it that they are disagreeing about? I suggest that disputes often turn not on statutory terms "themselves," but instead on the appropriate interpretive principles in cases in which, without some such principles, the process of interpretation cannot go forward. Once the relevant principles are made explicit, they sometimes appear highly contestable. In these circumstances, I argue, it is necessary to identify them, to subject them to scrutiny, and ultimately to develop principles of interpretation that grow out of, and do not collide with, the basic purposes of the constitutional framework, of existing institutional arrangements, and of social and economic regulation. Above all, it is important to develop principles that are consistent with the goals and improve the performance of the modern regulatory state, and that are not drawn from pre-New Deal perceptions, which sometimes seem to have overstayed their welcome.

The Anachronistic Legal Culture

To those with a sense of history, it will seem puzzling to suggest that courts might be hospitably inclined toward regulation and attempt to interpret statutes so as to ensure their success. In the early part of the twentieth century, courts often treated regulatory statutes as foreign substances. Starting from principles of laissez-faire, judges saw statutory protections of workers, consumers, and others as unprincipled interest-group transfers supported by theories that were at best obscure and more often disingenuous. By contrast, judge-made doctrines of property, contract, and tort seemed to create a system with enormous integrity and coherence. Nineteenth-century principles of private markets and private right provided the baseline against which regulatory measures were assessed and interpreted.

In this period, the basic role of the courts was one of damage control. The most important organizing principle for interpretation was that regulatory statutes should be construed narrowly—so as to harmonize with, and minimally to disrupt, the principles of common law

ordering. Traditional private law provided the backdrop for interpreting public law. This approach found its major locus in the principle calling for courts narrowly to construe "statutes in derogation
of the common law."[1] Under the guise of statutory interpretation,
courts limited the reach of statutes protecting workers, consumers,
and other intended beneficiaries of regulation. Silences were filled in,
and ambiguities resolved, by reference to common law principles.
Often such interpretations grossly distorted the meaning of the relevant statute.

Legal interpretation of regulatory principles can no longer be
understood in these terms. The period of aggressive judicial resistance
to statutory disruption of the common law ended in the 1930s. But
in many respects public law has not outgrown the assumptions that
account for the initial period of judicial antagonism. Above all, public
law lacks a sympathetic understanding of the functions of social and
economic regulation, a failing that accounts for the continued presence of private law principles in contemporary law. The initial period
of judicial resistance is unmistakably recalled by recent suggestions
that courts should indulge a presumption in favor of private ordering,
and that they should interpret regulatory statutes so as to intrude
minimally on the private market.[2] In this view, traditional private law
and laissez-faire should continue to provide the backdrop for public
law. Statutes protecting (for example) the environment and victims of
discrimination should thus be construed as narrowly as possible—
views supported by some recent judicial decisions.[3]

The original view that regulatory statutes should be seen against a
baseline of common law property and contract rights and hence as
naked wealth transfers also finds a modern home in the increasingly
prominent idea, growing out of the economic tradition, that statutes
should be understood as unprincipled "deals" among self-interested
private actors.[4] On this view, the role of the courts is to carry out the
deal, which is mere fiat, unsupported by intelligible policies or principles.

Others have emphasized the findings of public choice theory, which
suggest that legislative outcomes have a large degree of irrationality
built into them. Collective action problems, vote cycling, strategic and
manipulative behavior, and other difficulties make it hard to speak
sensibly of preferences aggregated through a multimember institution, or of a unitary, let alone public-regarding, legislative "pur-

pose."[5] In this view as well, courts should treat statutes as unprincipled interventions lacking coherent normative underpinnings.

Less obviously, the initial encounter between courts and the regulatory state is recalled by both poles of the contemporary debate over the possibility of constrained or objective interpretation of legal texts. At one extreme, some courts and observers contend that the "plain meaning" of statutory language[6] is the exclusive or principal guide to meaning. At the other extreme is the view that legal terms are quite generally indeterminate,[7] or have the meaning that those with authority impose on them.[8] But the two camps form an important alliance. Both treat the category of regulatory statutes as an undifferentiated and unprincipled whole, without distinct and accessible purposes. Both camps treat as inevitably unsuccessful the attempt to mediate the sharp ideological disagreements that sometimes underlie interpretive disputes. Both camps neglect the need for, and fail to supply, an understanding of the distinctive and separable functions of regulatory statutes and of the various ways in which such statutes tend to fail. It is the lack of understanding of the role of interpretive norms—and an emphasis on the inevitably value-laden or political character of those norms—that drive some commentators to the pretense that words have plain meanings before interpretation and outside of their context; others to the demonstrably false claim that statutes are generally indeterminate in meaning; and still others to the uninformative view that meaning is a function of authority.

Some of the most prominent commentators on statutory construction repudiate claims of plain meaning and indeterminacy and suggest that courts should fill interpretive gaps by "making sense" of statutes or by interpreting them so as to be "the best that they can be."[9] But even if unexceptionable, advice of this sort is simply too open-ended to be useful in difficult cases; and it fails to bring to bear on interpretive problems a conception of regulation and its pathologies that might give content to the idea that statutes should be interpreted so as to "make sense."

Finally, judicial interpretation of regulatory statutes has been influenced by misunderstandings of the nature and performance of regulatory agencies. Courts have, for example, demanded a showing of a sharp and clear relationship between regulatory measures and particular, identifiable, real-world harms—even though regulatory statutes frequently attempt to counteract environmental or other risks that are merely probable or systemic. Courts have also misunderstood the systemic effects of regulatory programs, effects that make the incidence of regulatory benefits and burdens far more complicated than they might at first appear. Incorrect judicial (or bureaucratic) assessments of these systemic effects have produced regulatory irrationality.

In short, the characteristics of the modern administrative state have been invisible in most discussions of statutory interpretation. It is thus not altogether surprising that recent arguments about statutory interpretation, in and out of the judiciary, have often dissolved into fruitless and unilluminating debates about the constraints supplied by language itself (as if such a thing could be imagined). The solution, or so I shall argue, lies in the identification and development of interpretive principles with which to approach regulatory statutes.

This book is organized in six chapters. In Chapter 1, I describe the history of regulation, the impact of the New Deal, and the rights revolution of the 1960s and 1970s. I also offer a general defense of regulatory initiatives, particularly against the claim that those initiatives represent unjustified meddling with private choice.

In Chapter 2 I deal more particularly with the reasons for regulatory statutes, distinguishing among their various functions. I suggest that it is possible to develop a quite general understanding of modern social and economic legislation, one that accounts for both the diversity of regulatory programs and the presence of recognizable patterns. Drawing on ideas associated both with the liberal republican tradition that lies at the center of the American constitutional order and with the New Deal and the Great Society, this understanding amounts to a sympathetic portrayal of the reasons for regulation. It rejects attacks on the regulatory state that are rooted in modern welfare economics and in pre-New Deal principles of private right.

In Chapter 3 I explore the record of recent regulatory programs, offering evidence of both success and failure. Many programs have brought about important improvements, but my emphasis is on the characteristic ways in which regulatory statutes fail. Statutes designed to promote various purposes have proved unsuccessful in identifiable ways, and the patterns of failure suggest a number of concrete reforms for the future. These reforms recall some of the goals of the original constitutional regime. They also suggest the need to attend to the inevitability of tradeoffs and the ways in which the market circumvents the goals of statutory programs.

In Chapter 4 I reject the usual understandings of how courts do and should construe statutes; I also propose an alternative view of current practice and a novel approach for the future. I attempt to understand statutory construction by means of a general defense of the much abused "canons" of construction, defined as background principles designed to resolve interpretive difficulties. I defend the use of background principles by disaggregating their various functions and by suggesting that the use of such principles is desirable and in any case inevitable. I also suggest that several current background principles can be defended as a means of combatting interest-group power, promoting deliberation in government, and incorporating New Deal reforms of the legal system. This claim has implications for interpretation in law quite generally, suggesting that background norms play a significant though usually overlooked role.

In Chapter 5 I set out a series of new interpretive principles in an attempt to serve the purposes of constitutional government after the rights revolution. I argue that many such principles can be traced to constitutional norms and to assessments of the performance of various governmental institutions; they can counteract many of the failings in regulatory systems. Although these suggestions are designed principally for reviewing courts, their implications extend as well to administrative agencies attempting to implement statutes, and also to Congress in its efforts to design and reform social and economic regulation.

In Chapter 6 I attempt to particularize this general claim, applying the interpretive techniques in Chapter 5 to a wide range of current disputes. Chapter 6 also seeks to develop an understanding of the implications of the New Deal and the rights revolution for the constitutional structure, arguing that a large task of modern public law is to synthesize elements of both developments with features of the original constitutional design that are still attractive.

The most general goal of this book is to help develop a better understanding of social and economic regulation and its relation to constitutional government—an understanding that has moved beyond the awkward reception that the legal system once accorded, and continues to accord, to regulatory legislation. Ideally, a fuller perception would account for the distinctive character of law in modern liberal democracies; repudiate the original and still persistent treatment of regulatory statutes as foreign bodies or as self-interested deals; reveal an awareness of the diverse functions and frequent failures of regulatory programs; acknowledge the inevitable role of background principles in the interpretive process; and use the process of interpretation as a corrective, albeit a partial one, against the occasional pathologies of regulatory legislation. In the process, it will be necessary to develop a distinctive understanding of the nature of legal interpretation and of the character of the modern regulatory state. As we will see, the two areas are closely related; they cannot be separated from one another.

CHAPTER

1

Why Regulation?

A general attack on collectivism promises to be a central distinguishing feature of the last quarter of the twentieth century. This is so in both political theory and political practice. Most conspicuously, influential movements in Eastern Europe and China have reflected mounting dissatisfaction with governmental controls and increasing interest in the use of the market to promote both private liberty and economic productivity. Large gains have already resulted from these movements, and there is reason to hope for future progress in the same direction. On a more modest scale, the deregulation initiatives of the 1970s and 1980s, emphasizing both private property and freedom of contract, have been highly influential in the United States and in Western European democracies. Here as well some significant improvements have resulted.

But the general attack on collectivism and the deregulation movement—salutary as these have generally been—have sometimes endangered desirable regulatory programs and at the same time thwarted governmental initiatives that would do much more good than harm. Indeed, crude or facile beliefs in private ordering and private markets have contributed to the rejection or nonenforcement of valuable public programs. There is a serious risk that if it is undiscriminating, an appreciation of the frequent advantages of markets will lead in extremely unfortunate directions.

In this chapter I describe the development of statutory programs in the twentieth century and defend the view that targeted regulatory interventions are desirable in many settings. My principal criticism is directed against the resilient and influential claim that a system having such interventions is inferior, in principle, to complete or near-complete reliance on freedom of contract, private ordering, and largely unfettered markets. If my argument is persuasive, it suggests that the modern regulatory state has a large degree of coherence and integrity, and that in many areas the problem is one of too little, rather than too much, in the way of collective controls.

The basic argument for regulatory regimes grows out of familiar notions of freedom or autonomy on the one hand and welfare on the other—notions deriving, respectively, from Kantian traditions respecting individual liberty and utilitarian traditions stressing the maximization of human happiness. As I understand them here, these notions are connected to two principal sources. The first is the liberal republicanism[1] of American constitutional thought—a set of ideas treating the political process not as an aggregation of purely private interests, but as a deliberative effort to promote the common good. Republican ideas played a substantial role in the development of the original constitutional framework, which is best understood as an effort to create a kind of deliberative democracy.[2] On the republican account, self-interest is an insufficient basis for political advantage; it must be translated into some broader conception of the public interest.

The second source is the New Deal reformation of the constitutional structure. As we will see, the rise of modern regulation owes a great deal to the New Deal reformation, whose transformative effects on American constitutionalism we have only started to recognize.[3] Ideas having roots in American republicanism and in the New Deal help explain a wide array of regulatory programs. In its best form, the modern regulatory system can be seen as a kind of post-New Deal republicanism. Its goal is to respect private property and freedom of contract, but also to permit a large range of governmental activity in the interest of economic productivity and protection of the disadvantaged—while simultaneously adhering to the original belief in the governmental process as one of deliberation oriented to the public good rather than as a series of interest-group tradeoffs.

A Historical Overview

Between the New Deal and the 1980s the United States witnessed a rights revolution—the creation by Congress of legal entitlements to freedom from risks in the workplace and in consumer products, from poverty, from long hours and low wages, from fraud and deception, from domination by employers, from one-sided or purely commercial broadcasting, and from dirty air, dirty water, and toxic substances. Building on the original Bill of Rights, and inspired by the civil rights movement, Congress created regulatory programs as a means of furnishing government protection against the multiple hazards of industrialized society. This development has been an exceptionally dramatic and important one. Indeed, it has renovated the original constitutional framework and the system of government under which the nation operated for most of its history.

Madison's Republic

For well over a hundred years the national government engaged in little regulation of the domestic economy, at least by modern standards. The development of a national bureaucracy and a centralized regulatory system came extremely late. The principal regulatory functions were performed by the states or by the operation of private markets. When it existed at all, the domestic business of the national government was intermittent and highly specialized.

To say this is not to say that there was no regulatory activity from Congress and the executive branch. The idea that the framers of the Constitution sought to ensure a system of laissez-faire is belied by their theory and their practice.[4] The various departments of the Cabinet—notably Commerce and Treasury—performed a variety of regulatory functions from the earliest days of nationhood. Alexander Hamilton's Treasury Department attempted to promote industrial development, indeed to engage in a limited form of national planning; and other important actors in the early period sought to employ the national government in the encouragement of transportation, land development, and a wide range of internal improvements. Significantly, the original constitutional structure was a rejection of the Articles of Confederation, which lacked an executive branch, in favor of a system that would ensure a more energetic national government. It was also, however, designed in large part as a limitation on domestic controls by that same government. The American Revolution had been largely a struggle against centralized governmental authority. A principal task of constitution-making was to overcome the defects of the Articles while remaining fundamentally faithful to the principles of the Revolution.

The original structure was powerfully influenced by James Madison's revision of classical republican thought and in particular by his conception of political representation. Madison's understanding was above all a reaction against the classical republican belief in small political units, in which citizens would participate actively in governmental processes during a continuous process of collective self-definition and self-governance. The founding period was one of active engagement with classical republican thought, with the antifederalists—opponents of the Constitution—invoking many of the traditional republican claims as the foundation for their criticism of the proposed Constitution. In the antifederalist view, a national system with remote national representatives would repudiate the principles for which the Revolution had been fought. In particular, local self-determination and self-government would be sacrificed by the creation of a powerful national government.

Madison's response started with the claim that the central danger for a political system lay in factionalism—the usurpation of government power by well-organized groups with interests adverse to those of the public as a whole.[5] Of special importance here was debtor-relief legislation—regulatory law which, by discouraging contractual arrangements, was a major obstacle to trade and furnished part of the impetus behind the Constitution itself. Madison believed that politics should not consist of a series of unprincipled tradeoffs among self-interested factions. The process should have a significant component of deliberation and dialogue. Thus far, Madison and his antifederalist adversaries were of one mind.

As Madison saw it, however, experience had proved that the classical republican belief in small-scale democracy, calling for active citizen participation in government, was unrealistic and counterproductive. In view of the self-interested character of much political behavior, efforts to promote decisions by the citizenry at large would produce factional warfare—a conclusion supported by the experience with various regulatory efforts in the states under the Articles of Confederation. These efforts included not only debtor relief legislation, but also paper money and various protectionist measures. Widespread citizen participation therefore would fail to serve the republican belief in deliberative government.

Madison's solution dramatically revised traditional republican thought. For classical republicans, only a small republic with direct self-rule could produce and benefit from a virtuous citizenry. Madison turned this idea on its head. In his view, it was a large republic, with comparatively insulated representatives, that would be uniquely able to produce a well-functioning deliberative democracy. While a small republic would be torn by factional warfare, the representatives of a large one would be able to escape the pressures of powerful groups and engage in the deliberative tasks of politics. Within a large republic the various factions would be so numerous that they would cancel each other out, making it more likely that representatives would serve the common good. It was therefore desirable to place decisions in the hands of representatives chosen from a large territory, "whose wisdom may best discern the true interest of their country and whose patriotism and love of justice will be least likely to sacrifice it to temporary or partial conditions."[6] Madison abandoned the classical republican belief in direct self-rule by the citizenry without rejecting the fundamental republican faith in deliberative democracy.

In the framing period there was an intimate connection among four central ideas: the fear of faction, the distrust of government, the belief in deliberation, and the protection of private ordering, particularly against certain kinds of redistributive measures. Deliberation was designed in large part as a check against popular passions for the counterproductive or illegitimate redistribution of wealth. Thus it was that Madison's revision of republican thought produced a system designed to ensure limitations on government regulation in the domestic arena.

This general understanding is confirmed by the five basic commitments of the original Constitution: the grant of enumerated federal powers; the system of checks and balances; federalism; judicial review; and individual rights. The allocation of powers to the federal government, and among its three branches, reflects considerable skepticism about national regulatory controls. Although the federal government was entrusted with a variety of regulatory tasks, its powers were enumerated rather than general, and many of those powers were in fact designed to ensure the free movement of goods. The commerce clause is by far the most important example, designed as it was not to permit national controls on the free market, but on the contrary to authorize Congress to overcome state barriers to free trade.

Moreover, and even more notably, the system of checks and balances provided a serious obstacle to national regulation. That system was self-consciously justified as an effort to allow each branch to prevent the others from embarking on unjustified interference with private behavior.[7] The major goal here was to preserve liberty by disabling government. Even the desire to ensure an energetic executive—partly designed to expedite government action, especially in foreign affairs—was intended to create a kind of government-checking friction among the branches. Under the constitutional plan, a measure of agreement among three differently constituted branches was necessary in order for government to act. In the framers' view, that constraint furnished an important safeguard against unwarranted governmental intrusions into the private sphere. The system of checks and balances enabled the sovereign people to pursue a strategy of "divide and conquer."

In these respects, the distribution of national powers served as a major guarantor of private ordering and also as a check against the twin dangers to a republic that Madison himself feared most. The first was factionalism: the usurpation of government by powerful and self-interested groups. The second was self-interested representation: the distortion of governance by the selfish motivations of public officials.[8] By requiring agreement among the branches and allowing one branch to disable the others, the system of checks and balances operated as a safeguard against both threats. The division of national powers was also a means of promoting efficiency through a healthy division of labor, particularly through a unitary executive branch capable of ensuring energetic and coordinated government. But the most important reason for the distribution of national powers was to diminish the risk of tyranny.

The commitment to federalism, allowing mutual checks by the states and national government, was similarly intended to discourage regulatory activity by national officials. The two governments would "control each other" through mutual jealousies and regulations from which the public as a whole would benefit.[9] "Control" was understood to mean constraints on unwarranted government action. In this respect, federalism provided a kind of vertical check and balance, supplementing the distribution of powers at the national level. Moreover, judicial review—interpretation of the Constitution by an independent judiciary—ensured that the various constraints on government would not be subject to override by public officials or even by the short-term desires of citizens themselves.

Finally, in the original conception of individual rights freedom tended to be seen as immunity from governmental constraints; under that view, domestic regulation was a potential threat to the basic system of private liberty and property. Perhaps the most important individual rights provisions of the original Constitution were the contracts clause—exempting freedom of contract from governmental interference—and the privileges and immunities clause, which entitled citizens of each state to be free from protectionist interference from the governments of other states. Moreover, the eminent domain clause, safeguarding private property, was a prominent part of the Bill of Rights, which has usually been thought, rightly, to find an organizing principle in the desire to prevent collective interference with private ordering. In these respects, the original constitutional rights were "negative" in character—rights to be free from governmental intrusion, rather than rights to affirmative governmental assistance.

An often overlooked qualification, however, is necessary here. The protection of life, liberty, and property was a central task of the federal and state governments in the framers' view; and that protection required governmental action. Under the social contract, government must protect citizens from private aggression by the provision and indeed redistribution of security, and that purpose could hardly be secured through immunity from governmental controls. For this reason it would be implausible to see such immunity as the only goal of the constitutional regime, or to understand the governmental structure as protecting only "negative" rights. Governmental protection of life, property, and contract can only be called affirmative in character.[10] Nonetheless, regulatory controls that went beyond the basic protection of these interests were not part of the original constitutional plan, and for this reason it is useful to understand the system as designed largely to protect rights against government.

The consequence of this system was that the vast majority of regulatory functions were undertaken by the common law courts, which elaborated the basic principles of property, tort, and contract. Public and private interactions were controlled largely through those principles. Governance was largely dependent on the states. As noted above, to say this is not to suggest that the national government entirely eschewed regulatory activity. Indeed, antecedents of the modern regulatory state can be found in a number of agencies designed to promote and develop the economy, including the Army Corps of Engineers (1824), the Patent and Trademark Office (1836), the Comptroller of the Currency (1863), and the Bureau of Fisheries (1883). But the range of domestic regulation was relatively narrow, and from President Andrew Jackson's presidency in the 1830s, an interest in states' rights merged with an interest in ensuring against federal regulatory controls. The principal governmental functions, including laws that imposed sanctions directly on citizens, were carried out by the states.

Most notably, the United States—unlike European countries—lacked a well-defined bureaucratic apparatus or centralized governing body. Its regulatory controls could be found principally in judge-made rules of the common law. From corporate and property law to family law, judges performed the basic regulatory functions that might otherwise have been carried out by bureaucrats.

By the late nineteenth century common law principles came to be treated as largely neutral and prepolitical, and indeed as purely facilitative—rather than constitutive—of private arrangements. These principles ultimately embodied much of the structure of laissez-faire, and they gave the nation a definite albeit misleading sense of statelessness. Moreover, they were fueled by one way of understanding the legacy of the Civil War. Thus it was that common law principles of laissez-faire came to be seen as part of liberty under the Constitution.[11]

On this view, the antislavery movement was animated by a quite general desire to protect self-ownership and self-direction—in short, freedom—in the employment market. Minimum wage and maximum hour legislation, and other regulatory measures, thus offended the same principle that doomed slavery. An alternative to this perception of the evil of slavery would point not to the need for unfettered markets in all contexts, but instead to a principle of nonsubordination that might in some settings find coercion and dominance in markets themselves. And if coercion were seen there, regulation would be a necessary corrective. On this view, free markets and freedom of contract were not the foundational principles, but instead second-order implementing devices, to be rejected when they failed to serve their purposes. On this alternative view, the lesson of the Civil War, rightly understood, would sometimes point toward the need for an active national government and for protection of employees and others from defects in markets. This lesson ultimately received vindication in the New Deal.

New Deal Constitutionalism

We have seen that the federal government embarked on various regulatory programs in the early period of nationhood. In the late nineteenth century, moreover, the chartering and supervision of national banks (in 1863) and the Interstate Commerce Commission (in 1887) produced national monitoring of private institutions that were critical to the domestic economy. The creation of the ICC—a response to the failure of both markets and state and judicial regulation—was an especially important development. The relevant legislation authorized the ICC to ensure "reasonable and just" rates and also prohibited rate discrimination, price-fixing, and rebating. Notably, the members of the ICC were to be independent of the President, in the sense that they could not be fired at his whim. Following this pattern, Congress enacted the Federal Reserve Act in 1913 and created the Federal Trade Commission in 1914. The pre-New Deal period, fueled by the progressive movement, also saw the strengthening of the ICC (1920) and the creation of the Commodities Exchange Authority (1922), the Federal Radio Commission (1927), and the Federal Power Commission (1930). Responding to the rise of industrialism, the country embarked for the first time on the large-scale development of a national bureaucracy.

Despite these various antecedents, the rise of modern social and economic regulation should be seen as part of the New Deal reformation of the American constitutional structure.[12] The pre-New Deal developments were extremely timid, at least in comparison with what followed. The New Deal reformation had two principal components. The first, substantive in character, consisted of a wholesale assault on the system of common law ordering. The basis of the assault was a conviction that that system reflected anachronistic, inefficient, and unjust principles of laissez-faire—principles that had, in the early part of the twentieth century, been treated as a part of the federal Constitution.[13] Seeing the common law status quo as prelegal and neutral, judges (and many others) did not recognize its principles as a part of a regulatory system at all, but regarded them instead as the state of nature. Ideas of this sort underlay a number of constitutional decisions, which saw departures from common law principles as constitutionally suspect, and treated interference with market ordering as impermissible government "subsidies" to powerful or favored factions.[14]

Under this framework, courts regarded government decisions disturbing market ordering under the common law as partisan and active, whereas adherence to common law categories appeared neutral and inactive. It was on this view that market prices received constitutional protection and that market wages were treated as an antecedent entitlement for employers. In the Supreme Court's view, minimum wage and maximum hour legislation were an unjustifiable compulsory exaction from the employer on behalf of employees and the public at large. Since the employer had committed no common law wrong in obtaining an agreement on market wages and market hours, there was simply no predicate for governmental intervention. Regulation was permitted only if it fell within the "police power"—an imperfectly defined authority that included the prevention of harms to the public as a whole, but that largely proscribed paternalism and redistribution through regulation. If redistribution was to occur, it would have to be through the tax system rather than through regulatory controls. The result of all this was a system of public law that was built directly on private law principles.

For the New Deal reformers, by contrast, the common law was hardly neutral or prepolitical, but instead reflected a set of explicit regulatory decisions. In this view, the law of tort, contract, and property—actually encompassing a wide range of social choices or government intervention concerning the duties citizens owed to one another—did not have any special status. The existing distribution of wealth and entitlements was hardly the state of nature or freedom from governmental constraint; it consisted of a range of controversial, substantive, official decisions. Even market prices were therefore a construct of the legal system. It was in this spirit that President Roosevelt defended social security as necessary in this "man-made world of ours," [15] and suggested that "We must lay hold of the fact that the laws of economics are not made by nature. They are made by human beings." [16] Market ordering and market values were made subject to politics out of a recognition that they had always been a political product in reality.[17]

In the New Deal period, then, the common law no longer provided the baseline from which to distinguish between government action and inaction, or partisanship and neutrality. The shift was signaled not merely in political debate, but also in a number of Supreme Court decisions treating the common law as a controversial regulatory system and as subject to democratic change.[18] The resulting regime of public law rapidly departed from private law principles.

These considerations of course supplied no affirmative reason for statutory intervention. To say that a system of law is a social construct may remove some persistent arguments in its favor, to the effect that it is natural or inevitable, or impossible to alter, or to be respected unless there is unanimous consent for change. But systems that are socially constructed are not for that reason either good or bad. A substantive theory is necessary in order to evaluate them; and in developing such a theory the nonnatural character of the status quo is unhelpful, indeed it is entirely neutral from the moral point of view.

The New Deal reformers thought that the common law was inadequate as a system of regulation not because it was a governmental choice as such, but because it was economically disastrous, insulated established property rights from democratic control, failed to protect the disadvantaged, and disabled the states and the national government from revitalizing or stabilizing the economy. These claims of course took on central importance in the face of the Depression, with a substantial part of the population facing long hours, low wages, or unemployment. They were fueled by the rise of Keynesian economics, which saw governmental spending and taxing decisions as inevitably tied up with economic performance and treated spending in particular as a means of eliminating economic stagnation.

On the view that emerged, governmental decisions inevitably constituted the private sphere; they were prior to it rather than vice versa. Thus a minimum wage law could be seen not as a compulsory subsidy at all, but instead as the fulfillment of an antecedent obligation that the employer owed to both the employee and the public at large.[19] And governmental interventions of various sorts—including regulatory cartelization of industry to promote business confidence, to increase employment, and to counteract the pervasive problems of excessive capacity and insufficient demand—appeared necessary in the interest of economic productivity and greater employment.

Ideas of this sort found their culmination in President Roosevelt's endorsement of a "second Bill of Rights" designed to protect rights to housing, welfare, employment, education, and food. Roosevelt's catalogue included "the right to a useful and remunerative job in the industries or shops or farms or mines of the Nation; the right to earn enough to provide adequate food and clothing and recreation; the right of every farmer to raise and sell his products at a return which will give him and his family a decent living; the right of every businessman, large and small, to trade in an atmosphere of freedom from unfair competition and domination by monopolies at home or abroad; the right of every family to a decent home; the right to adequate medical care and the opportunity to achieve and enjoy good health; the right to adequate protection from the economic fears of old age, sickness, accident, and unemployment; the right to a good education." [20]

Protection of rights of this sort of course extended the reach of the government in altogether different directions from those marked out by the original property and contract interests. There was in this sense a significant break between the conception of protected interests in the founding and the New Deal periods. To be sure, there is a commonality as well. The interests protected in the New Deal might be seen as the equivalents under new conditions of the original rights of property and contract; and as we have seen, those rights were also "affirmative" in character. But in its nature and scope, the New Deal conception of governmentally protected rights represented a novel development in American government.

The second component of the New Deal reformation was institutional, and dramatic institutional innovations grew directly out of the substantive critique of the common law. The New Deal reformers were skeptical of the original systems of federalism and checks and balances, believing that those systems impeded necessary action by the national government. States were weak and ineffectual, unable to deal with serious social problems. The Madisonian idea that the states would check the federal government—if true—was perverse in light of the need for national action. States hardly seemed to be a forum for democratic self-determination; they were instead peculiarly subject to the power of faction. By contrast, the presidency seemed uniquely responsive to the public as a whole. By making the presidency, rather than states and localities, the focal point for self-determination, the New Dealers in a single stroke linked the Hamiltonian belief in an energetic national government with the Jeffersonian endorsement of citizen self-determination. The New Deal thus democratized Hamiltonian ideas through novel conceptions of the presidency.

As regulators of the economy, moreover, the state and federal courts were grossly inadequate. Their capacities were outstripped by the need for managerial sophistication, public initiative, flexibility in procedure and over time, continuous powers of supervision and coordination, and accountability to the democratic process and to shifting public desires.[21] New entities were necessary to restore the securities markets, to protect agriculture, and to safeguard the banking and financial system in general. Thus it was that between 1933 and

1939, the civil service expanded from 572,000 to 920,000 employees, and the budget grew from $4.6 to $8.8 billion—huge increases in comparison to previous administrations.

In short, a system of centralized and unified powers, bypassing the states and the judiciary, seemed indispensable to allow for dramatic and frequent governmental regulation. In the new circumstances the system of checks and balances no longer appeared to be a necessary safeguard of private property and liberty from factionalism, but instead—and this was the crucial point—a faction-driven obstacle to social change in the public interest. The complicated character of modern problems vastly increased the need for technical expertise and specialization in making regulatory decisions. None of the original institutions had the necessary qualities. To the extent that the branches would limit each other, the system of checks and balances aggravated rather than solved the problem of factionalism. As Roscoe Pound wrote, in the early part of the twentieth century, "No one will assert at present that the separation of powers is part of the legal order of nature or that it is essential to liberty." [22]

The ultimate consequences of these attacks were a transfer of power from the states to the federal government, a massive growth in the national bureaucracy, a weakening of the judiciary and of legal controls on politics and administration, and the grant to the President of powers that had formerly been exercised by Congress, the states, and the common law courts. The federal government came to act directly, with its own sanctions, on the citizenry. Although Roosevelt's plan to "pack the Court" failed, the general attack on the laissez-faire Supreme Court was ultimately successful. The Court upheld a wide range of national regulatory controls in the face of previously plausible arguments invoking contractual freedom, property rights, state authority, and separation of powers. [23]

The resulting range of administrative activity was extraordinary. The new agencies often combined the traditionally separated powers of legislation, adjudication, and execution; and they often were given broad policymaking authority by Congress. They included such employment agencies as the Civil Works Administration, the Public Works Administration, the Tennessee Valley Authority, the Works Progress Administration, and the Civilian Conservation Corps; such risk-pooling or redistributive agencies as the Farm Security Administration, the Farm Credit Administration, the Social Security Administration, the Federal Deposit Insurance Corporation, and the Home

Owners Loan Corporation; and regulatory measures including the National Labor Relations Act, the Securities and Exchange Act, the Agricultural Adjustment Act, amendments to the Food and Drug Act and the Federal Trade Commission Act, the Federal Power Act, the Fair Labor Standards Act, and the Public Utility Holding Company Act. The 1930s saw the rise as well of such entities as the Maritime Administration, protecting the merchant marine and the nation's ocean commerce; the Civil Aeronautics Authority, to regulate airlines; and the Federal Communications Commission, to consolidate regulation of communications, including radio, telephone, and telegraph. (See Table 1 for a catalogue.)

The rise of these entities produced a dramatic change in the fabric of the national government, as well as in the basic conception of the relationships between the states and the federal government and the citizen and government in general. Consider the fact that eleven agencies were created between the framing of the Constitution and the close of the Civil War; six were created between 1865 and the close of the century; nine more were created between 1918 and the Depression; and no fewer than 17 were created in the decade between 1930 and 1940. (See Appendix C.)

We might use the term "New Deal constitutionalism" to describe the resulting structure of social and economic regulation—a structure that renovated the original constitutional regime in favor of new understandings of individual rights, checks and balances, the role of the judiciary, and federalism. The preexisting category of individual rights seemed to encompass too much and too little, especially in its exclusion of new regulatory rights; the systems of checks and balances and federalism imposed limitations on necessary governmental action, which a unified national government was uniquely able to provide; and legal controls surrounded the regulatory process with anachronistic limitations. Almost every subsequent development in public law has been a reaction, favorable or unfavorable, to the New Deal reformation.

The Rights Revolution

The most notable set of initiatives since the New Deal period occurred during the 1960s and 1970s.[24] This period marked a revolution in the category of legally protected rights—a revolution that built on and materially expanded the New Deal. Congress and the

Table 1. Representative Agencies Created in the 1960s and 1970s and in the
New Deal Period

1960s and 1970s

Department of Energy (1977)
Office of Surface Mining (1977)
Nuclear Regulatory Commission (1975)
Materials Transportation Board (1975)
Mine Safety and Health Administration (1973)
Occupational Safety and Health Administration (1973)
Consumer Product Safety Commission (1972)
National Highway Traffic Safety Administration (1970)
Environmental Protection Agency (1970)
Equal Employment Opportunity Commission (1964)
United States Commission on Civil Rights (expansion; originally created in
1957) (1960)

New Deal

Food and Drug Administration (expansion) (1938)
Federal Trade Commission (expansion) (1938)
Federal Communications Commission (1936)
Soil Conservation Service (1935)
Social Security Administration (1935)
Federal Power Commission (1935)
Securities and Exchange Commission (1934)
National Labor Relations Board (1934)
Federal Housing Administration (1934)
Public Works Administration (1933)
Tennessee Valley Authority (1933)
Civil Works Administration (1933)
Rural Electrification Administration (1933)
Civilian Conservation Corps (1933)
Federal Deposit Insurance Corporation (1933)
Federal Home Loan Bank Board (1932)

President invoked the rhetorical power of the civil rights movement
on behalf of causes involving not only discrimination on various
grounds, but also the environment, workers, the poor, and even consumers. In this period, the Supreme Court also used the Constitution
to protect against race and sex discrimination, and recognized broad
rights of free speech, voting, and criminal procedure. But the rights
revolution of the 1960s and 1970s was mostly the work of Congress
and the President.

The period was marked by bold regulatory initiatives in a number

Table 2. Occupational Safety

Black Lung Benefits Act (1989)
Contract Work Hours and Safety Standards Amendments (1983)
Black Lung Benefits Revenue Act (1977)
Federal Mine Safety and Health Act (1977)
Occupational Safety and Health Act (1970)
Mine Safety and Health Act (1969)
Metal and Nonmetallic Mine Safety Act (1966)
Service Contract Act (1965)
National Foundation on the Arts and the Humanities Act (1965)
Contract Work Hours and Safety Standards Act (1962)
Longshoremen's and Harbor Workers' Compensation Act, Section 41 (1958)
Walsh-Healey Public Contracts Act (1936)

of new areas, most prominently involving air and water pollution, discrimination, and management of social risks in general. (See Table 1.) The highly influential environmental movement led to a wide variety of regulatory measures, including the Clean Air Act, the Clean Water Act, the Ocean Dumping Act, the National Environmental Policy Act, the Safe Drinking Water Act, and various other laws regulating noise, pesticides, and other toxic substances. The initial, and still the most important, burst of federal antidiscrimination law was enacted in the middle and late 1960s. Eventually Congress created legal entitlements to be free from discrimination on the basis of race, sex, handicap, and age. In 1970 the national government enacted its first major occupational safety and health law. The consumer movement helped produce automobile safety legislation in 1966, a consumer product safety act in 1973, and an agency regulating transportation of hazardous materials in 1975. Various bodies controlling energy were created and eventually consolidated, in 1977, as the cabinet-level Department of Energy. Still other statutes in this period were designed to protect endangered species. (See Tables 2, 3, and 4 for chronologies of measures dealing with the environment, occupational safety, and discrimination.)

In this extraordinary era—a period that prominently displayed President Johnson's Great Society—a number of redistributive programs were also enacted, including the Food Stamp Act, Head Start, Medicare, and Medicaid, and existing welfare programs were significantly supplemented. The new agencies included the Environmental Protection Agency (EPA), implementing the Toxic Substances Control

Table 3. The Environment

Shore Protection Act (1988)
Pesticide Monitoring Improvements Act (1988)
Emergency Planning and Community Right-to-Know Act (1986)
Water Resources Research Act (1984)
Nuclear Waste Policy Act (1982)
Comprehensive Environmental Response, Compensation, and Liability Act
    (1980)
Fish and Wildlife Conservation Act (1980)
Aviation Safety and Noise Abatement Act (1979)
Port and Tanker Safety Act (1978)
National Ocean Pollution Planning Act (1978)
Soil and Water Resources Conservation Act (1977)
Clean Air Act (1977)
Safe Drinking Water Act (1977)
Clean Water Act (1977)
Surface Mining Control and Reclamation Act (1977)
Resource Conservation and Recovery Act (1976)
Toxic Substances Control Act (1976)
Deepwater Port Act (1974)
Safe Drinking Water Act (1974)
Energy Supply and Environmental Coordination Act (1974)
Endangered Species Act (1973)
Federal Water Pollution Control Act (1972)
Coastal Zone Management Act (1972)
Noise Control Act (1972)
Marine Protection, Research, and Sanctuaries Act (1972)
Marine Mammal Protection Act (1972)
Federal Insecticide, Fungicide, and Rodenticide Act (1972)
Clean Air Act Amendments (1970)
Endangered Species Conservation Act (1969)
National Environmental Policy Act (1969)
Wild and Scenic Rivers Act (1968)
Clean Air Act (1967)
Water Resources Planning Act (1965)
Clean Air Act (1963)
Fish and Wildlife Coordination Act (1958)

Act, the Resource Recovery and Conservation Act, the Clean Air Act, and the Clean Water Act along with numerous others; the Occupational Safety and Health Administration (OSHA); the Materials Transportation Board; the Office of Surface Mining Reclamation and Enforcement; the Consumer Product Safety Commission; the Equal Employment Opportunity Commission; the Federal Highway Traffic

Table 4. Civil Rights: The "Second Reconstruction" and After

Americans with Disabilities Act (passed the Senate; expected passage in 1990)
Developmentally Disabled Assistance and Bill of Rights Act (1975)
Age Discrimination Act (1975)
Rehabilitation Act (1973), barring discrimination against the handicapped
Education Amendments (1972), forbidding sex discrimination in education
Civil Rights Act (1968), with Fair Housing provisions
Age Discrimination in Employment Act (1967)
Voting Rights Act (1965)
Civil Rights Act (1964), forbidding discrimination in employment, public
    accommodations, and institutions receiving federal funds, on grounds of
    race, religion, sex, national origin
Equal Pay Act (1963), forbidding unequal pay between men and women
Civil Rights Act (1960), strengthening Civil Rights Commission and imposing
    limited criminal sanctions for racially motivated bombings and arson
Civil Rights Act (1957), creating U.S. Commission on Civil Rights, with
    investigatory responsibilities

Note: A number of civil rights statutes were enacted during the Reconstruction period,
in the aftermath of the Civil War.

Safety Administration; the National Transportation Safety Board; the
Mine Safety and Health Administration; and the Employment Standards Administration, one of whose purposes was to protect the disabled.

The 1970s saw an enormous expansion in expenditures for the major regulatory agencies, growing from $866 million in 1970 to more
than $5.5 billion in 1979. The daily Federal Register, containing pro-
posed and actual administrative regulations, was subject to a similar
growth, from 9,562 pages in 1960 to 74,120 pages in 1980. The budget of the OSHA increased from $37 million in 1973, to $109 million
in 1976, to $178 million in 1980; it climbed to over $240 million in
1989. The budget of the EPA, only $70 million in 1962, increased to
$303 million in 1969, to $1.1 billion in 1973, to $3.1 billion in 1976,
and ultimately to $5.6 billion in 1980; it ranged between $4 and $5.5
billion from 1980 to 1990. All in all, the budgets of the major regulatory agencies grew by 537 percent and employment by 216 percent
between 1970 and 1979. (See Appendix C.)

The rhetoric of rights was frequently invoked as justification for
initiatives of this sort. Building on Roosevelt's Second Bill of Rights,
and associating highly diverse causes with the civil rights movement,
legislation protecting interests in environmental quality, occupational

safety, antidiscrimination, and risks in consumer products was said to vindicate rights held by the citizenry at large. In a characteristic formulation, President Richard Nixon proclaimed, "Clean air, clean water, open spaces—these should again be the birthright for every American."[25]

. As we will see, the assimilation of interests of this sort to rights has raised a number of difficulties. The contexts involved affirmative governmental protection rather than a mere veto on public officials. The relevant harms were not suffered by individuals alone but were necessarily felt in common by all or many citizens; the rights were collective rather than individual in character. Moreover, the possibility of injury could be reduced but not eliminated. The government was thus managing risks rather than vindicating individual rights. All of these difficulties have affected regulatory performance.

Regulation in the 1960s and 1970s differed both substantively and institutionally from that of the 1930s. In the later period, the purpose of governmental controls was not primarily to stabilize the economy or to provide price and entry controls in the interest of restoring business confidence. Excess capacity, insufficient demand, and resulting unemployment were the principal problems in the period during and after the Depression; they were not an issue in the 1960s and 1970s. The more recent goals of Congress have been to protect public health and safety from risks of various sorts—at work, in the air and water, and in consumer products—and to counteract the social subordination of disadvantaged groups. The substantive themes of risk management and antisubordination were the principal ones in this period.

Moreover, in the 1960s and 1970s Congress largely abandoned the New Deal faith in administrative autonomy. Bureaucracy was the problem rather than the solution. Congress often refused, for example, to provide the characteristic New Deal blank checks to regulatory agencies by allowing them to prevent "unreasonable" behavior, or to act "in the public interest." Experience had shown that administrative autonomy often gave rise to precisely the risks of self-interested representation and factionalism that the original constitutional framework was designed to prevent. As we will see, the result of open-ended delegations has frequently been misdirected regulation, as well as under- or overregulation.

Rejecting such delegations, Congress sometimes enacted quite precise guidelines that compelled agencies to undertake specified actions within specified times. This amounted to a dramatic reassertion of legislative primacy in the regulatory process. In this respect, Congress rejected the institutional learning of the New Deal and produced a partial revival of original notions of checks and balances. It did so, however, without rejecting the New Deal belief in active governmental controls in the interest of economic productivity and protection of the disadvantaged.

In the same period both the President and the courts repudiated the New Deal belief in agency autonomy. Federal courts no longer assumed the deferential posture of the 1930s and 1940s. Solicitous of the interests Congress sought to protect through regulatory statutes, and fearful of agency "capture," courts took on a far more aggressive role, sometimes compelling governmental action.[26] Here judicial controls were very much on the side of regulatory intervention—a most ironic reversal of the New Deal belief in the inevitable incompatibility between active administration and legalism.

At roughly the same time, American presidents asserted increasing power over administrative agencies. Most notably, President Ronald Reagan issued two important executive orders that concentrated regulatory policymaking within the Office of Management and Budget. The President's claims frequently invoked the original constitutional decision to create a unitary executive and the policies that undergirded that decision: coordination, expedition, and accountability in the execution of the laws. All of these policies took on special importance in a period in which major decisions were made by numerous unaccountable agencies in a sprawling and highly bureaucratic national government. One goal of presidential control, at least in the 1980s, was to reduce regulatory controls—this too an ironic reversal of the institutional learning of the New Deal.

The assumption of greater roles by Congress, the courts, and the President amounted to a large-scale revival of checks and balances at the expense of administrative autonomy. These developments signaled a diminishing faith in "expertise" in regulation, and greater suspicion about the democratic pedigree of the administrative arm of government. In some quarters, enthusiasm for the rights revolution was coupled with distrust of regulatory administration; a greater role for Congress and the courts seemed only natural.

In the late 1970s and 1980s, however, an economic recession was combined with high inflation, the energy crisis, and sharp decreases in international competitiveness, productivity, and employment. The result was a period of severe protest against regulatory controls, which appeared to contribute to at least some of these developments. The protest produced two concrete developments. The first was the enactment, in the late 1970s and early 1980s, of legislation calling for deregulation, especially in the area of transportation (including airlines, railroads, and trucking) and energy (including the removal of controls on oil pricing).

The second development consisted of unilateral action by the Reagan administration, producing deregulation by way of elimination or reduction of agency-initiated regulatory controls coupled with sheer inaction. The goal was to promote economic productivity through increased reliance on private markets and private enterprise. The presidential initiatives, fueled by two executive orders calling for cost-benefit analysis and for attention to private markets,[27] were often controversial. In the aggregate, they proved of enormous importance in limiting or redirecting regulation in areas involving communications and broadcasting, discrimination, endangered species, occupational safety and health, and the environment.

The 1980s also witnessed considerable dissatisfaction with legal controls on administration. Belief in the courts' lack of accountability and expertise, as well as perception of their slow pace, seemed to point to a more modest judicial role. Here the institutional learning of the New Deal was usually invoked by those seeking to scale back regulation—a final illustration of the reversal of the institutional understanding of the New Dealers. Thus it was that judicial review of regulatory decisions became more deferential.[28]

In the New Deal period, as during the Great Society and after, it was clear that promotion of economic productivity and protection of the disadvantaged were the principal goals of regulatory legislation. The various justifications for regulatory statutes have not always been sharply distinguished or even articulated, however, and the absence of clear justifications has helped produce too many, too few, and misdirected regulatory controls. After more than a half-century of experience with regulation, it is possible to be quite explicit about its diverse functions. First, however, it is important to understand in more general terms the case for and against market ordering, and the antagonism to governmental interference with the market.

Public and Private Ordering

First Principles

In recent years regulatory programs have been attacked on a variety of grounds. The critics have claimed that regulation amounts in practice to unjustified interference with freedom of choice and is frequently a usurpation of private decisions in violation of government's first obligation, which is neutrality among competing conceptions of the good. Only purportedly in the public interest, regulation turns out on inspection to be interest-group transfers designed to protect well-organized private groups—such as business interests or unions—at the expense of the rest of the citizenry. Governmental controls impose partial, narrowly held views of what is right and just, views held by elite or parochial interests.

Many of the most powerful attacks on regulation are empirical; they include a range of complaints. Regulation has imposed huge costs on the economy. The result has been decreased productivity, unemployment and inflation, and threats to international competitiveness. Moreover, regulatory programs often aggravate the very problems they are intended to solve. The minimum wage has increased unemployment; environmental regulation of new sources has kept old, dirty machinery on the market even longer; civil rights legislation has discouraged employers from hiring blacks and women. Regulation has thus been ineffectual and even counterproductive, imposing costs not only on those who are regulated, but on its intended beneficiaries as well.

Criticisms of these sorts have been invoked against governmental efforts to require high-quality or nonentertainment broadcasting on radio and television, sometimes at the expense of private choice; to protect environmental diversity and purity and endangered species, sometimes at the expense of the poor in particular and economic productivity in general; to control children's advertising, violence on television, and pornography, frequently at the expense of the desires of viewers and listeners; to reduce risks in consumer products, nuclear power, and on the job, often at high cost to the economy and to people who would voluntarily incur those risks if they were permitted to do so; and even to antidiscrimination programs, which (on one view) interfere with freedom of association. All of these criticisms have played an important role in discouraging the enactment and implementation of programs protecting these sorts of interests.

Here and in the next chapter, I explore the theoretical issues; Chapter 3 examines the facts. We might begin the inquiry with an approach that takes seriously some of the components of both American republicanism and the New Deal reformation. This approach has the advantage of being congenial to many varieties of modern political thought—particularly to Rawls's *A Theory of Justice*,[29] but also to some of Rawls's critics.

Let us imagine a group of citizens concerned to set out the basic rules controlling governmental power in a newly formed but highly industrialized democracy. The citizens intend to ensure economic growth and productivity; they are for that reason well disposed toward freedom of contract and private markets. They will also be inclined in that direction as a result of their awareness that people have different tastes and conceptions of the good, their belief that such differences are desirable for individuals and for society as a whole, and their commitment to individual freedom and self-development, which argue in favor of respect for privately held plans of life. At the same time, the citizens are fearful that governmental impositions may be oppressive or counterproductive, especially as a result of the power of well-organized factions and the self-interest or venality of their representatives.

But the citizens are aware that nongovernmental action may cause a range of problems as well, quite outside the usual settings of private force and fraud. They know that environmental harms are highly likely; that risks to health and safety result from employment, automobiles, and other consumer products; that there are dangers of monopoly and cartelization; that the wholly private management of important industries, including energy and agriculture, may produce serious risks; that, in short, many people will be hurt by exclusive reliance on market ordering pursuant to conventional rules of contract and property.

The citizens are concerned, too, that there will be significant disparities in wealth and power within their country, and in particular that some people may be homeless, hungry, or otherwise lack the necessities of life. They are also aware of their differences in terms of race, sex, ability, handicap, sexual orientation, and basic tastes and life plans. They know that certain groups may be subject to discrimination. Individuals, however, have no clear sense of the particular harms that may befall them or their descendants after they have put the basic rules into effect.[30]

If citizens of this sort are deciding on the appropriate nature and scope of regulation, what sorts of criteria might they invoke? The most likely, and most familiar, are welfare on the one hand and autonomy on the other. The pursuit of both of these is informed and constrained by conceptions of justice as defined by the original position.[31]

On the first view, associated with utilitarianism and some forms of contractarian thought, regulation should be designed so as to maximize social welfare. We might distinguish between two variants of this view. According to the first, the government should ensure satisfaction of whatever preferences people actually have. The goal of preference satisfaction is closely associated with the Pareto criterion, which has achieved immense currency among welfare economists and which provides some of the foundations for freedom of contract. Under that criterion, a change from an existing social state is desirable—Pareto-superior—if at least one person is made better off without making anyone else worse off. Almost by definition, a voluntary contract produces a Pareto improvement. A system has become Pareto-optimal if it is not possible to make any change in the status quo without making at least one person worse off. Some forms of contemporary regulation are justifiable as a means of making Pareto improvements; most are not, because they produce losers as well as winners.

The current prominence of a conception of welfare based on satisfaction of existing preferences—a quite modern idea—is partly a function of the difficulty of making interpersonal comparisons of utility. It is also a product of the epistemological difficulties in assessing preferences in terms of their true connection with individual welfare, and the perceived political dangers of allowing government to engage in such inquiries.

On a second variation on the welfarist view, the process of maximizing social welfare should take place, not by satisfying current preferences, but by promoting those preferences and satisfying them to such an extent as is consonant with the best or highest conception of human happiness. This view, connected with older forms of utilitarianism,[32] does not take existing preferences as given, and it does not put all preferences on the same plane. The criterion of welfare remains the ultimate one, but the system is not focused solely on preference satisfaction. We will see this view at work in several areas of regulation.

On a quite different view, drawn broadly from the deontological tradition and also associated with contractarianism, regulation should be based on a norm of autonomy or freedom. Here too we might distinguish two variations. The first is focused on individuals. It sees the goal as one of ensuring, to the extent possible, opportunities for individual self-determination and individual self-rule. This is itself an ambiguous concept. It appears to point toward little in the way of collective controls, but as we will see, this is a controversial understanding.

A different conception of autonomy places an emphasis on the freedom of collectivities or communities—a freedom embodied in decisions, reached by the citizenry as a whole, about what courses to pursue. This view is closely associated with traditional republicanism, but it has resonances in Madisonian thought as well. On this view, political autonomy can be found in collective self-determination, as citizens decide, not what they "want," but instead who they are—what their values are and what those values require. What they want must be supported by reasons. An important form of freedom may consist in precisely these processes of collective self-determination. Of course there are serious dangers here, and there must be some constraints—usually denominated rights—on this process. But citizens in a new polity would be likely to make some space for processes of this sort, which are embodied in (for example) modern environmental and antidiscrimination law.

Thus far we have several sets of ideas, mostly quite general and abstract, with which to approach questions of governmental regulation. How will those ideas work in particular settings? What sort of orientation do they provide toward questions about the acceptable scope of regulatory controls?

Autonomy, Welfare, Democracy, Regulation

Freedom of Contract and the Minimal State. It is tempting to suggest that they provide a formidable basis for antagonism to the sorts of social and economic regulation that I intend to defend. Such antagonism can be traced to three ideas. The first is a belief in individual autonomy, freedom, or rights; the second refers to utilitarian or welfarist concerns; the third invokes, somewhat loosely, fears of self-interest and factionalism in governmental processes. All these are closely connected to the welfarist and nonwelfarist criteria for assessing governmental performance.

Liberty. A belief in individual liberty often underlies antagonism toward government intervention into the marketplace. The understanding here is that if there is no harm to others, government ought to respect and even encourage divergent conceptions of the good life, as they are expressed in private conduct and contractual arrangements. There is no reason to suppose that government knows better than individuals do what is in their interests, and considerable reason to suspect the opposite. This is so especially in cases involving large numbers of people, and strangers rather than intimates. In any case, individual liberty includes the freedom to make mistakes, which is an important part of self-development. Respect for private choice is sometimes described as government neutrality, which is seen as an important guarantor of private liberty.

On this account, there is simply no reason for collective intervention if the relevant actors are content. If there is harm to others, of course, government action might be permissible; but that category must be kept relatively small. Ideas of this kind provide the foundation for the idea that modern regulation is, almost by definition, illegitimate paternalism, or imposition of a parochial position by one group on others, or reflection of the self-interest of the politically powerful.

A related view has been expressed quite prominently in the writings of Nobel Prize winner James Buchanan and of some others operating within the increasingly influential tradition of public choice theory.[33] On this view, any change from the status quo must receive unanimous consent from the public. If it does not, it operates as a kind of "taking," or theft, from one group for the benefit of another. For Buchanan and his followers, the principal purpose of constitutionalism is to limit this form of theft. On Buchanan's account, a departure from the criterion of unanimous consent to arguments about welfare, autonomy, or justice, "seems to be purse escapism; it represents retreat into empty arguments about personal values which spells the end of rational discourse."[34] This may sound extreme. But the same ideas underlie widespread antipathy to regulatory programs that seem to have redistributive features or to be based on public aspirations. Indeed, the basic Paretian criterion—allowing a change from an existing social state if and only if at least one person might be made better off without making any one else worse off—has a similar foundation. A belief in liberty, in short, might be taken to argue against a wide range of regulatory programs.

Welfare. A related but distinct set of objections is based on utilitarian or welfarist concerns. The basic position is that people know what is in their own best interests and that respect for private preferences, as expressed in market transactions, is the best way to promote aggregate social welfare.[35] Government cannot, it is said, disrupt advantageous relations without producing some kind of welfare loss. In accordance with the Paretian criterion, the foundational idea behind freedom of contract, voluntary agreements (by definition) make both parties better off. In these circumstances, a decision to block the exchange will lead to individual harm by preventing people from making deals that will benefit them, and to collective harm by eliminating efficiency gains.

Moreover, governmental disruptions of such relations will, in this view, prove futile. The desires and preferences whose expression is suppressed by regulation are likely to manifest themselves in other, more destructive forms; thus regulation will be counterproductive as well as inefficient. This is the basis for the claim that the minimum wage has increased unemployment by making it more expensive for employers to hire unskilled workers; or that rent control has diminished the amount of housing available for the poor by decreasing incentives to invest in the housing market; or that antidiscrimination law has harmed blacks and women by making employers more reluctant to hire them in the first place. The central argument here is that interference with voluntary transactions will both produce welfare losses and, in the end, hurt the very people that intervention is intended to help.

The market, in short, is quite agile at counteracting well-intended efforts to redistribute resources through regulation. People at the very bottom of the economic ladder are often the victims. On this view, a collective decision to block an exchange, though frequently grounded in a laudable desire to protect one side from what seems like a harsh bargain, will fail to promote its own purposes. If members of one group—the poor, for example—make bad bargains because of their poverty and their powerlessness, the solution is to give them more money and more power, not to prevent them from entering into an agreement that they deem in their best interests. Frequently regulation that does the latter is said also (and by virtue of that fact) to do the former; but this is a fundamental mistake. Many regulatory controls will thus diminish economic productivity and at the same time fail to carry out their redistributive goals.

Government Failure. A final argument serves to account for some of the remaining intuitions behind the idea that government should respect private ordering. The concern here is that social and economic regulation introduces a grave danger of distortion. This is because of the government's own incentives, which may be parochial or perverse. Public decisions may be infected by factional pressures from narrow or regional interests or by the self-interest, venality, or confusion of public officials—a central theme during the founding period. Even without such pressures, governmental decisions may be mistaken or ill-informed.

For example, if government is permitted to regulate the consumption of sugar, salt, or alcohol, interest groups may influence regulatory decisions in such a way as to undermine whatever gains the system of regulation might provide if it were operating optimally. This position finds some (though far from complete) support from empirical work on the regulatory process discussed in Chapter 3. It is also supported by social choice theory, which has revealed that majoritarian processes have a high degree of arbitrariness built into them, that collective action problems aggravate the problem of accurately reflecting citizen desires through law, and that, in general, government is a highly imperfect mechanism for aggregating preferences.[36] In this view, the best approach is a bright-line rule or at least a strong presumption against government intervention into voluntary arrangements. Such a rule or presumption would provide protection against interest-group pressures and the occasional arbitrariness of majoritarianism.

Aspirations, Collective Action, and the Dependence of Preferences on Context. These factors provide solid reasons for a presumption in favor of protecting voluntary agreements and behavior from collective control. They help to explain the increasing disenchantment with collectivism in socialist and communist countries and supply reasons to understand and approve aspects of the movement toward deregulation in the liberal democracies as well. They do not, however, prove nearly as much as they purport to do.

An initial set of responses would point to the possibility that both liberty and welfare might be promoted, not undermined, by government action. The most conventional example here involves the problem of market failures or harms to third parties—a point to which we will return. But a more general response would begin by suggesting that governmental rules are implicated in, indeed constitute, the distribution of wealth and entitlements in the first instance. A system that required unanimous consent for redistribution would be understandable only if the existing distribution seemed prepolitical, or just, or supported by unanimous consent at some privileged earlier stage not later disturbed by injustice. If the existing distribution is in fact none of these, Buchanan's notion that something called "constitutionalism" should be designed to bar redistribution that does not have unanimous consent seems exceedingly peculiar.

In short, market outcomes—including prices and wages pursuant to a system of freedom of contract—are affected by a wide range of factors that are morally arbitrary. They include, for example, supply and demand at any particular place and time, unequally distributed opportunities before people become traders at all, existing tastes, the sheer number of purchasers and sellers, and even the unequal distributions of skills. There is no good reason for government to take these factors as natural or fixed, or to allow them to be turned into social and legal advantages, when it is deciding on the appropriate scope of regulation. If this is so, governmental efforts to interfere with market outcomes, at least if they can be made to accomplish their intended purposes (an important qualification), would seem to be required rather than proscribed.

This problem infects considerable work in public choice theory. In its normative capacity, and in the hands of some of its proponents, the field seems built on the (implicit and unjustified) assumption that the status quo itself is in no need of defense. The same point applies to Paretian criteria if they are presented as the exclusive reasons for social change. A Pareto improvement is generally[37] a sufficient condition for change; but it is an altogether different thing to suggest that it is a necessary condition as well. A distribution in which one person owns everything, and everyone else nothing, is Pareto-optimal; but it would not for that reason be uncontroversial on moral grounds.

Moreover, the welfarist and nonwelfarist arguments for freedom of contract and private ordering seem to depend on crude understandings of both liberty and welfare.

Liberty. The most obvious problem with the objection from liberty is that difficulties in coordinating the behavior of many people, and problems of collective action, sometimes make private ordering coercive or unworkable. Here government regulation prevents coercion or chaos, and thus promotes liberty by making it easier for people to do or to get what they want. For example, the rules of the road, regulation of airplane traffic, controls on polluting behavior, and governmental allocation of broadcast licenses do not interfere with freedom, rightly understood. I take up this point in more detail below.

Moreover, the satisfaction of private preferences, whatever their content, is an utterly implausible conception of liberty or autonomy. The notion of autonomy should be taken to refer instead to decisions reached with a full and vivid awareness of available opportunities, with all relevant information, or, most generally, without illegitimate constraints on the process of preference formation. When these conditions are not met, decisions might be described as unfree or nonautonomous.

Above all, the mistake here consists in taking all preferences as fixed and exogenous. This mistake is an extremely prominent one in welfare economics and in many contemporary challenges to regulation. If preferences are instead a product of available information, of existing consumption patterns, of social pressures, and of legal rules, it seems odd to suggest that individual freedom lies exclusively or by definition in preference satisfaction. It seems even odder to suggest that all preferences should be treated the same way, independently of their origins and the reasons offered in their support.

Consider, for example, a decision to purchase dangerous foods, consumer products, or cigarettes by someone unaware of the (serious) health risks; an employer's decision not to deal with blacks because of the background of public and private segregation or racial hostility in his community; a decision of a woman to adopt a traditional gender role because of the social stigma of refusing to do so; a decision not to purchase cars equipped with seatbelts or to wear motorcycle helmets because of the social pressures imposed by one's peer group; a lack of interest in environmental diversity resulting from personal experiences that are limited to industrialized urban areas; a decision not to employ blacks at a restaurant because of fear of violence from whites. In all of these cases, the interest in liberty or autonomy does not call for governmental inaction, even if that were an intelligible category. Indeed, in all of these cases regulation removes a kind of coercion.

One goal of a legal system, in short, is not merely to ensure autonomy by allowing satisfaction of preferences, but also and more fundamentally to promote autonomy in the processes of preference formation. The view that freedom requires an opportunity to choose among alternatives is supplemented by the view that people should not face unjustifiable constraints on the free development of their preferences and beliefs, although it is not altogether clear what such a view would require. At the very least, such a view would see a failure of autonomy, and a reason for collective response, in beliefs and preferences based on the absence of information or available opportunities—as, for example, in the case of members of disadvantaged groups who accept their subordinate position because the status quo seems intractable, or in the case of people who are indifferent to high-quality broadcasting because they have experienced only banal situation comedies and dehumanizing, violence-ridden police dramas.

The point suggests more fundamentally that it is incorrect to claim that something called the market, or respect for private arrangements, embodies governmental "neutrality." Private preferences are partly a product of available opportunities, which are a function of legal rules. Those rules allocate rights and entitlements; that function is simply unavoidable (short of anarchy). The allocation will in turn have a profound effect on and indeed help constitute the distribution of wealth and the content of private preferences.

Whether someone has a preference for a commodity, a right, or anything else is in part a function of whether the legal system has allocated it to him in the first instance. For example, a decision to give employees a right to organize, or women a right not to be subject to sexual harassment, will have a significant impact on social attitudes toward labor organization and sexual harassment. The legal allocation helps to legitimate or delegitimate the relevant rights. It therefore has an effect on social attitudes toward them, and on their valuation by both current owners and would-be purchasers.[38]

In addition, the government's allocation will affect the ways in which preferences are manifested in markets, which rely on the criterion of private willingness to pay. Willingness to pay is a function of ability to pay, and an actor's ability to pay is a function of the amount of goods that have been (legally) allocated to him. In these circumstances, it is hard to see neutrality in governmental respect for preferences, whatever their content and consequences.

To put the point most simply: when preferences are a function of legal rules, the rules cannot, without circularity, be justified by reference to the preferences.[39] It should be a familiar point that government is responsible for the allocation of wealth and entitlements in the first instance—a major underpinning of New Deal constitutionalism. The decision to permit market ordering pursuant to that allocation represents a controversial choice about competing values.

To say this is not to say that the government ought generally to be free to override preferences on the ground that they are a function of the existing social order. Such a view would be a license for tyranny. It is to say, however, that the concept of autonomy will call not merely for the satisfaction of whatever preferences people currently have, but more generally, or instead, for protection of the processes of preference formation. We will deal with the point more particularly in Chapter 2.

The discussion thus far suggests that if individual freedom is the goal, laissez-faire is not the solution. Government action might also be justified on grounds of autonomy when the public seeks to implement, through democratic processes culminating in law, widely held social aspirations or collective "preferences about preferences." Individual consumption choices often diverge from collective considered judgments:[40] people may seek, through law, to implement their reflective, democratic decisions about what courses to pursue. If so, it is no violation of autonomy to allow those considered judgments to be vindicated by governmental action. Consider a law calling for protection of the environment or support of high-quality broadcasting, wanted by a majority of the population and creating opportunities insufficiently provided through market ordering. Ideas of this sort can be connected to the original constitutional belief in deliberative democracy, a belief that, as we have seen, grew out of republican conceptions of politics, which place a high premium on political deliberation. Collective aspirations or considered judgments, produced by a process of deliberation in which competing perspectives are brought to bear, reflect a conception of political freedom having deep roots in the American constitutional tradition.

Welfare. With respect to welfare, the response to the case for respecting voluntary agreements would begin by pointing to the existence of coordination and collective action problems, which make the ordinary model of contractual freedom, built on two-party transactions, far less attractive when large numbers of people are involved. Rules regulating automobile or airplane traffic are necessary to prevent chaos. Frequently, moreover, a group of people in a position to contract with one or many firms face a prisoner's dilemma:[41] a situation in which market pressures, and sheer numbers, prevent them from obtaining their preferred solution, which will result only if all cooperate, and are indeed constrained to do so. It is in this sense that markets can be genuinely coercive. On utilitarian grounds, they are not the realm of freedom at all.

A simple case here is that of littering in a park. It may well be in everyone's self-interest to litter, since the individual benefits may outweigh the individual costs. But if everyone litters, the aggregate costs may dwarf the aggregate benefits. If this is so, the preferred outcome, for most or all citizens, is a situation in which everyone can be assured that no one will litter. It is possible that this solution may be obtained through social norms, which sometimes solve dilemmas of this sort,[42] but when such norms are absent or weak, legal controls are the only solution. Here the force of law is necessary to allow people to obtain what they want. The example of pollution is a clear one, but the need for legal coercion to ensure the satisfaction of individual preferences comes up in more surprising contexts.

Consider, for example, laws prohibiting employers from refusing to hire or discharging workers who have declined to sign a pledge not to join labor unions. It may be individually rational for each worker to sign such a pledge. Each worker may be better off with the job and the pledge than without either. But laws prohibiting an employer from requiring the pledge are in the interest of employees as a whole, since they bar the employer from taking advantage of the employees' need to compete among themselves. That competition works to the collective detriment of employees. Regulation is the solution.

Such problems often characterize the situation of workers, victims of discrimination and pollution, and consumers. Workers will, for example, fail to seek safer places of employment if market pressures make it economically irrational for each individual worker to do so. The worker who asks for a safer workplace may find himself without a workplace at all. But regulation requiring safer workplaces might be in the interest of most employees. (The qualification is necessary because regulatory controls of workplace hazards will have a range of ancillary costs for consumers, employers, and even employees, possibly including increased unemployment and lower salaries.)

Phenomena of this sort severely complicate the idea that respect for voluntary transactions is always justified on grounds of welfare. Here regulation is not a paternalistic measure to override people's expressed desires, but instead a necessary mechanism for allowing people to get what they in fact want. The market does not provide the preferred option. Regulation has a facilitative function—ironically, facilitative by virtue of its coercive quality.

As we have seen, those who object to social and economic regulation tend to assume that preferences are static and fixed. The falsity of this assumption undermines not only the objection from liberty, but welfarist complaints as well. Preferences are shifting and endogenous rather than exogenous—endogenous to, or a function of, existing information, consumption patterns, legal rules, and social pressures most generally. Because preferences are shifting and endogenous, legal rules that treat them as fixed will lose important opportunities for welfare gains.

For example, legal rules prohibiting or discouraging addictive behavior may have significant advantages in terms of welfare. Regulation of heroin or cigarettes—at least if the regulation does not have unanticipated side effects and can be made effective—might well increase aggregate social welfare by decreasing harmful behavior, removing the secondary effects of those harms, and producing more healthful and satisfying lives. Or government regulation of the environment or broadcasting—encouraging or requiring, for example, protection of pristine areas, nonentertainment broadcasting, or high-quality programs—may in the end generate new preferences, providing increased satisfaction and consequently producing considerable welfare gains. The same may well be true of antidiscrimination measures, which affect the desires and attitudes of discriminators and victims alike. A system that takes private preferences for granted will sacrifice large opportunities for social improvement on welfarist criteria. This point was a crucial one in the early stages of utilitarian thought; it has been lost more recently with the shift from older forms of welfarism to Paretianism.[43]

The fact that preferences are shifting and endogenous also weakens the objection that legal disruption of voluntary transactions will be futile. If the preference is itself a function of the legal rule, or of current consumption patterns, legal barriers will not be circumvented, for the preference in question will be diminished or eliminated. Thus, for example, a law preventing sexual harassment is designed to (and may in fact) reduce the desire of employers and teachers to harass employees and students. If so, the law will not be evaded by contracting parties. Similar points apply both to laws prohibiting discrimination on various grounds and to regulations calling for environmental protection or broadcasting controls. Such laws are designed to alter preferences and beliefs as well as actions. All of these are welfarist reasons, ranging from solid to plausible, for much modern regulation.

Government Failure. The argument from factional intrigue and self-interested representation also depends on empirical judgments and contingencies that are highly speculative. It is both true and important that government regulation may be distorted by irrelevant or impermissible considerations and that it may make things worse rather than better; we will discuss this risk in several places below. Considerations of this sort suggest that the possibility of identifying welfarist and nonwelfarist reasons for governmental interference with voluntary behavior creates only a prima facie case. Just as government action might not be on balance justifiable to correct a market failure—because of the danger that such action may make the situation even worse than the status quo—the existence of deficiencies in voluntary behavior may be on balance an insufficient reason for collective control. But the risk that intervention will make things worse rather than better is a prudential concern that bears on implementation. It does not provide a general basis for antagonism to social and economic regulation. In some circumstances, interference may produce significant benefits for trivial costs.

In sum: the case against the so-called minimal state, and in favor of a relatively large set of regulatory programs, is grounded in three principal points. The first is that the minimal state, distributing basic entitlements, has a range of consequences for, indeed constitutes, the distribution of rights, wealth, and power. That distribution in turn affects private preferences and beliefs. In this respect, it is not neutral in any global sense. Indeed, it is hardly minimal. This point does not provide a broadside attack on freedom of contract, and the argument does not furnish the affirmative case for regulatory controls. It does suggest, however, that a frequently voiced argument against regulation is misconceived.

The second point is that sometimes regulatory programs are necessary to solve collective action and coordination problems. Programs responsive to such problems facilitate the satisfaction of private desires, and do not override them at all. Here the justification lies in arguments from both autonomy and welfare. Ironically, coercion is necessary to allow people to achieve what they want. This position does not depend at all on controversial views about whether private desires, as expressed in markets, should be the only basis for social choice.

The third point is that private preferences should not always be respected: (a) far from being fixed and exogenous, they adapt to and indeed are a function of existing circumstances, which may include injustice, in the form (for example) of limitations in both available opportunities and information; and (b) they might be overridden by collective aspirations or considered judgments. In the former case, regulation might counteract poor information or unjustified limitations in opportunities. In the latter case, arguments from democracy suggest that private arrangements should not be respected. In both cases, the status quo is an inappropriate baseline for assessing change, and regulation is justified even if some people are made worse off as a result. It is in these cases that criteria drawn from welfare economics, public choice theory, and pre-New Deal principles of private right are most fundamentally wrong.

To make these claims is emphatically not to deny that democratic societies should make much room for private property, freedom of contract, and other voluntary arrangements. Indeed, a system having all of these has the crucial advantage of respecting and fostering diverse conceptions of the good, an important part of individual freedom; it will promote economic productivity as well. A presumption in favor of a system of voluntary arrangements, operated within the basic institutions of private property, tort, and contract, thus emerges quite naturally from the guiding criteria of autonomy and welfare. The presumption is, however, only that, and it hardly provides a decisive reason to reject a wide array of regulatory initiatives. In many cases, considerations of autonomy and welfare will argue for rather than against such initiatives. It is time, however, to explore these problems in more particular settings.

CHAPTER

2

The Functions of Regulatory Statutes

The discussion in Chapter 1 suggests that powerful claims can be made, in principle, for social and economic regulation. In this respect, the relatively well-understood phenomenon of "market failure" is supplemented by a range of other defects in market ordering. A general regime of deliberate preference-shaping through governmental control of desires and beliefs is of course a central characteristic of totalitarian regimes. No one should deny that such a regime would be intolerable. But it would be most peculiar to take that point as a reason to deprive citizens in an electoral democracy of the power to implement collective aspirations through law, or to counteract, by providing information and opportunities, preferences and beliefs that have adapted to an unjust or otherwise objectionable status quo.

The origins of regulatory statutes can be discussed in terms of either explanations or justifications. An explanation attempts to account for the existence of the statute; a justification attempts to say why the statute is a good idea. Happily, an explanation is sometimes a justification as well. A statute might prevent monopoly, and its enactment might be attributable to a legislative understanding to that effect. Conversely, an explanation of a statute might fail to justify it, and even go a long way toward discrediting it. Statutes are often explained as "mere" interest-group transfers, and except on highly artificial assumptions[1] explanations of that sort undermine rather than justify the relevant measures. Almost every issue of the *Journal of Law and Economics* has a contribution arguing that apparently public-spirited regulation—including protection of the environment and of safety in the workplace—is actually an effort to benefit a powerful industry or to create a cartel; or that it merely reflects what is described as "rent-seeking," the dissipation of otherwise productive energies through wasteful, self-interested political behavior.[2] The following discussion outlines a variety of explanations for regulatory statutes, most of which amount to justifications.

A few disclaimers are necessary here. Many statutes will fall in more than one category; different provisions of the same statute might be put in different categories; particular claims about categorization will depend on contestable normative and empirical grounds; and it is impossible to make claims about the precise scope and nature of regulation without knowing a lot about the facts. My purpose is to suggest that in spite of these difficulties, regulatory statutes can be distinguished according to function; they should not be treated as undifferentiated wholes; they fall into recognizable patterns; they are often subject, at least in principle, to a powerful defense.

Market Failures

Many statutes respond to market failures, as that concept is understood in neoclassical economics. It will be sufficient here to outline some conventional examples.[3]

Monopoly. Regulatory statutes are, least controversially, a response to the risks of monopoly. Government regulation preventing monopolistic behavior or cartels—like the basic rules of contract, tort, and property—is designed to ensure a well-functioning market. Far from being an unjustified constraint on private decisions, regulation of this sort has a facilitative or constitutive function. Sometimes governmental controls take the form of civil and criminal sanctions for monopolistic behavior. The Sherman and Clayton acts, as well as most of the rest of the law of antitrust, fall in this category, though there is dispute in some circles about whether such laws actually promote efficiency when their costs are taken into account.

Legal controls on monopolistic behavior are a poor solution when there is a natural monopoly, found in areas in which economies of scale enable a large firm to drive out competitors because of its lower costs. In such cases, the ordinary remedy consists of ceilings on prices and perhaps of quality controls as well. The basic goal is to provide goods and services at the competitive level. The Federal Communications Act and the Natural Gas Act are efforts to deal with the problem. The size of the category of natural monopoly is highly disputed, however, and technological changes can convert markets that once seemed to involve natural monopoly into highly competitive arenas.

Collective Action Problems, Coordination Questions, and Transactions Costs. It is a familiar point that individually rational private behavior may produce collective or public irrationality.[4] If everyone acts in his self-interest, serious harm will sometimes result. Clear cases here involve public or collective goods, which are characterized by two features: nonrivalrous consumption and nonexcludability. The standard example is the system of national defense: when it is in place, no one can be excluded from it; national defense cannot be provided to one without simultaneously being provided to all. Moreover, the fact that one person is protected does not diminish the protection of others. In cases of this sort, each person, acting rationally, is tempted to "free-ride" while others pay, the consequence being that the good would not be provided at all. Government regulation is needed to eliminate the free-rider problem and to ensure that public goods will be created.

Environmental law is a good illustration, since clean air and clean water have the characteristics of public goods. The social costs of polluting activity may dwarf the social benefits, but the costs are so diffused, and so small in the individual case, that the market will not force individual polluters to take those costs into account. Each polluter will engage quite rationally in conduct that will make society as a whole worse off. Because of the individually high costs and low benefits of seeking redress, each victim[5] will attempt to take a free ride on the remedial efforts of other victims, and will quite rationally refuse to bring suit. The result is that neither the polluter nor any of its victims will limit the harmful effects of the activity, which will therefore be far higher than the optimal point. Environmental regulation is characteristically a response to this problem.

Similarly, a group of people may face a "prisoner's dilemma" in which rational individual behavior makes the relevant actors worse off than they would be if they could act cooperatively.[6] In the prisoner's dilemma, two prisoners are suspected of a crime, placed in separate cells, interrogated separately, and offered the same deal by the prosecutor. The prosecutor says: "If you confess to the crime, and if the other prisoner does not confess, you will be a witness for the prosecution, and freed; but if you confess and the other prisoner also confesses, you will be convicted of the crime and receive a five-year sentence. If you do not confess, and if the other prisoner also does not confess, you will both be convicted of a lesser crime, carrying a one-year sentence, on which there is now sufficient evidence. But if you do not confess, and the other prisoner does, you will receive the maximum sentence of ten years."

For each prisoner, deciding independently, the best strategy is to confess. Whatever the other prisoner does, the payoff from confessing is clearly better than that from not confessing. But if both follow that strategy, the outcome, which is a five-year sentence, is worse for both than if neither confesses, in which case they would receive only one year of imprisonment. Cooperative behavior ensuring against defections would be necessary in order to achieve the best result. And even if the prisoners could speak with each other, their problem would not be solved. Each prisoner would have a strong incentive—his freedom—to breach the agreement; and with the decision whether to breach, the dilemma will rematerialize. What is necessary is assurance of compliance, in the form of a coercive enforcement mechanism.

Parallel problems arise in many settings. Indeed, markets are prisoner's dilemmas for both sellers and purchasers, who would be better off with a cooperative solution. At least with respect to sellers, there is a consensus that a prisoner's dilemma is socially desirable, and the antitrust laws are designed to ensure that consumers and society as a whole benefit from it. But sometimes a prisoner's dilemma produces general harm, and regulatory solutions are necessary. Here too, for example, legal control of pollution can be understood as a response. Each person who pollutes or litters may be acting in his rational self-interest, but the aggregate level of polluting and littering will be well above the social optimum, which can be achieved only through collective action, including coercion, which guarantees cooperation. A central problem here is that a market often carries high transaction costs for the achievement of desired social states. It is expensive for people to make cooperative arrangements on their own, and in any case external coercion may be indispensable, at least in the absence of strong social norms.

Ideas of this sort help justify regulatory controls that appear to intrude on private choice, but that actually facilitate an outcome that people want and cannot obtain without governmental assistance. A prohibition on littering is an example. A related phenomenon is the legal ban on racial discrimination in restaurants, which, paradoxically, was sought by restaurants themselves. The force of the law was needed in order to remove pressures imposed by white customers and thus to enable restaurants to serve people as they chose. Fear of reprisal from whites could find a remedy in legal protection permitting a business to do what it already, in an important sense, wants to do.

Similarly, compulsory seatbelt laws might be understood as a device to overcome the social pressures imposed on (especially young) people not to buckle up. Here the shield of the law removes psychological pressures and thus helps people do what in fact they want to do.[7] A restriction on smoking might also be justified as a response to a prisoner's dilemma faced by young people facing peer pressure. Such a regulation need not be seen as paternalistic at all; instead it enables people to reach the cooperative solution.

There is a general lesson here. Some governmental controls commonly regarded as unjustified paternalism can be understood instead as an effort to facilitate the satisfaction of private desires. The phenomenon suggests one explanation for the striking fact that people's preferences, in their capacities as voters or citizens, are quite different from what they are when people act in their purely private or market capacities. A majority of citizens might support regulation that would prevent them from engaging in the very conduct which, in an unregulated system, they are led to choose because of a prisoner's dilemma or a collective action problem. People might prefer a system in which all are prevented from (for example) littering or driving without seatbelts even if they would personally rather litter or drive without belts than be the only nonlitterers or beltbucklers.

An analogous problem is that of coordination: the arrangement by government of private behavior in such a way as to satisfy private desires which, if left to individual decision, would produce chaos or disorder.[8] Either a social norm or legal constraint is necessary to solve the problem. Unlike in a prisoner's dilemma, a coordination problem presents no incentive to defect once the solution is in place. An agreement to solve a coordination problem is stable; an agreement to solve a prisoner's dilemma is not.

Coordination problems are omnipresent. Government regulation of airplane or automobile traffic, undertaken by federal and state governments, provides a familiar example. So too with the allocation of broadcasting licenses over various frequencies. In this case, regulation "is not really forcing people to do what they don't want to do, but rather enabling them to do what they want to do by forcing them to do it."[9] The category is a large one. Here as well, coercion has an often overlooked facilitative function.

Inadequate Information. People often lack information. This problem is of particular importance in the area of safety and health. For example, workers do not have the tools by which to assess the risks posed by carcinogens in the workplace; the information is simply unavailable. So too, purchasers of various products, including food and drugs, are often unaware of the relevant dangers.

The absence of information may be a result of market failures of various sorts.[10] For example, information might be a public good. Suppose a test of the safety of cigarettes reported facts from which, postpublication, nonpaying companies and citizens (free riders) could not be excluded. In such circumstances, smokers and others might in the aggregate place a high positive value on the information, but each individual smoker would find it too costly, in light of the free-rider problem, to pay for it. The result is too little information.

There will also be a market failure in the case of manufacturers who have poor incentives to provide information about hazardous products. Competition over the degree of dangerousness may decrease total purchases of the product rather than help any particular manufacturer to obtain greater sales. If so, too little information will come out. Finally, producers sometimes know which products are safe, but consumers cannot tell. This asymmetry in information may force safe products out of the market because (1) safe products will sell for no higher price than dangerous ones, (2) safe products will be more expensive to produce, and (3) consumers will not be able to know the difference.[11]

The extent of these phenomena is sharply disputed. Moreover, the absence of information may be a result of market success rather than failure. Information is costly to produce and process, and the market may be providing the optimal level of information even if that level is relatively low. But if information is inadequate, government regulation is a sensible response. The best remedy here is usually to furnish the information if the market fails to do so rather than to ban the transaction. In the interest of both autonomy and welfare, the regulatory presumption should be in favor of disclosure rather than prohibition.

Sometimes, however, the provision of information will itself be so costly that it is undesirable for government to intervene at all; and sometimes a disclosure remedy will be both expensive and ineffective in comparison to a flat ban, which is therefore the best approach. If the relevant behavior involves risks that no reasonable and informed person would undertake, and if the provision of information is costly, it would be entirely appropriate to proscribe the conduct rather than simply to require disclosure. Some regulation of dangerous food and drugs, consumer products, and workplace risks can be understood in these terms.

Disclosure remedies are especially troublesome in view of the enormous difficulties people face in dealing with low-probability events.[12] People tend to rely on heuristics that lead to systemic errors in assessing probability, by misunderstanding the phenomenon of regression to the mean, giving too much weight to recent catastrophes, or starting from a general initial expectation that is insufficiently adjusted to take account of the particular problem at hand.[13] The result is that popular understandings of the risks posed by low-probability events are seriously distorted. There is also evidence that the provision of information is unhelpful when views about risk are deeply engrained. People may be accustomed to believing that a risk is low, or want to believe that they are not subject to danger; it is difficult to dislodge that belief. If people seek to reduce cognitive dissonance, information campaigns may not alter beliefs at all.[14]

For these reasons, it is not always useful, in cases of inadequate information, for government to rely on disclosure remedies. As noted, direct prohibitions are a natural response. Much of modern safety regulation—protecting against harms from nuclear power, toxic substances in the workplace, dangerous food and drugs and consumer products—can be understood as a response to the absence of information (for example, the Occupational Safety and Health Act, the Food and Drug Act, the Consumer Product Safety Act, and the Nuclear Power Act). It is probable, however, that these statutes would be more effective and less burdensome if disclosure remedies were used more often.

The category of inadequate information includes the problems of impulsive behavior and regret: the possibility that ex ante choices will disregard or undervalue the likelihood of ex post harm or dissatisfaction. A rationale of this sort supplies the basis for a mandatory "cooling off" period in certain consumer transactions. It also bears on such issues as surrogate motherhood, whose regulation might depend on a belief that, through a kind of myopia, contracting parties underestimate the real costs of the arrangement.

Externalities. A wide range of private conduct has external costs that are not adequately taken into account by private markets. The decision to offer employment in a dangerous workplace or one producing dangerous products may affect not only the relevant workers and purchasers, but a wide variety of strangers as well—people in the vicinity of production and use, their family members, participants in insurance markets, and taxpayers who must support those who are injured. These costs are external because they are not "internalized" to the employer through the operation of the market. Governmental controls involving such issues as narcotics, energy use, the environment, nuclear power, and pension plans can be understood as a response.

In industrialized democracies with large interdependencies between those who are injured and the public at large, externalities are nearly everywhere. To take a perhaps surprising example, the protection of endangered species can be understood as a recognition of the large external benefits that come from preserving biological diversity. Species of various sorts have genetic endowments that provide the raw materials for a wide range of useful materials, including medicines and pesticides. For example, about 25% of prescription drugs now sold in the United States come from chemicals originally derived from wild plants. The Endangered Species Act was partly a product of this concern.

The simplest cases of externality involve straightforward harms to third parties, as in the case of a nuclear power plant endangering those who live in the vicinity. Somewhat more controversially, externalities may call for apparently paternalistic health and safety regulations. Often injuries must ultimately be paid for by taxpayers, and the costs of death, injury, and disease are imposed on spouses and children as well as on those most directly affected. Ideas of this sort played a role in the creation of the Occupational Safety and Health Act.

Two often overlooked qualifications are necessary here. First, the idea that the producer of harmful products has "caused" adverse effects purports to be purely descriptive, but in fact it has a large normative dimension. Whether harms materializing from dangerous products should be attributed to the acts of the producer, of the consumer, or of some third party requires a moral theory. Such harms could with plausibility be treated as a function of the acts and omissions of a range of people.[15]

Second, private conduct has an extraordinarily wide range of external consequences on others, and those consequences often count as injuries, many of which people would be willing to pay to prevent. Such injuries include the moral offense or injury to self-respect caused by (for example) environmental degradation, racial discrimination, risk-taking, racial intermarriage, and pornography. Any workable theory of externalities must describe and limit the category of effects that count as regulable injuries to third parties; and that theory must partake of political theory rather than science or even economics.

Public-Interested Redistribution

Many statutes are designed to redistribute resources from one group to another. Some respond to a widely held or easily defended view that the benefited groups have a legitimate claim to the relevant resources. Statutes directly transferring resources to the poor or the disadvantaged, such as the Social Security Act, the Food Stamp Act, and Aid to Families with Dependent Children all fall in this basic category.

Often redistributive measures do not directly transfer resources to disadvantaged people or to those whom we wish to subsidize, but instead attempt to deal with coordination or collective action problems faced by large groups. As we have seen, statutory protection of workers can be understood as efforts to overcome the difficulties of organization of many people in the employment market. Suppose, for example, that numerous employees prefer a nine-hour to a twelve-hour day. Suppose as well that many or most or all of them would prefer working twelve hours to not working at all. Workers may not be able to rely on the labor market to achieve their favored alternative. Individual workers will compete against each other to their collective harm. If their preferred solution is to be provided, it must be as a result of statutes that eliminate the option of unlimited working hours.[16]

Because of the collective action problem, regulatory statutes must make the relevant rights inalienable. If workers are left free to trade these rights, the collective action problem will rematerialize. Labor markets create a prisoner's dilemma that is soluble only through governmental action. Ideas of this sort help justify minimum wage and maximum hour legislation and indeed the Fair Labor Standards Act in general—though the distributional consequences here are complex, and there are many losers as well as winners, even within the group of workers.[17] This kind of collective action problem produces a rationale for regulation that is based on redistribution rather than on economic efficiency. It is not at all clear that it is efficient to allow the creation of cartels among workers, even if it is in the interest of those thus authorized; and this latter point is not entirely clear in light of the fact that (for example) the minimum wage increases unemployment.

Regulation is often an attempt to redistribute resources to certain groups. Health and safety regulation is sometimes justified as a means of transferring resources to workers and consumers at the expense of employers and producers, whether or not there is a collective action problem. But redistributive rationales for regulation are heavily contested, and for good reason. In general, regulatory strategies are inferior to direct transfer payments as a means of redistributing wealth.[18] One of the paradoxes of the regulatory state is that efforts to redistribute resources through regulation tend to hurt the least well-off, and in any case to have complex effects, many of them unintended and perverse. The market is extremely creative in overcoming efforts to transfer resources through regulation.

Consider, as particular examples, minimum price supports for farmers and rent control. It is by no means clear either that these regulations benefit a class with a strong claim to the public fisc, or that the intended redistribution will really occur. Rent control, for example, has not served as a direct transfer of resources to the disadvantaged. On the contrary, it has discouraged new investment in housing, decreased the available housing stock, and benefited existing tenants, many of them financially well-off, at the expense of others, many of them poor.

There is a general lesson here. People often think that regulation produces a simple redistribution from one class to another, but the distributive effects of regulation are complex and sometimes unfortunate, in light of the flexibility of the market in ensuring ex ante adjustments to regulatory controls. Thus, for example, minimum wage legislation reduces employment, and some occupational health legislation decreases both salaries and employment. (To say this is not to say that such legislation should be repealed; it is necessary to know the magnitude of all of these effects in order to make such a judgment.) A related problem is that regulation sometimes benefits groups that might not deserve the help; it is not easy to argue that farmers as a class should receive the massive and varied subsidies embodied in federal law.

Collective Desires and Aspirations

Some statutes should be understood as an embodiment not of privately held preferences, but of what might be described as collective desires, including aspirations, "preferences about preferences," or considered judgments on the part of significant segments of society. Laws of this sort are a product of deliberative processes on the part of citizens and representatives. They cannot be understood as an attempt to aggregate or trade off private preferences. This understanding of politics recalls Madison's belief in deliberative democracy.[19]

Frequently, political choices cannot easily be understood as a process of aggregating prepolitical desires. Some people may, for example, want nonentertainment broadcasting on television, even though their own consumption patterns favor situation comedies; they may seek stringent environmental laws even though they do not use the public parks; they may approve of laws calling for social security and welfare even though they do not save or give to the poor; they may support antidiscrimination laws even though their own behavior is hardly race- or gender-neutral. The choices people make as political participants are different from those they make as consumers. Democracy thus calls for an intrusion on markets. The widespread disjunction between political and consumption choices presents something of a puzzle. Indeed, it sometimes leads to the view that market ordering is undemocratic and that choices made through the political process are a preferable basis for social ordering.

A generalization of this sort would be far too broad in light of the multiple breakdowns of the political process and the advantages of market ordering in many arenas. But it would also be a mistake to suggest, as some do, that markets always reflect individual choice more reliably than politics, or that political choices differ from consumption outcomes only because of confusion, as voters fail to realize that they must ultimately bear the costs of the programs they favor. Undoubtedly consumer behavior is sometimes a better or more realistic reflection of actual preferences than is political behavior. But since preferences depend on context, the very notion of a "better reflection" of "actual" preferences is a confused one. Moreover, the difference might be explained by the fact that political behavior reflects a variety of influences that are distinctive to the context of politics.

These include four closely related phenomena. First, citizens may seek to fulfill individual and collective aspirations in political behavior, not in private consumption. As citizens, people may seek the aid of the law to bring about a social state in some sense higher than what emerges from market ordering. Second, people may, in their capacity as political actors, attempt to satisfy altruistic or other-regarding desires, which diverge from the self-interested preferences characteristic of markets.[20] Third, political decisions might vindicate what might be called meta-preferences or second-order preferences. A law protecting environmental diversity and opposing consumption behavior is an example. People have wishes about their wishes; and sometimes they try to vindicate those second-order wishes, or considered judgments about what is best, through law. Fourth, people may precommit themselves, with regulation, to a course of action that they consider to be in the general interest; the story of Ulysses and the Sirens is the model here. The adoption of a Constitution is itself an example of a precommitment strategy.

For all these reasons people seem to favor regulation designed to secure high-quality broadcasting even though their consumption patterns favor situation comedies—a phenomenon that helps justify certain controversial regulatory decisions by the Federal Communications Commission requiring nonentertainment broadcasting and presentations on issues of public importance. The same category of aspirations or public spiritedness includes measures designed to protect endangered species and natural preserves in the face of individual behavior that reflects little solicitude for them.

The collective character of politics, permitting a response to collective action problems, helps to explain these phenomena. People may not want to satisfy their meta-preferences, or to be altruistic, unless they are sure that others will be bound as well. More simply, people may prefer not to contribute to a collective benefit if donations are made individually, but their most favored system might be one in which they contribute if (but only if) there is assurance that others will do so. The collective character of politics might also overcome the problem, discussed below, of preferences and beliefs that have adapted to an unjust status quo or to limits in available opportunities. Without the possibility of collective action, the status quo may seem intractable, and private behavior will adapt accordingly. But if people can act in concert, preferences might take a quite different form; consider social movements involving the environment, labor, and race and sex discrimination.

In addition, social and cultural norms might incline people to express aspirational or altruistic goals in political behavior but not in markets. Such norms may press people, in their capacity as citizens, distinctly in the direction of a concern for others or for the public interest. The deliberative aspects of politics, bringing additional information and perspectives to bear, may also bring out or affect preferences as expressed through governmental processes.

Government action is a necessary response here. Possible examples include recycling programs, energy conservation programs, and contributions to the arts, to the poor, and to environmental protection. The collective action problem interacts with aspirations, altruistic desires, second-order preferences, and precommitment strategies; all of these are most likely to be enacted into law in the face of a question of collective action. Moreover, consumption decisions are a product of the criterion of private willingness to pay, which contains distortions of its own. Willingness to pay is a function of ability to pay, and it is an extremely crude proxy for utility. Political behavior removes this distortion (which is not to say that it does not introduce distortions of its own).

These general considerations suggest that statutes are sometimes a response to a considered judgment on the part of the electorate that the choices reflected in consumption patterns ought to be overcome. A related but more narrow justification is that statutes safeguard noncommodity values that an unregulated market protects inadequately.[21] Social ordering through markets may have long-term, world-transforming effects that reflect a kind of collective myopia in the form of an emphasis on short-term considerations at the expense of the future. Here regulation is a natural response. Examples include promoting high-quality programming in broadcasting, supporting the arts, and ensuring diversity through protection of the environment and of endangered species. In all of these respects, political choices are not made by consulting given or private desires, but instead reflect a deliberative process designed to shape and reflect values.

Arguments from collective desires are irresistible if the measure at issue is adopted unanimously. But more serious difficulties are produced if (as is usual) the law imposes on a minority what it regards as a burden rather than a benefit. Suppose, for example, that a majority wants to require high-quality television and to ban violent and dehumanizing shows, but that a significant minority wants to see them. (I put the first amendment questions to one side.) It might be thought that those who perceive a need to bind themselves, or to express an aspiration, should not be permitted to do so if the consequence is to deprive others of an opportunity to satisfy their preferences.

The foreclosure of the preferences of the minority is unfortunate, but in general it is hard to see what argument there might be for an across-the-board rule against collective action of this sort. If the majority is prohibited from vindicating its second-order or altruistic preferences through legislation, its own desires will be frustrated. The choice is between the preferences of the majority and those of the minority, although the foreclosure of the minority should probably be permitted only when less restrictive alternatives, including private arrangements, are unavailable to serve the same end.

The argument for regulation embodying collective desires is much weaker in three categories of cases. First, if the particular choice foreclosed has some special character—for instance, some forms of intimate sexual activity—it is appropriately considered a right, and the majority has no authority to intervene. Second, some collective desires might be objectionable or distorted. A social preference against racial intermarriage could not plausibly be justified as reflecting an aspiration or a precommitment strategy—though to explain why, it is necessary to offer an independent argument, challenging that preference and invoking a claim of justice. Third, some collective desires might reflect a special weakness on the part of the majority; consider a curfew law, or perhaps prohibition. In such circumstances, a legal remedy might remove desirable incentives for private self-control, have unintended side-effects resulting from "bottling up" desires, and prove unnecessary in light of the existence of alternative remedies. When any of these three concerns arise, the case for protection of collective desires is much less powerful. But in many cases these concerns are absent, and regulatory programs initiated on these grounds are justified.

Diverse Experiences and Preference Formation

Some regulatory programs should be understood as an attempt to foster and promote diverse experiences, with a view toward providing broad opportunities for the formation of preferences and beliefs, and for distance from and critical scrutiny of existing desires. This rationale supports private ordering and freedom of contract as well. But it calls for regulatory safeguards when those forces push toward homogeneity and uniformity, as they often do in industrialized nations.

For example, the Prevention of Significant Deterioration (PSD) program of the Clean Air Act protects pristine areas from environmental degradation. The goal is to ensure that in a period of increasing urbanization and homogenization, federal law ensures the preservation of unspoiled areas. This goal would be a worthy one even if private preferences, as expressed in markets, would not protect such areas. The Endangered Species Act is a similar effort to ensure that current and future generations will be able to explore diverse species of animals and plants.

Regulation of broadcasting—subsidizing public broadcasting, ensuring a range of disparate programming, or calling for high-quality programming largely unavailable in the marketplace—can be understood in similar terms. Indeed, the need to provide diverse opportunities for preference formation suggests reasons to be quite skeptical of unrestricted markets in communication and broadcasting. There is a firm theoretical justification for the much criticized and now largely abandoned "fairness doctrine," which required broadcasters to cover controversial issues and to ensure competing views.[22] The fairness doctrine operated as an exceptionally mild corrective to a broadcasting market in which most viewers see shows that rarely deal with serious problems; are frequently sensationalistic, prurient, dehumanizing, or banal; reflect and perpetuate a bland, watered-down version of the most conventional views about politics and morality; are influenced excessively by the concerns of advertisers; and are sometimes riddled with violence, sexism, and racism. In view of the inevitable effects of such programming on character, beliefs, and even conduct, it is hardly clear that governmental "inaction" is always appropriate in a constitutional democracy; indeed the contrary seems true.

Social Subordination

Some regulatory statutes attempt not simply to redistribute resources, but to eliminate or reduce the social subordination of various social groups. Much of antidiscrimination law is designed as an attack on practices and beliefs that have adverse consequences for members of disadvantaged groups. Discriminatory attitudes and practices result in the social subordination of blacks, women, the handicapped, and gays and lesbians. Statutes designed to eliminate discrimination attempt to change both practices and attitudes. The motivating idea here is that differences that are irrelevant from the moral point of view ought not to be turned into social disadvantages,[23] and they certainly should not be permitted to do so if the disadvantage is systemic. In all of these cases, social practices turn differences into systemic harms for the relevant group. Such measures as the Equal Pay Act, the Civil Rights Act of 1964, and the Developmentally Disabled Assistance and Bill of Rights Act attempt to supply correctives. As we will see, measures of this sort might be seen as a fulfillment of constitutional duties imposed by the fifth amendment on the Congress; and this is so even if those duties are not enforced by constitutional courts.

It is sometimes suggested that market pressures are sufficient to counteract social subordination, and that statutory intervention is therefore unnecessary. Businesses that discriminate will ultimately face economic pressure from those that do not. The refusal to hire qualified blacks and women will result in competitive injury to discriminators, who will therefore face higher costs and ultimately be driven from the marketplace. This process is said to make markets a good check on discrimination and on caste systems.[24] Although such a process does occur in some settings, market pressures constitute, for several reasons, an inadequate constraint.

First, third parties might impose serious costs on those who agree to deal with members of disadvantaged groups; customers and others sometimes withdraw patronage or services. Consider, for example, the risks sometimes faced by firms that employ blacks, women, the disabled, and gays and lesbians. By their ability to impose costs, customers and others are well situated to prevent elimination of discriminatory practices. In these circumstances market pressures do not check discrimination, but instead guarantee that it will continue. A caste system of some sort is the predictable result. Undoubtedly such pressures have contributed to the perpetuation of discrimination in many settings.[25]

Second, discriminatory behavior is sometimes a response to generalizations or stereotypes that, although quite overbroad and even invidious, provide an economically rational basis for market decisions. Because the behavior is economically rational, not based on a competitively harmful racial animus, it will persist as long as markets do. For example, an employer might act discriminatorily not because he hates or devalues blacks or women, or has a general desire not to associate with them, or is "prejudiced" in the ordinary sense, but because he has found that the stereotypes have sufficient truth to be a basis for employment decisions. Of course it will be exceptionally difficult to disentangle these various attitudes, and they will frequently overlap; but in light of the history of discrimination against both blacks and women, it would hardly be shocking if stereotyping was sometimes economically rational.

This form of discrimination is objectionable not because it is a reflection of ordinary bigotry or even irrationality, but because it works to perpetuate the second-class citizenship of members of disadvantaged groups. Markets will do nothing about such discrimination; civil rights legislation reduces it. The example suggests that the line between antidiscrimination laws and affirmative action is far thinner than is generally believed.[26]

Third, private preferences of both beneficiaries and victims of discrimination tend to adapt to existing injustice, and to do so in such a way as to make significant change hard to undertake.[27] People often have a "taste" for discrimination, and one of the purposes of antidiscrimination law is to alter that taste. The beneficiaries of the status quo take advantage of strategies that reduce cognitive dissonance, such as blaming the victim. The victims also reduce dissonance by adapting their preferences to the available opportunities or by adapting their aspirations to fit their persistent belief that the world is just.[28] Psychological mechanisms of this sort furnish a formidable barrier to social change.

In a closely related phenomenon, members of disadvantaged groups faced with widespread discrimination on the part of employers may well respond to the relevant signals by deciding to invest less than other people in the acquisition of the skills valued by the market. Individual and group productivity is a function of demand; it is not independent of it. Members of a group that is the object of discrimination may therefore end up less productive, not only because their skin color or gender is devalued, but also because the market sends signals that it is less worthwhile for them to develop the skills necessary to compete.

Fourth, and most fundamentally, markets incorporate the practices and norms of the advantaged group. Conspicuous examples include the multiple ways in which employment settings, requirements, and expectations are structured for the able-bodied and for traditional male career patterns. In such cases, markets are the problem, not the solution. One goal of the advocates of antisubordination is to restructure market arrangements so as to put disadvantaged groups on a plane of equality—not by helping them to be "like" members of advantaged groups, but by changing the criteria themselves. A law cannot make it up to someone for being deaf or requiring a wheelchair; but it can aggravate or diminish the social consequences of deafness and lameness. Regulation requiring sign language and wheelchair ramps ensures that a difference is not turned into a systemic disadvantage. Here the conventional test of discrimination law—is the member of the disadvantaged group "similarly situated" to the member of the advantaged group?—itself reflects inequality, since it takes the norms and practices of the advantaged group as the baseline against which to measure inequality.[29]

Statutes protecting the handicapped are the best example here. To say this is not to suggest the nature or degree of appropriate restructuring of the market—a difficult question in light of the sometimes enormous costs of adaptation to the norms and practices of disadvantaged groups. But it is to say that markets are far from a sufficient protection against social subordination.

Endogenous Preferences

Some statutes interfere with market behavior when preferences are a function of, or endogenous to, legal rules, acts of consumption, or existing norms or practices. In these circumstances, the purpose of regulation is to affect the development of certain preferences. Regulation of addictive substances, of myopia, and of habits is a familiar example. For an addict, the costs of nonconsumption—of living without the good to which he is addicted—increase dramatically over time, as the benefits of consumption remain constant or fall sharply. The result is that the aggregate costs over time of consumption exceed the aggregate benefits, even if the initial consumption choice provides benefits that exceed costs. Behavior that is rational for each individual consumption choice may ultimately lead people into severely inferior social states. In such cases people would in all likelihood not want to become involved with the article of consumption in the first place. Regulation is a possible response.

Menahem Yaari offers the example of a group of traders attempting to induce alcoholism in an Indian tribe.[30] At the outset alcoholic beverages are not extremely valuable to consumers. The consumers are willing to buy only for a low price, which the traders willingly offer. But as a result of past consumption, the value of the beverages to the consumers steadily increases, to the point where they are willing to pay enormous sums for them. Thus the traders are able "to manoevre the Indian into a position where rationality conflicts with Pareto-efficiency, i.e., into a position where to be efficient is to be irrational and to be irrational is to be inefficient . . . The disadvantage, for an economic unit, of having endogenously changing tastes is that, even with perfect information and perfect foresight, the unit may find itself forced to follow an action which, by the unit's own standards, is Pareto-dominated."

Because of the effect of consumption, over time, on certain preferences, someone who is addicted to heroin is much worse off in the long run—even though the original decision to consume was not irrational if one looks only at immediate costs and benefits. Statutes that regulate addictive substances respond to a social belief that the relevant preferences should not be formed in the first place.

We might describe this situation as involving an intrapersonal collective action problem,[31] in which the costs and benefits of engaging in the relevant activity change dramatically over time for a particular individual. The central point is that consumption patterns induce a significant change in preferences. An addiction is the most obvious case, but it is part of a far broader category. Consider, for example, the sort of myopic behavior, defined as a refusal—because the short-term costs exceed the short-term benefits—to engage in activity having long-term benefits that dwarf long-term costs. Another kind of intrapersonal collective action problem is produced by habits people follow because of the subjectively high short-term costs of changing their behavior even when the long-term benefits exceed the short-term benefits. Akrasia, or weakness of the will, has a related structure,[32] and some laws respond to its individual or collective forms.

For the most part, problems of this sort are best addressed at the individual level or through private associations, which minimize coercion; but social regulation is a possible response. Statutes that subsidize the arts or public broadcasting, or that discourage the formation of some habits and encourage the formation of others, are illustrations. So too are legal requirements to install seatbelts or have people buckle them. The subjective costs of buckling decrease over time. Once people are in the habit of buckling, the costs become minimal. The fact that the costs shrink rapidly after the habit of buckling has formed counts in favor of regulation, certainly on welfare grounds, and perhaps on autonomy grounds as well.

Moreover, market behavior is sometimes based on an effort to reduce cognitive dissonance by adjusting to current practices and opportunities. The point has large implications. For example, workers may underestimate the risks of hazardous activity partly in order to reduce the dissonance that would be produced by an understanding of the real dangers of the workplace.[33] In these circumstances, regulation might produce gains in terms of both welfare and autonomy.

Similar ideas help account for antidiscrimination principles. Most generally, the beliefs of both beneficiaries and victims of existing injustice are affected by dissonance-reducing strategies.[34] The phenomenon of blaming the victim has distinct cognitive and motivational foundations. A central point here is that the strategy of blaming the victim, or assuming that an injury was deserved or inevitable, tends to permit nonvictims or members of advantaged groups to reduce dissonance by assuming that the world is just—a pervasive, insistent, and sometimes irrationally held belief.[35] The reduction of cognitive dissonance is a powerful motivational force, and it operates as a significant obstacle to the recognition of social injustice or irrationality.

Victims also participate in dissonance-reducing strategies, including the lowering of self-esteem to accommodate both the fact of victimization and the belief that the world is essentially just. Sometimes it appears easier to assume that one's suffering is warranted than that it has been imposed cruelly or by mere chance. Consider here the astonishing fact that after a draft lottery, many of those with both favorable and unfavorable results decided that the outcomes of the purely random process were deserved.[36] Blaming the victim also reflects the "hindsight effect," through which people unjustifiably perceive events as more predictable than they in fact were, and therefore suggest that victims or disadvantaged groups should have been able to prevent the negative outcome.[37]

There is suggestive evidence in the psychological literature to this effect. Some work here reveals that people who engage in cruel behavior change their attitudes toward the objects of their cruelty so as to devalue them; observers tend to do the same.[38] Such evidence bears on antidiscrimination law in general. Aspects of American labor and race discrimination law can be understood as a response to the basic problem of distorted beliefs and preferences.[39] There are implications here for sex discrimination as well. The movement for the elimination of sex discrimination is informed by an understanding that many women—as well as many men—have adapted to an unjust status quo.

Standing by itself, the observation that preferences are shifting and endogenous is hardly a sufficient reason for regulation. All preferences are to some degree dependent on existing law and current consumption patterns, and that cannot be a reason for government action without creating a license for tyranny. The argument for government action in the face of endogenous preferences must rely on a belief that welfare or autonomy will thereby be promoted. The most powerful cases here involve collective efforts to prevent addiction, to overcome myopia, and to eliminate practices that are the result of adaptation to an unjust status quo. A good prima facie case can be made that significant gains, in terms of welfare and autonomy, will result from programs designed to prevent addictive behavior, at least when information is absent. When preferences have adapted to the absence of available opportunities, there is a solid argument for collective action as well. Its actual content, however, will be controversial, and it probably should begin and usually end with efforts to provide information and to increase opportunities. Thus, for example, governmentally required disclosure of risks in the workplace is a highly plausible strategy. In a few cases, however, these milder strategies may be inadequate, and coercion is necessary.

The category of statutory responses to endogenous preferences overlaps with that of antisubordination statutes and measures that attempt to protect collective aspirations and noncommodity values. Antisubordination statutes, for example, are an effort to overcome interest-induced beliefs and adaptive preferences. Frequently aspirations form the basis for laws that attempt to influence processes of preference formation. For the most part, endogeneity of preferences does not stand alone, but is part of a complex argument for collective intervention.

Irreversibility, Future Generations, Animals, and Nature

Some statutes are a response to the problem of irreversibility—the fact that a certain course of conduct, if continued, will lead to an outcome from which current and future generations will be able to recover not at all, or only at very high cost. Since markets reflect the preferences of current consumers, they do not take account of the effect of transactions on future generations. The consequences of reliance on market ordering will sometimes be an irretrievable loss. The protection of endangered species stems in part from this fear. Much of the impetus behind laws protecting natural areas is that environmental degradation is sometimes final or extraordinarily expensive to repair. Protection of cultural relics stems from a similar rationale.

To a large degree, social and economic regulation of this sort is produced by a belief in obligations owed by the present to future generations. Current practices may produce losses that might be acceptable if no one else were affected, but that are intolerable in light of their consequences for those who will follow. Effects on future generations thus amount to a kind of externality.[40] Such externalities might include limitations in the available range of experiences or the elimination of potential sources of medicines and pesticides; consider the Endangered Species Act.

In more complex forms, arguments of this sort emphasize the multiple values of protecting species, animals, and nature. Some of these arguments are "anthrocentric," in the sense that they focus on the ultimate value of such protection to human beings. For example, many people enjoy seeing diversity in nature; and plants and animals furnish most of the raw materials for medicines, pesticides, and other substances with considerable instrumental worth to humanity. On this view, the loss or reduction of a species is a serious one for human beings. It is hard to monetize these values because of the difficulty of ascertaining, at any particular time, the many uses to which different species might be put.

A related but somewhat different argument emphasizes the value of natural diversity for the transformation of human values and for deliberation about the good. On this view, the preservation of diverse species and of natural beauty serves to alter existing preferences and provides an occasion for critical scrutiny of current desires and beliefs. Aesthetic experiences play an important role in shaping ideas and desires, and regulation may be necessary to ensure the necessary diversity.

On a different account, the elimination of a species, particular animals, and perhaps of waters and streams is objectionable quite apart from its effects on human beings, and indeed for its own sake. This

ular settings will be controversial. For purposes of categorization, the principal problem is to elaborate a full-fledged theory to distinguish between the various justifications discussed above on the one hand and interest-group transfers on the other. Theory and facts must be assembled to explain why (for example) regulation of broadcasting, public support for the arts, environmental controls, and antidiscrimination statutes are public-regarding whereas various banking controls and agricultural subsidies are simple responses to the power of self-interested private groups—if indeed these are the appropriate conclusions. If the discussion thus far is persuasive, it provides reasons to believe that the former measures are justified, at least in principle. The category of interest-group transfers should therefore be seen as a residual one, used for regulation that cannot be persuasively justified on independent grounds.

Sometimes the problem of identifying interest-group transfers is solved by treating the existing distribution of wealth, the existing set of preferences, and existing entitlements as exogenous variables. On this view, which has become prominent in the economic and public choice literature on regulation, any change of the status quo should be seen as the product of "rent-seeking."[43] In this context, rent-seeking might be defined as the dissipation of wealth through efforts to redistribute resources by way of politics, rather than the production of wealth through markets. Political activity designed to bring about change of the status quo is thus objectionable—even, perhaps, changes that result in deregulation or economic efficiency, and certainly if they redistribute resources. Rent-seeking is objectionable because it produces "dead-weight losses," in the form of expenditures on politics that should be used for productive activity. The intended meaning of rent-seeking, as applied to politics, is not entirely clear. At any rate it incorporates exceedingly peculiar ideas about the role of government. Even if it is sometimes useful for purposes of positive social science, it is hard to take seriously as a normative proposition, and for two separate reasons.

First, such a view would assimilate to the class of interest-group transfers a wide range of measures that are generally supported and easily justified. The very notion of redistribution (if it is used as a pejorative) depends on a belief that the existing distribution of property and entitlements should be taken as neutral and prelegal—in any case just. This position cannot be defended in light of the numerous ways in which existing distributions are a product of law, and in view

account itself takes various forms. Sometimes the argument is a democratic one: most people believe that obligations are owed to nonhuman objects, and the majority deserves to rule. Sometimes the invocation of the rights of nonhuman creatures and objects can best be understood as a rhetorical device designed to inculcate social norms that will overcome collective action problems in preserving the environment—problems that are ultimately harmful to human beings. In many hands, however, the argument, sounding in what is sometimes called "deep ecology," does not even refer to human desires. The idea here is that animals, species as such, and perhaps even natural objects warrant respect for their own sake, and quite apart from their interactions with human beings. Sometimes such arguments posit general rights held by living creatures (and natural objects) against human depredations. In especially powerful forms, these arguments are utilitarian in character, stressing the often extreme and unnecessary suffering of animals who are hurt or killed. The Animal Welfare Act reflects these concerns.

Interest-Group Transfers and "Rent-Seeking"

Many statutes result from efforts by self-interested private groups to redistribute wealth in their favor. Purportedly public-spirited regulation in fact helps narrow or parochial interests, a topic taken up in some detail in Chapter 3. Considerable work in the public choice tradition has explored structural characteristics of the legislative process that aggravate this effect. Collective action problems and opportunities for strategic behavior are principal culprits here. Above all, groups that are able to organize at minimal cost can exert disproportionate influence on legislators. Relatively diffuse and unorganized groups are frequently unable to counteract their power.

Interest-group transfers, by definition, do not serve the public welfare on any plausible view. Many aspects of the extensive network of federal controls of the banking industry are hard to understand as anything other than an effort to protect banks from competition; consider the prohibition on interstate and branch banking.[41] The public is the loser. The enormous federal subsidies, direct and indirect, to large agricultural interests belong in the same category.[42] Regulation of the transportation industry, now substantially reduced in the United States, was originally justified on flimsy public interest grounds; in fact it created partial cartels at public expense.

The same is true of other programs, though conclusions in partic-

of the powerful moral criticisms directed at those distributions from a wide variety of foundations. And we have seen that the New Deal reformation represented a societal rejection of the view that all forms of redistribution should be taken as a whole, and condemned as such.

Second, the notion of rent-seeking rejects, as unproductive, nearly all of the basic workings of politics. It treats citizenship itself as an evil. Efforts to enact public aspirations, to counteract discrimination, to protect the environment—all these are seen as the diversion of productive energies into a wasteful place. This view represents a peculiar reversal of the liberal tradition, which has seen political behavior not as an evil, but as an important arena for education, for deliberation and discussion about the nation's direction, for the development of the faculties, and for the cultivation of aspirations and feelings of altruism.[44] On all of these scores, the liberal tradition remains extremely vibrant in the United States; and it continues to describe a wide range of individual and collective behavior. It would of course be foolish to deny that much political conduct is wasteful or an effort to use governmental power to serve selfish ends. But to collapse all political behavior into the category of objectionable rent-seeking is grotesquely to devalue the activities of citizenship.

The Problem of Categorization

It is possible, then, to connect regulatory statutes to a variety of identifiable rationales for disruption of market ordering, and regulation in modern liberal democracies tends to include a relatively small number of categories. For this reason, regulatory statutes should not be treated either as an undifferentiated whole or as a series of highly particularistic intrusions into a general backdrop set by the common law. Moreover, the contemporary legal fabric in liberal democracies owes more to the various understandings I have set out than it does to pre-New Deal notions of private right or to common law standards—a fact that, as we will see, has not entirely made its way into contemporary public law.

It should also be clear, however, that the appropriate nature and scope of regulation cannot be decided on without knowing a good deal about the facts, including above all the practical effects of various regulatory strategies (discussed in Chapter 3). Moreover, the problem of characterization is not always a simple one, and many statutes fall quite plausibly into more than one category. How are we to categorize statutes that might be thought to fit within one or another category?

The answer will vary with the purpose of the question. One approach would be to look to effects. A statute apparently designed to bring about public-interested redistribution might in fact distribute resources to well-organized groups. A statute defended as a means of promoting public aspirations might serve in reality as an interest-group transfer that is difficult to justify on any view.

Another approach might attempt to characterize statutes by asking the value-laden question about what is the best—most attractive—conception of the statutory scheme.[45] Thus, for example, the toxic substances provision of the Occupational Safety and Health Act might be characterized as a response to lack of information on the part of workers if that characterization made the best sense of the provision, and if other understandings appeared less defensible to those attempting to make a characterization.

Yet another approach would rely on the reasons explicitly invoked by public officials for legislative action. Thus statutes could be characterized by reference to the legislative purpose, broadly defined. As we will see, this is a problematic concept, but perhaps purpose could be derived from an examination of the problems and forces that gave rise to the measure and the relevant legislative history.

A related but distinct approach would attempt to explain the actual rather than articulated motivations for legislative behavior, focusing, for example, on the roles of relevant interest groups. Here the goal would be to generate predictions about the circumstances in which social and economic regulation is forthcoming, and the shape that it is likely to take. The purpose of the characterization would be to understand the forces and pressures, often perhaps objectionable or morally neutral, that gave rise to the statute. Much of economic analysis of legislation follows this strategy.

A final option would depend neither on statutory purposes nor on effects, but more fundamentally on the broadest view about the proper tasks of government in a liberal democracy. Here the effort is to develop and apply first principles about the regulatory state. This approach is taken both by those defending statutes designed to protect social aspirations and by many of those assimilating much social and economic regulation to the class of "rent-seeking."

There is a place for all of these approaches, and as I have noted, their applicability depends on the purpose for which the task of categorization is undertaken. For present purposes, it is unnecessary to deal with the alternatives in much detail. I have attempted to portray the functions of regulation in a way that suggests that a wide array of governmental programs can be justified by reference to quite conventional understandings of social welfare and individual or collective autonomy. But whether or not the portrayal is persuasive, the issue is considerably simplified for courts and agencies dealing with questions of interpretation. Both administrators and judges face institutional constraints that argue powerfully against some of these approaches. For example, an assessment of regulation from first principles is beyond the appropriate province of the executive and judicial branches. In a constitutional democracy, courts have no warrant for categorizing statutes as (say) interest-group transfers merely because they disagree with the legislature's desire to protect (say) collective aspirations. The task of interpretation calls for sympathetic engagement with the modern regulatory state, not for the use of principles conspicuously rejected by the rise of regulation—an idea with significant implications for judicial and administrative practice. Similarly, effects may be relevant to interpretation for many purposes, but it would be most peculiar for courts to make interpretive strategies depend crucially on complex, case-by-case empirical inquiries for which the judiciary is ill-suited. The same concerns argue against a judicial effort to explain regulation in terms of its causes; this is a difficult task for which courts lack the necessary tools.

For the most part, then, interpretive approaches should be based on sympathetic engagement with the statute, putting it in its most favorable light. Often, of course, there will be ambiguity here; one of the goals of what follows is to give more content to this claim. The inquiry into regulatory function will not simply be a reconstruction of the facts, but instead a product of an inescapably normative inquiry into what sort of problem the statute is most sensibly understood as addressing, and how the problem can most sensibly be resolved. But in many cases regulatory statutes—viewed sympathetically as they must be in courts in a constitutional democracy—will fit quite naturally in one or another category. We will return to this point in further chapters.

CHAPTER

3

How Regulation Fails

To say that the modern regulatory state has a certain coherence and rationality, or that it responds to persuasive conceptions of autonomy and welfare, is not to say that it has been a complete or even partial success. Theoretical justifications are one thing; reform in the real world is another. Indeed, it has become fashionable in recent years to argue that social and economic regulation has been generally unsuccessful, imposing large costs for uncertain or nonexistent gains.[1]

Such conclusions are far too crude. The regulatory state has not been a failure. On the contrary, regulatory statutes have brought about significant improvements in a variety of areas, including the environment, energy conservation, automobile safety, endangered species, and discrimination on the basis of race and sex. At the same time, however, some statutes have produced benefits that are dwarfed by the costs, had unanticipated adverse side effects, or have in any case been far less successful than their advocates had hoped. Moreover, the entire area is pervaded by what we might call *paradoxes of regulation:* regulatory strategies that are self-defeating in the sense that they bring about results precisely opposite to those that are intended.

As we will see, many forms of regulatory failure implicate original constitutional goals. The lack of coordination in the executive branch; the absence of political deliberation or accountability; the influence of factional power and self-interested representation—these problems of the regulatory state suggest that it has fallen prey to a number of dangers against which the founding document was designed to guard.

My goals in this chapter are to give some examples of regulatory success; to provide a brief diagnosis of the sources and nature of regulatory failure; and to connect that failure to the confrontation between modern regulatory institutions and the constitutional regime. I conclude by suggesting a number of reforms for the regulatory state.

Severe difficulties stand in the way of those who would assess the real-world consequences of regulation. The most fundamental difficulty is that even if the facts could be accurately established, one person's failure might be another's success. Moreover, it is hard to develop criteria for distinguishing between the two. A few examples will explain the point. If the toxic substances provisions of the Occupational Safety and Health Act are thought by some observers to impose huge costs for trivial gains, administrative inaction will, for them, represent the best possible outcome. Enforcement of the civil rights laws that lead to strict racial quotas will, for some, represent a conspicuous failure. More broadly, if agencies fail to enforce regulatory statutes because they deplore the misconceptions, poor value judgments, or private interest-group deals that underlie them, government inaction might well be deemed a success from the standpoint of the public interest.

Conversely, if Congress intended the Interstate Commerce Act to create a cartel helping railroads to increase prices and decrease quality at the expense of consumers and the economy as a whole, perhaps conduct by the ICC that achieves precisely that goal constitutes success. If Congress intends statutes to be unprincipled efforts to transfer resources from one group to another, regulation might be successful even if it does not—indeed, precisely because it does not—benefit the public as a whole.

A judgment about success or failure will depend, then, on a view about the appropriate goals and scope of regulation. Even if a consensus were achieved on that question, extremely serious methodological problems would remain. Above all, efforts to estimate the costs and benefits of regulation have led to sharp disputes of both value and fact. Should the measurement be based on private willingness to pay for regulatory goods? If so, it will be necessary to decide whether we should look to the willingness of the beneficiaries to pay for regulation (the "offer price") or instead to what the beneficiaries will require to relinquish regulatory protection (the "asking price"). There could be a substantial difference between offer and asking prices. Employees might, for example, require an enormous sum before they give up a right to a certain level of safety, even though they would not be willing to pay nearly so much to obtain that right in the first place.

Even if this problem were resolved, it would be necessary to decide whether the willingness-to-pay criterion should be controlling. That criterion might well be questioned in light of its crudeness as a proxy for utility, its inevitable dependence on ability to pay, the controversial use of it to value life and health, and its vulnerability, discussed in chapters 1 and 2, to a variety of moral objections. Unfortunately, rejection of the willingness-to-pay criterion leaves no obvious alternative, so the calculation of costs and benefits will remain as difficult as ever.

Additional problems plague efforts to assess the costs and, even more, the benefits of regulation. In many cases it is difficult to make confident statements about causation. Scientific uncertainty is pervasive in this context. Postregulation decreases in accident and death rates may, for example, be attributable to factors other than regulatory controls. It is necessary to look at (among other things) economic, industrial, and demographic trends preceding regulatory intervention. Moreover, it is extremely hard to control for possible confounding variables.

Regulation might also have a range of ancillary or incidental costs and benefits that must be taken into account, but that are easy to disregard and difficult to measure. For example, the introduction of seat belts might make drivers less careful and thus produce an increase in injuries to pedestrians;[2] or the control of new sources of pollution might keep old, dirty sources on the market for especially long periods. On the benefit side, the government's requirement of technological development to control pollution might spur valuable advances in other areas as well. It is hard to hold everything else constant in attempting to measure the impact of regulation.

Notwithstanding these disclaimers, it is possible to make some general comparisons between the state of the world postregulation and its likely state if regulation had never been introduced. Moreover, uniform measurements of costs and benefits might yield a sense of how various regulatory programs compare with one another. And while the conclusions are not uncontested, an approach of this sort reveals that some regulation has produced significant benefits. I offer a few examples here.

The United States faced an enormous problem of air and water pollution in the 1960s, posing a variety of short-term and long-term threats to safety and health. Largely as a result of environmental controls in the 1960s and 1970s, the problem has been substantially reduced. Statutory programs have resulted in decreases in most of the important air pollutants. Early studies suggested savings from the Clean Air Act of between $5.1 to $15.9 billion as a result of reduced mortality, and of $28.4 to $58.1 billion from reduced morbidity.[3] One study found annual health benefits in 1978 of $5.1 to $16 billion as a result of a 60% reduction in air pollution in urban areas with a total population of 150 million.[4] These studies, now quite old, undoubtedly underestimate the benefits because they disregard the large gains since 1980.

Although the problems of measurement produce severe methodological difficulties, progress since that time appears to have increased. Over 2,600 of the 3,151 counties in the United States are now in compliance with air quality goals. Between 1975 and 1986 regulation has contributed to large decreases in pollution of the air by sulfur dioxide, carbon monoxide, ozone, lead, and nitrogen dioxide. The national Pollution Standard Index reveals dramatic downward trends in air pollution. These reductions are partly attributable to federal controls on emissions of carbon monoxide from automobiles and pollutants that contribute to ozone. National ambient concentrations of the most serious pollutants have all significantly decreased.[5]

In 1975, for example, 54.2 million metric tons of carbon monoxide were emitted from highway vehicles, a figure that by 1984 had been reduced by 59.2%, to 41.4 million. The aggregate decreases are quite dramatic: total suspended particulate levels decreased 20% between 1975 and 1986, while emissions were reduced by about a third; annual mean sulfur dioxide concentrations have declined 36%, with emissions decreasing by 17%; carbon monoxide emissions have decreased by 25%; nitrogen oxide levels decreased by 10%.

Although the reduction of water pollution is far less impressive than that of air pollution, here too there have been important advances. The five Great Lakes are substantially cleaner than they were in 1965, when hundreds of lake beaches had to be closed. Governmental efforts are largely responsible. Thus, for example, phosphorus loadings into Lake Michigan were cut nearly in half, from 6,656 to 3,956 metric tons between 1976 and 1985; in Lake Ontario, the decrease in the same period was from 12,695 to 7,083 metric tons. Similar patterns can be found for the other lakes. Even more dramatic is the extraordinary reduction in levels of DDT, PCB, and dieldrin contaminants in Great Lake fish in the same period—for example, the PCB level in Lake Michigan trout declined from 18.68 parts per million in 1976 to 4.48 in 1984, and DDT levels in Lake Michigan salmon decreased from 14.03 in 1970, to 4.48 in 1973, to 0.19 in 1984. Many rivers are also substantially cleaner, including the Potomac, the Hudson, and parts of the Mississippi. Certain harmful nutrients, including phosphate and sewage-borne bacteria, have been reduced by 46% nationally.

The minimum treatment requirements of the Clean Water Act have significantly expanded secondary sewage treatment, from 85 million plants in 1972 to 127 million plants in 1986. These plants remove at least 80% of suspended solids and oxygen-depleting substances. Effluent discharges from pulp and paper mills were reduced by more than half from 1974 to 1984. In general, the Clean Water Act has produced improvements in water quality through reductions in nitrates, lead, and other substances.[6]

Other areas of environmental controls show large gains. There have been huge reductions in emissions of hydrocarbons and nitrogen oxides, although the aggregate miles driven have substantially increased. Lead emissions from almost all sources have been dramatically lowered. In transportation, lead emissions were reduced from 122.6 million metric tons in 1975 to 3.5 in 1986; in industrial processes, from 10.3 to 1.9; in total, from 147 to 8.6—truly impressive improvements. Ambient concentrations of lead declined by over 85% between 1975 and 1986, with a 78% reduction in the use of lead in gasoline as a result of regulation between 1977 and 1982 alone. The percentage of DDT in body fat has declined by 79%; mercury in lake sediments is 80% lower; PCBs in body fat have been cut by 75%. Protection of endangered and threatened species, and of wildlife in general, has increased as a result of regulatory controls.[7] Many species of birds that had become almost extinct as a result of DDT and other pesticides have begun to reproduce at a healthy rate; these include the bald eagle and the brown pelican.

Most generally, the health and safety problems resulting from industrial pollution have been significantly reduced. To say this is emphatically not to deny that extremely serious environmental problems remain. Aggressive regulatory controls will be necessary to deal with such problems as solid waste disposal, hazardous substances, and water pollution. With respect to air pollution, there has been significant noncompliance with federal standards. Much of the country is in violation of federal health standards for carbon monoxide, ozone, and particulates.[8] A high ozone level, contributing to smog, is a particular problem. The government has only begun to deal with the problem of acid deposition, and long-term issues involving destruction of the ozone layer and the greenhouse effect remain in the most preliminary of regulatory stages. Cleanup work on the nearly 1,000 abandoned hazardous waste dumps in the United States has barely started. No more than 1,500 of the 70,000 registered and potentially toxic chemical compounds have been completely tested. Oil spills and hazardous waste spills have been increasing in both numbers and volume, from, for example, 57 spills producing .85 million pounds of hazardous waste in 1977 to 1,433 spills producing 3.80 million pounds in 1984. Over half of all water pollution, produced by 65,000 industrial polluters and by run-off from farms and streets, is substantially uncontrolled. But environmental problems would be far worse if not for the environmental regulation of the 1970s.

In the area of automobile safety, the initiatives of the late 1960s and early 1970s produced significant gains as well, often at relatively low cost. Some estimates show that highway fatalities would have been about 40% greater in 1983 without automobile safety regulation—an impressive illustration of regulatory success.[9] Automobiles are substantially safer for occupants, with one estimate of total benefits of $10.59 billion per year (in 1981 dollars), including reduced deaths and injuries.[10] Between 1966 and 1974, 28,000 lives were saved as a result of a series of occupant protection standards.[11] Both the seatbelt requirement and the fifty-five mile per hour speed limit significantly reduced deaths and injuries from accidents. Improvements can also be attributed to head restraints, energy-absorbing steering columns, and interior protection and windshield requirements.

The general record of the Consumer Product Safety Commission is quite poor, but according to one estimate, crib safety regulations have reduced crib-related infant injuries by 44%; and drug packaging rules prevented 34,000 injuries as a result of accidental drug ingestion between 1973 and 1976 alone.[12] As we will see, the record of the Occupational Safety and Health Administration has been the farthest thing from a universal success in light of the high costs and relatively low benefits of much of its activity. But a number of OSHA initiatives have proved beneficial: its regulation of asbestos, for example, saves an estimated 396 lives per year.[13] There is also evidence, though it is contested, of gains from safety regulation.[14] Total domestic energy consumption decreased from 78.90 to 74.26 quadrillion Btu in the period from 1979 to 1986, despite substantial increases in population, automobiles, and other likely sources of energy consumption; the decrease is at least partly attributable to federal efforts to promote energy conservation.

In the area of racial discrimination major benefits are manifest as well. The Voting Rights Act of 1965 has broken up the white monopoly on electoral processes in many states. In the eleven southern states, the number of registered blacks increased from 1.5 million to 2.8 million—an increase of almost 90%—only two years after passage of the Act. A large part of the increase is unquestionably attributable to the statute. No comparable increase appeared at any time before its enactment.

The Civil Rights Act of 1964 has produced significant gains in overcoming discrimination in both education and employment.[15] Here the results are disputed, but the economic achievement of blacks shows great improvements relative to whites, and statistical measures show a clear shift after 1964.[16] An early study suggested that federal pressures raised black male employment in specific companies by 12.9%;[17] other studies show increases of between 5.6% and 10.4%.[18] Moreover, and strikingly, the gains in the relative income of blacks did not erode as a result of the severe recession in the mid-seventies.[19]

These improvements appear attributable in large part to changes in educational and personnel policy brought about by government action in the employment market. In the view of one observer, antidiscrimination policies "have revolutionized personnel and employment selection practices. Unless company personnel policies are totally ineffective or a complete sham, there would appear to be a substantial upward shift in demand for black labor as a result of these changes."[20]

A dramatic recent study of the manufacturing sector of South Carolina shows that the proportion of black employees grew rapidly in 1965. Notably, the share of blacks had remained constant between 1910 and 1965 despite a wide range of changes in the relevant market. "Suddenly in 1965 the black share in employment begins to improve when Title VII legislation becomes effective and the Equal Employment Opportunity Commission begins to press textile firms to employ blacks and when Executive Order 11246 forbids discrimination by government contractors at the risk of forfeit of government business." [21] Other explanations for the change seem weak.

Studies of Executive Order 11246, requiring affirmative action and nondiscrimination by those who contract with the federal government, show especially large effects.[22] The prospect of federal enforcement activity has dramatically altered employer practices in a range of areas. Similar gains occurred in combating discrimination on the basis of sex and disability.[23] The evidence shows favorable effects on both the earnings and occupational position of women. Moreover, there have been dramatic increases in the representation of female workers in firms subject to reporting requirements from the Equal Employment Opportunity Commission.

More generally, even conventional studies of the costs and benefits of regulatory initiatives often show considerable success. To be sure, one must be cautious about the estimates here, but one examination of fifty-seven lifesaving programs revealed that thirteen programs had net costs of *zero*. This finding means that the gains from greater health and associated savings—entirely apart from lives saved—justified the costs. The significant gains in reduced mortality were therefore costless.[24] These programs included initiatives by the National Highway Traffic Safety Administration, including roadside hazard removal, the fifty-five mile per hour speed limit, and vehicle inspection. Also in this category were mandatory smoke detectors, parts of the 1970 Clean Air Act standards, and clothing flammability controls. Many programs required extremely low expenditures per life saved, with twenty-four programs saving a life at the cost of $300,000 or much less. Here too automobile regulation is especially well represented. (See Appendix B.)

The regulatory process has not, however, always produced good results. Often statutes are poorly designed; sometimes they aggravate the very problem they are intended to solve; at times they are under-enforced or have unanticipated consequences; they may do much less good than they should; they impose costs that exceed any benefits. Consider, for example, that between 1972 and 1985 the United States spent a total of no less than $632 billion for pollution control. Regulation of the environment is much more costly than it might be. Some studies suggest that the least-cost solution—discussed in some detail below and involving incentive systems in the place of command and control regulation—could produce the same results at more than a 400% decrease in cost.[25] Almost all studies show huge wasted resources in pollution control. At the same time, many environmental problems have only begun to be met at all, including regulation of pesticides and other toxic substances.

Emissions and safety regulation of automobiles has produced an increase in cost of between $1,200 and $2,200 (in 1981 dollars) per vehicle.[26] Automotive emissions controls have yielded benefits estimated at $0.3 billion annually, and perhaps exceeding $5 billion, but they cost probably over $15 billion per year. The program's exclusive focus on new vehicles has produced a range of harmful unanticipated consequences, including lower replacement of old vehicles and automobiles whose emissions performance deteriorates quickly over time.

The EPA's fuel economy standards have produced uncertain gains in light of the fact that manufacturers were moving in any case to smaller and more efficient cars. The program appears to have had few beneficial effects and indeed has caused significant losses in lives as a result of producing more dangerous vehicles. Much regulation of the airline industry was decidedly harmful; it led to both higher costs and less convenience.[27] Likewise, the regulation of trucking and related industries created a cartel benefiting companies at the expense of the public at large.

The Consumer Product Safety Commission issued only three standards in its first four years, and consumer product-related injuries requiring emergency medical treatment increased by 44% in its first five years. The commission has often imposed large costs for speculative gains.[28] Perhaps most egregious of all, by delaying and preventing many valuable drugs from getting on the market, the Food and Drug Administration has sometimes impaired safety and health and has had serious adverse effects on innovation and research as well.[29]

Much of the work of the Occupational Safety and Health Administration has also been ineffective. For example, OSHA's vinyl chloride regulation saves about one life a year, at a cost of no less than $40 million.[30] OSHA's extremely elaborate (and essentially unenforced) design standards for the workplace have sometimes had little real effect in increasing workplace safety.[31] On the other hand, OSHA does not regulate at all a number of toxic substances, including carcinogens, that pose significant risks.[32] Similarly, discrimination against blacks and women has persisted against the background of inadequate regulatory controls.

Perhaps worst of all, much of the so-called economic regulation of the last few decades has had perverse consequences. Overall, airline regulation produced overcharges probably amounting to several billion dollars per year; and new competition, which would have benefited consumers, was discouraged. In transportation generally, deregulation has been a substantial success, significantly reducing prices and costs, increasing convenience, rewarding efficient firms, and doing all this without producing overall decreases in safety or quality of service.

The Natural Gas Act, allowing government control of prices of gas, might well have caused and certainly worsened the dangerous gas shortages of the late 1970s. In this period hundreds of thousands of jobs were lost; industrial production was scaled back; businesses transferred to the south to find fuel; and gas supply was reduced for millions of Americans. All this was largely a result of severe government control of interstate prices, which led producers not to search for new gas at all, and of a system that created artificially low prices for old gas and thus produced significant shortages. Here too deregulation, in the form of a return to market ordering, is a large success. In many cases of economic regulation, the rationale for governmental controls is weak, and such controls have often been implemented in such a way as to make things worse rather than better.

All this should suffice to show that even when it is possible to identify a good reason for statutory intervention, governmental regulation may not be successful. The statutory solution might be poorly designed, producing a "government failure" parallel to or more costly than the market failure that gave rise to regulation in the first instance.

Even when well designed by the legislature, statutes can be subverted in the implementation process. Ignorance, misdiagnosis, poor incentives for administrators, misunderstanding of the market, and pressures from powerful private groups incline enforcement of the law in unproductive or perverse directions. A wide range of empirical work shows that regulatory programs have often failed even in cases when the prima facie case for government intervention is quite powerful.[33]

For reasons explored above, the claim that a regulatory statute has failed, like the claim that it has succeeded, cannot be solely empirical and descriptive. A claim of failure must depend on some view about the nature of a well-functioning regulatory regime, and such views are controversial. For present purposes, I will assume that statutes are successful to the extent that they carry out the basic goals described in Chapter 2, and do so at the lowest possible cost. I will treat as a failure a statute that does not carry out any such purpose; that does so with significant perverse side-effects; that has costs that dwarf benefits on any plausible view of both; or that embodies an interest-group deal not defensible in terms of public-regarding purposes.

In order to disaggregate the various reasons for statutory failure, it will be useful to distinguish between failures that inhere in the original statute and failures that are attributable to poor implementation. As we will see, both forms of failure recall original constitutional themes, including federalism, checks and balances, unity in the executive branch, and the risks posed by self-interested private groups and public officials themselves.

Failures in the Original Statute

Regulatory failure often results from mistakes on the part of the enacting legislature. Faithful implementation of a bad statute will inevitably make things worse rather than better. No matter how able and well-motivated, administrators cannot be successful unless they decide not to enforce the law at all. In other cases, faithful implementation of regulatory statutes will lead to some social improvements, but it will also impose unnecessary costs, create ancillary irrationality or injustice, or confer benefits significantly lower than a well-functioning regulatory system would produce. A number of problems fall in this category.

Interest-Group Transfers

Statutes that amount to private wealth transfers should be understood as failures per se. By hypothesis, such statutes do not promote a public purpose, whether characterized in terms of redistribution, economic productivity, social aspirations, or otherwise. When statutes fall in this category—as noted, a difficult question—the only issue is the amount of the damage.

Frequently the decision to create a regulatory program cannot be treated as a mere interest-group transfer, because there is a genuine problem with relying on the market, yet the content and reach of the program are adversely affected by the power of well-organized private groups. Regulation of the environment provides many examples. Consider, for example, the subtitle of a recent book on the subject: *How the Clean Air Act Became a Multibillion Dollar Bail-out for High-Sulfur Fuel Producers.*[34] The book demonstrates that certain provisions of the Clean Air Act were far more costly and far less effective than they might have been, because of a peculiar alliance between environmental groups and Eastern high-sulfur coal producers. The basic question was whether to rely on clean, low-sulfur coal (most of it Western) or to impose technological requirements on all coal producers. The dirty coal-clean air alliance produced an exceptionally expensive "scrubbing" requirement for new sources of coal.

This requirement was designed to and did in fact put Western, low-sulfur coal producers at a serious economic disadvantage, by forcing them to scrub their already clean coal with the same technology required of dirty Eastern producers. The consequences of the program were to prevent the (entirely sensible) use of low-sulfur fuel as an antipollution strategy; to ensure that regulation would not be a result of an inquiry into how to clean the air at the lowest possible cost; to create large financial incentives to keep existing dirty plants on the market as long as possible because of the stringent scrubbing requirements for new plants; and to deflect attention from the problem of acid deposition. All this produced a series of additional threats to the environment. The scrubbing program accomplished the unusual feat of increasing environmental degradation, at least in some parts of the country, while imposing large economic costs.

The power of well-organized interests is also reflected in the Prevention of Significant Deterioration (PSD) program of the Clean Air Act. The PSD program is designed to ensure that in all parts of the country existing air quality will not be made worse by additional pollution. This is a salutary goal, especially insofar as it protects beautiful or pristine areas from degradation. But the program was sponsored, molded, and expanded not by environmentalists, but by Eastern interests seeking to prevent the exodus of their own industries to clean areas. The program emerged from a heated regional battle in which Eastern interests sought to retain industrial polluters, in especially dirty areas, as against clean air regions attempting to attract business.[35]

All in all, the PSD program is not a sensible antipollution scheme. The exodus of dirty industries from dirty areas to clean ones is in some settings a low-cost and quite appropriate strategy for reducing pollution in the most heavily polluted areas. Probably the PSD program should be limited to the protection of currently pristine areas; it should not prevent all deterioration in relatively clean but not pristine areas so long as the deterioration does not prevent those areas from maintaining a safe and healthful environment.

Other areas of regulation also reflect the problem of interest-group power. The OSHA statute's draconian provision for regulation of toxic substances, producing costs not plausibly commensurate with the benefits, is in part a consequence of the lobbying efforts of unions. Similar problems are at work in the civil rights context, where employer pressure produced a variety of severe procedural limitations on private enforcement actions. A final and especially pernicious example, characteristic of modern regulatory law, is the stringent regulation of new environmental or occupational risks, combined with minimal regulation of existing risks. This approach not only perpetuates old risks but also insulates current industries from new entry; it should come as no surprise that it has proved so popular. Bizarrely, the focus on new risks turns regulatory controls into a device for immunizing existing industries from fresh competition.

Misdiagnosis and Poor Policy Analysis

Sometimes statutes fail because they are based on a misdiagnosis of the problem, on poor policy analysis, or on inadequate information. Difficulties of this sort are especially likely to occur when Congress is responding rapidly to a single event or to an intense but short-term public outcry—involving anecdotes rather than sustained analysis— or when it attempts to legislate with great particularity in technically complex areas.

Automobile Emissions. Regulation of exhaust emissions suffered because of haste and complexity.[36] The regulation was a rapid response to widespread publicity about air pollution, producing a kind of public panic. The consequence was the 1970 Clean Air Act Amendments, which included rigid "technology-forcing" legislation designed to reduce emissions of hydrocarbons and carbon monoxide by 95% between 1968 and 1975, and to reduce nitrogen oxide emissions by 90% between 1970 and 1976. The relevant deadlines proved impossible to meet, and manufacturers responded in part by producing cars that were quite expensive, performed poorly on the road, were far worse than their predecessors in terms of fuel economy, and whose antipollution devices deteriorated sharply over the life of the vehicles. One consequence of the increased cost of new vehicles was that old, relatively dirty cars continued on the roads for an especially long period. The aggregate costs of the program were high, exceeding $10 billion per year. To be sure, the program did have a substantial impact on emissions levels, but the resulting regime was only modestly successful in cleaning the ambient air. By almost any measure, the program was poorly conceived.

More generally, regulatory programs have been impaired by three pervasive forms of poor policy analysis: a reliance on command-and-control rather than more flexible strategies that allow for market incentives; a refusal to take account of the side-effects of apparently salutary regulation; and a failure to match regulatory function with regulatory strategy.

Command and Control and the Unsuccessful BAT. Congress has often employed command-and-control strategies to accomplish various regulatory goals, most notably to clean the air and water. Command-and-control strategies seek to direct private behavior through centralized national bureaucracies. Often they require all or most industries to adopt inflexible, legally identified methods of achieving compliance within specified times.

In the environmental area, command-and-control approaches typically take the form of regulatory requirements of the "best available technology" (BAT) for pollution sources. It is important to acknowledge that such approaches, focused on means of pollution reduction rather than the goal of clean air and water, have some advantages. For administrators, they have the large virtue of easy and simple application. But they also have multiple defects, and the defects far outweigh the advantages.[37]

An important problem with technology-based strategies is that they ignore the enormous differences among plants and industries and among geographical areas. In view of these differences, uniform technological requirements are exceptionally inefficient. It makes no sense to require the same technology in diverse areas—regardless of whether they are polluted or clean, populated or empty, or expensive or cheap to clean up. Antipollution strategies should be more finely tuned to variations in the costs and benefits of antipollution strategies in different contexts. Perversely, BAT strategies also impose enormous burdens of enforcement and information-gathering on a centralized federal agency.

By requiring all new industries to adopt costly technology, BAT strategies penalize new products, thus discouraging investment and perpetuating old, dirty production; they also fail to encourage new pollution control technology and indeed actually discourage it by requiring its adoption for no financial gain. The BAT approach also inhibits the government from developing a sensible system of setting priorities, since it requires regulation of whatever pollutants happen to get on the agenda, and aggravates the problem of bureaucratic inaction by requiring stringent regulation for possibly little advantage. This is additional confirmation of the view, noted above, that overregulation produces underregulation.

There is considerable evidence that the government could accomplish its antipollution goals far more effectively through decentralized, incentive-based strategies that are focused on pollution reduction rather than on the means of achieving that end, and that also rely on market incentives.[38] Government might, for example, require polluters to pay for the right to pollute, and then allow them to trade that right. Such a strategy would encourage the development of antipollution technology and at the same time ensure that pollution abatement will be undertaken by those who can do it most cheaply. Recent years have seen considerable movement in this direction.[39]

Similar problems have developed in the area of occupational safety and health, where regulations have imposed detailed standards for workplace design, compiled in no less than 4,000 industry standards taking up 250 pages of the Federal Register. At one point the relevant standards governed the shape of toilet seats and the precise height of fire extinguishers; over 900 have been repealed on the ground that they were unrelated to job risks. Moreover, many standards are haphazardly enforced. OSHA would have done far better to concentrate on employers' performance in promoting safety rather than on uniform design standards.

Side-Effects. Often regulation has unintended adverse side-effects. The Delaney Clause, prohibiting all carcinogens in food additives, is a conspicuous example. The Clause prohibits the FDA from permitting a food additive as safe "if it is found to induce cancer when ingested by man or animal, or if it is found, after tests which are appropriate for the evaluation of the safety of food additives, to induce cancer in man or animal." Because some carcinogens are quite weak, the ban has led in two unfortunate directions. Vastly improved modern detection techniques prevent basically safe but carcinogenic substances from coming on the market, whereas cruder and older technology used to test previously authorized substances allowed them to be approved; the result is less rather than more safety. Moreover, some producers use food additives that are actually more dangerous than low-risk carcinogenic substances. For this reason the Clause may well cause more deaths than it prevents. Another example is the environmental strategies of the 1960s and 1970s which, by focusing on levels of pollution in the ambient air, encouraged industries to use techniques that put pollutants high in the atmosphere, thus contributing to acid deposition.

Mismatch of Regulation to Problem. Sometimes Congress will respond to a genuine problem in the private market with a regulatory tool that is ill-matched to it. To speak in rough and general terms, natural monopoly is most sensibly controlled through cost-of-service ratemaking; externalities are best regulated with incentive systems that rely on the marketplace; anticompetitive behavior should be handled through the antitrust laws; in the presence of inadequate information, disclosure and screening are the best responses.[40] But in many areas Congress has designed regulatory strategies that are not linked to the particular market breakdowns that it is attempting to remedy.

For example, the government responded to problems in the airline industry—which should have been controlled through the antitrust laws—with price and allocation controls. This strategy led to excessive costs, high profits for the industry, and a range of inconveniences and other disadvantages to consumers. As we have seen, the command-and-control strategies typical of the environmental area are inferior to approaches that take advantage of the flexibility of market systems. Natural gas regulation was undertaken through price controls, which caused a serious shortage of an indispensable commodity. The government would have been far better advised to rely on the tax system.

Risk Management versus Rights

Many regulatory statutes are insensitive to a variety of obstacles to the achievement of regulatory goals: regional and industrial variations; the inevitable problem of trading off various social goals in designing successful regulation; and limitations in methodology.

A particular culprit here is the idea that the interest in clean air and water, and in a safe workplace, should be seen as a "right" in the sense of something that will not be balanced against other social interests. As we have seen, the conception of regulatory interests as rights to be vindicated rather than risks to be socially managed was common in the 1970s. Reacting against the New Deal model of administrative autonomy and building on the civil rights movement, Congress sometimes appears to have assumed that noncompliance with (for example) environmental requirements is systematically a consequence of intransigence on the part of the agency or the industry. In fact, however, noncompliance might be a result of the enormous difficulties of changing the world in the way that is statutorily specified. The larger point is this: when a regulatory program attempts to diminish risks facing huge numbers of people, it is foolish to conceive of the program as creating individual entitlements that cannot ever be compromised.

Flexibility. Congressional insensitivity to regional and industrial variations is reflected in the many environmental statutes that impose uniform national standards. Because the costs and benefits of antipollution strategies will vary in different parts of the nation, uniform standards are likely to cause serious inefficiencies. Tastes vary greatly; the costs of cleanup perhaps even more so. The result of uniformity will be both higher costs and less environmental protection than might otherwise be possible. Nor is there good reason to impose the same requirements for design of the workplace on companies operating under enormously different conditions. Current regulatory policies in many areas of safety suffer from a form of centralized planning.

The Misleading Rhetoric of Rights. Regulatory legislation of the 1960s and 1970s has often been indifferent to cost, on the theory that no price tag should be put on life and health, which are "inalienable rights." Thus statutes protecting clean air and water are sometimes "health-based"; they call for protections to which cost is utterly irrelevant.

No sensible regulatory program, however, can be indifferent to cost. Regulatory expenditures, if sufficiently high, will endanger the economy, increase unemployment and poverty, and eventually risk both life and health as a result. Programs that seem to be indifferent to cost are in fact influenced by the need for balancing. For example, the exercise of prosecutorial discretion by administrative agencies deciding which substances to regulate will reflect a form of cost-benefit balancing even if the substantive statute prohibits such balancing once regulation has begun. If they are rational, agencies will bring enforcement actions against the most dangerous violators. It would be far better for Congress to recognize the inevitability of tradeoffs and to make the basic value judgment itself.

Methodology. Sometimes information is simply unavailable, and regulators must do the best they can in the face of uncertainty. For example, Congress has failed in the environmental area to understand that the methodology for determining existing levels of air quality in many regions is frequently unreliable. To require good monitoring of data is to require something that cannot yet be provided. To say this is not to say that "technology-forcing" through regulation is always undesirable; it is to say that sometimes the technology is not available, and cannot be made so in the immediate future.

Complex Systemic Effects and Unanticipated Consequences

A related and frequent source of regulatory failure is Congress' failure to understand the complex systemic effects of regulatory interventions. These may include circumvention by the market and unanticipated perverse consequences. The problem is especially severe when Congress attempts to transfer resources from one group to another. As we have seen, the redistributive impact of the minimum wage law is quite complex, in spite of the expectation on the part of its proponents that it would produce a simple transfer of wealth from employers to employees. Likewise, Congress appears to have thought that extremely aggressive protection of workers through the Occupational Safety and Health Act would produce a simple redistribution from employers to employees, a far too simple way of understanding the effects of regulatory intervention.

Both OSHA and environmental regulation reflect a legislative belief that extremely stringent regulatory requirements will automatically bring about the desired ends, in this case worker safety and clean air and water. But in both contexts stringent requirements have, paradoxically, brought about underregulation. They are therefore self-defeating. Under OSHA, once the Department of Labor has initiated a proceeding to regulate a toxic substance, the law requires it to promulgate a rule imposing controls even when the costs are enormous and the health benefits relatively small. Because regulation, once undertaken, must be draconian, the government avoids regulating many substances at all.[41] Ironically, the consequence of a stringent statutory standard is underprotection of workers. The fact that many workers continue to face threats from toxic substances is attributable at least in part to an excessive regulatory standard.

The same result can be found in the environmental area. Under the BAT approach, if a nontrivial risk is produced by some industrial process, the offending plant or industry must install whatever technology is available to reduce the risk, even up to the point where the plant or industry might be shut down. This requirement produces an "all-or-nothing" approach that leads the EPA to forgo altogether the regulation of many substances. The ultimate consequence is a serious distortion of the process of priority setting and, again, both over- and underregulation. In the area of hazardous substances, the consequences of underregulation have been particularly severe. The EPA has issued rules for only seven toxic substances—five as a result of a court order.

A recurrent problem in federal regulation stems from the different treatment of new and old industries. Congress has frequently responded to the problem of risk by imposing especially severe standards on new sources. This approach is understandable in light of the large expense and arguable unfairness of retroactive controls. But a predictable consequence of the old risk-new risk distinction is to put new enterprises at a severe financial disadvantage in comparison to old ones. This phenomenon retards innovation and has the unintended and potentially disastrous consequence of maintaining especially harmful older products—cars, industrial products, and others—on the market for a long time. As we have seen, this strategy is partly attributable to the political power of existing industry using regulatory strategies to close out potential new entrants.

In the environmental area, for example, current law imposes severe controls on new sources of air and water pollution, but has a variety of lenient rules and escape hatches for existing sources. Another illustration is provided by the automobile emissions controls imposed on new vehicles, which discouraged the process of removing relatively dirty old cars from the market.

To say this is not to deny that many of the intended effects of regulation will come about. Indeed, even some of the hoped-for redistributive effects do actually occur. The forces of supply and demand may prevent regulated companies from passing their costs onto others. In the labor setting, for instance, employers are unable to pass all of the costs of safety regulation onto the employees. If workers are at or near the minimum wage, the imposition of health and safety requirements on employers will not lower employees' salaries. The idea that statutory efforts at redistribution will always fail is as myopic as the claim that they will always succeed. But the effects tend to be much more complex than the legislature anticipates, and frequently they are perverse.

Failures of Coordination

Some statutes fail because they fit awkwardly or not at all with other statutes regulating the same subject. The result is inconsistency and incoherence in the law. In many areas the lack of coordination decreases accountability and responsiveness, increases internal struggles over turf, and prevents the government from setting out cohesive regulatory programs. The problem is pervasive in federal regulation.

Federal policy for the disabled is a conspicuous example. The diffusion of responsibility among various federal agencies guarantees confused and chaotic regulation. The beneficiaries of regulation and regulated parties are unable to understand the crazy-quilt of regulatory impositions; no single institution is responsible for introducing coherence. One commentator observes that "America has no disability policy. It maintains a set of disparate programs, many emanating from policies designed for other groups, that work at cross-purposes." [42] National energy policy suffers from a similar problem. The diffusion of responsibility among multiple entities, with various mandates and agendas, has made it difficult to set out rational policy. [43]

The multiple overlapping and inconsistent efforts to regulate carcinogens provide what may well be the most egregious example of failed coordination. No fewer than twenty statutes, administered by more than a dozen agencies, govern the regulation of carcinogens. It is unsurprising that the result is a pattern so peculiar—ranging from draconian regulation to no regulation at all—that it could not plausibly be justified. [44]

More generally, extraordinary disparities arise among agencies in terms of expenditures per life saved. [45] The methodological difficulties are serious here, and some disparities might reflect reasonable societal assessments of the different risks, including the voluntariness of exposure and the nonmonetary value of the underlying activity. Nonetheless it is possible, using uniform measurements, to produce some extremely revealing numbers. Thus the Consumer Product Safety Commission's regulation of unvented space heaters saves a life for only $70,000; some regulations of the automobile have required expenditures ranging from $3,600 to $408,000 per life saved; OSHA's carcinogen regulations impose expenditures of as much as $169,200,000 per life saved; and the FDA's ban on DES in cattle feed costs no less than $132,000,000 per life saved. (See Appendix B.)

The current allocation of authority between the Department of Justice and the Federal Trade Commission provides another example of the coordination problem.[46] It is hard to see a good reason to entrust two government agencies with the responsibility of enforcing the antitrust laws. A closely related problem occurs within a single agency charged with administering more than one statute. This problem has come up, for example, in the EPA's regulation of "multimedia pollutants" (including lead, cadmium, and various pesticides), which migrate through the air, soil, and water and which must be regulated in accordance with sharply divergent statutory mandates addressed to these media. The same problem applies to FDA's efforts to regulate carcinogenic substances. All of these problems recall the original constitutional effort to create a unitary executive branch, which would promote coordination, expedition, and accountability.

Changed Circumstances and Obsolescence

Regulatory statutes may fail because circumstances have changed. Provisions that once sensibly addressed a social problem become obsolete. Changing technology and new policies and laws undermine the assumptions under which the statute was written. Congress is frequently unable to respond to the problem of obsolescence. Other issues occupy the legislative agenda; changed circumstances rarely produce high drama or mobilized groups; and reform sometimes seems to amount to the politically risky "watering down" of regulatory protections. Here the problem is not with the behavior of the enacting legislature, but it is not a question of improper implementation either.

The problem of changed circumstances is common. An example is the regulation of the telecommunications industry. A rapidly changing market has made the statutory framework anachronistic in numerous respects. Originally designed for a system with scarce broadcasting facilities, the regime is ill-adapted to a system which, as a result of cable television and other innovations, has enormous potential for a vast number of stations.

A similar problem hampers banking regulation, where new technology has also altered the premises underlying the original statute.[47] The authors of the regulatory system could not have anticipated the rise of money market funds, insurance companies performing banking services, and mechanical tellers. These innovations make it easy to evade the regulatory controls of the original statute—for example, to limit branch banking and to separate investment and banking activities—and it is highly uncertain how statutes imposing the original controls should be understood in the changed circumstances.

The Delaney Clause is an illustration here as well. An across-the-board prohibition of carcinogens in food additives is difficult to defend in light of new technology making it possible to identify carcinogens that are present in such minute quantities as to be virtually harmless. The drafters of the Clause assumed that a few chemical additives caused cancer and presented a significant health risk. By the 1980s it was clear that numerous food additives included carcinogenic substances, but many of the relevant risks were trivial. As noted above, one consequence of the Clause has been to encourage manufacturers to use food additives that were not carcinogenic, but that produced greater health risks than would low-level carcinogens. In these circumstances, mechanical application of the Clause—prohibiting trivial risks at significant cost—produces senseless regulation.

Changing knowledge about carcinogens has made statutory standards obsolete in other areas as well. A particular problem here is that the assumption of "safe thresholds"—an important one in the 1970s, when many environmental statutes were enacted—can no longer be sustained. There are no such thresholds for many carcinogens, which present at least some danger at any level. It is not a question of when exposure levels are safe, but of what levels are tolerable in light of the degree of the risk and the costs of eliminating it.

There are parallels in antidiscrimination law, prominently on the question of affirmative action. It is plausible to suggest that when the Civil Rights Act of 1964 was enacted, Congress regarded the Act's antidiscrimination principle as equivalent to a prohibition on any form of differentiation on the basis of race. It is surely possible that

Congress did not clearly choose between such an antidifferentiation principle and (for example) an antisubordination principle that would freely permit race-conscious efforts to increase the numbers of blacks and women in the workforce. But the period since the Act was passed has given rise to an unanticipated event: the voluntary use, by private employers, of affirmative action in order to increase the otherwise trivial numbers of blacks and women in the workforce or to fend off quite plausible claims of past discrimination.

Some observers claim that the evidence since 1964 has shown that affirmative action is necessary to counteract unconscious discrimination and thus to implement the nondiscrimination principle under current conditions. More broadly, some believe that affirmative action is required to promote the purposes of the Act—the incorporation of blacks into the workforce—in view of the difficulty of accomplishing a great deal through race-neutral policies alone.[48] The basic problem is that the statutory prohibition of discrimination, as originally understood, has become problematic in light of new developments.

Statutory obsolescence takes numerous forms. Most simply, changed circumstances may affect the factual assumptions that underlay the original statute, as in the cases of new knowledge about carcinogens. But obsolescence may result as well from changes in existing social values or in the fabric of the law as a whole; and in these cases as well, statutory failure is a predictable result. Consider, for example, a statute putting a high premium on commercial development in a period in which environmental concerns have come to the fore—or vice-versa.

The Substitution of Technocratic for Political Judgments

We have seen that regulatory programs pose serious difficulties in trading off various variables: economic performance, environmental degradation, energy conservation, employment, lives and health, and so forth. Congress has sometimes responded to these complexities by substituting a technocratic or engineering decision for the political one. This strategy masks the real stakes and forces someone else, usually the regulatory agency, to make the decision.

A striking example is provided by a critical contemporary problem: the dispersion of pollutants into the atmosphere. From one point of view, to allow such dispersion, through tall stacks or technological devices, is highly desirable. Dispersion to cleaner areas protects localities from high concentrations of pollutants, which can be especially harmful. On the other hand, dispersion adds to the problem of atmospheric loading, which causes acid rain, a major current problem of long-distance transport of pollutants. Acid rain can damage plants, reduce marine growth, acidify lakes and streams, kill fish, and have a variety of indirect and possibly harmful effects on human health.

Congress attempted to solve the problem of tall stacks by disallowing state pollution control plans from obtaining credit for "so much of the stack height of any source as exceeds good engineering practice." Good engineering practice is in turn defined as "the height necessary to insure that emissions . . . do not result in excessive concentrations of any air pollutant in the immediate vicinity of the source."[49] The assessment of what is an "excessive concentration" is of course not an engineering judgment at all. It calls for a complex political choice trading off the costs of controls, the risks of atmospheric loading, and the dangers of increasing local concentrations. Congress should have made that choice rather than disguising it in technocratic terms.

The BAT strategy characteristic of modern air and water pollution law is another example. To require adoption of the best technology may not be to bring about significant environmental improvements, or to do so at the appropriate cost. For example, the use of low-sulfur coal or of environmentally sensitive relocation policies for polluting industries may be a far better way of cleaning the air than the adoption of the most advanced equipment. Congressional focus on the question of the best available technology deflects attention from the inevitable political tradeoffs involved in environmental policy.

Implementation Failure

Many examples of statutory failure are problems in implementation. In such cases the statute is drafted in response to a serious problem in the marketplace, and a well-functioning regulatory system would prove beneficial. The reason for failure is that public officials have chosen an unsuccessful strategy for implementation.

The kinds of regulatory failure described above occur in the implementation process as well. Interest-group pressures often distort regulatory incentives, producing perverse outcomes. The failure to improve automobile safety is at least partly attributable to the power of industry over the National Traffic Safety Administration.[50] Excessive

regulation of certain carcinogens probably reflects the power of organized labor over OSHA.[51] Similar problems have sometimes hampered the performance of the Federal Trade Commission.[52] In 1963,
for example, over 95% of the FTC's orders involved allegations under
the Robinson-Patman Act, a statute producing little or no public benefit. Indeed, much of the FTC's activity appears to have been a product of complaints by unsuccessful competitors unsupported by any
plausible theory of consumer welfare.[53]

Administrative officials frequently act on the basis of inadequate
information or poor analysis. The EPA's implementation of the scrubbing stipulations of the Clean Air Act, referred to above, confirms the
point. It would have been possible to administer the 1977 amendments in such a way as to diminish its pathologies, to protect the
environment, and to impose lower costs; the EPA failed to do so.[54]
There is evidence as well that administrators take insufficient account
of the systemic effects of regulatory controls, and the absence of coordination of the regulatory process has produced striking anomalies.
Finally, once sensible regulatory strategies become obsolete over time.

But there are other failures in implementation as well. For every
justification for statutory intervention, there is a corresponding story
of statutory failure as a result of poor implementation.

Inadequate Protection

Some statutes fail because they are insufficiently implemented; their
protections amount to mere words and symbols and do not yield results in the real world. The result is frustration with the bureaucratic
process and a defeat for the rule of law. Much of modern administrative law has been concerned with the failure to carry out legislative
instructions in areas including the environment, occupational safety
and health, and discrimination.

Inadequate implementation occurs for many reasons. It is a familiar point that administrators are sometimes "captured" by groups
that they are charged with regulating. When that complex phenomenon occurs, it has multiple causes.[55] But there is no question that well-
organized groups have often exerted a disproportionate influence
over the regulatory process, partly because of their political capital
and organizing capacities, partly because of the agencies' ultimate dependence on good relations with them and on the information that
only they can provide. In this respect the New Deal belief in admin-

istrative autonomy has produced serious pathologies, including a failure to implement statutes—a situation that helped account for the strict legislative controls and deadlines in the regulatory statutes of the 1960s and 1970s.

The problem of factionalism is complemented by that of self-interested representation. The incentives to bureaucrats include the aggrandizement of bureaucratic self-interest and the preservation of individual agency autonomy.[56] In some circumstances administrators seek above all to increase their own power and prestige, and in any case there are multiple failures, sometimes called "agency costs," in representative processes. Administrative officials are often resistant to change as well, tending to resolve conflicts among competing groups not necessarily in favor of those with the best arguments, but instead those whose demands require the least drastic departures from established responses.[57] The result can be irrational and overzealous regulation; but it can also be inadequate protection. Inadequate protection may also be a product of a perceived but unrealistic need for complete information clearly linking regulatory controls to public benefits, or to a draconian statute that makes the agency reluctant to act at all.

Numerous regulatory systems are influenced by factors that incline them against adequate implementation. Among these agencies OSHA, for example, has failed to regulate a range of dangerous carcinogens that pose serious risks.[58] The EPA has failed to deal at all with many toxic and hazardous substances notwithstanding ample statutory authority. Statutes forbidding race and sex discrimination are also inadequately enforced.[59] President Reagan's head of EEOC had effectively abdicated enforcement activity in a range of areas.[60] The same problem can be found in automobile safety regulation, which has seen exceptionally limited activity since the middle 1970s.[61]

The efforts of the Federal Communications Commission have also been hampered by the power of well-organized private groups. The FCC has done exceedingly little to implement its statutory mandate, especially in recent years.[62] One consequence has been a wholesale movement toward deregulation, including repeal of the fairness doctrine—a strategy that is not without some justification in light of the large number of participants in the current market, but that entirely disregards the aspirational and other goals that have motivated FCC efforts in the past. A similar example is the failure of the FCC to regulate children's advertising, a failure produced by the power of well-organized groups over Congress.[63]

A closely related problem is administrative delay and torpor. Delay is usually caused by the same factors that account for inaction, but sometimes it is a product of rigid procedural requirements, which make it costly and time-consuming for an agency to issue a rule. Sometimes delay results from excessive caution in the face of incomplete information—caution that can have significant costs of its own.

Increasing Inefficiency and Excessive Controls

Some statutes are targeted at a genuine market failure, but in the implementation process they create more serious inefficiencies than those in an unregulated market. Food and drug regulation provides examples. Consumers have imperfect information with which to evaluate dangerous food and drugs, but as we have seen, the FDA's controls are sometimes counterproductive. Most generally, the FDA is reluctant to allow possibly dangerous substances on the market because of the extraordinary political costs imposed on the agency in the event of a mistaken approval. The FDA does not face comparable public scrutiny if it refuses to permit substances onto the market that are extremely beneficial. The result of this ratchet has been severely to bias the FDA against the introduction of valuable drugs. Sometimes the result has been significant harm to the public, with restrictive approvals providing modest health gains in comparison with the large health losses from regulatory disapprovals and delays.[64] More lenient practices in other countries appear far superior.

Similar results can be found in the environmental area, where some regulation has been far too costly.[65] As we have seen, controls of automobile emissions and the "scrubbing" strategy are examples. There are market breakdowns in the energy field as well, but regulatory strategies have often been unsuccessful.[66] Sometimes statutes are administered so as to impose costs that are exceptionally high in comparison to the benefits.[67] A prominent recent response has been deregulation.[68]

Skewed Redistribution

Some regulatory statutes are designed to produce redistribution that appeals to widely held or highly plausible social norms, but in the implementation process the redistribution is skewed or perverse. The minimum wage increases unemployment, thus harming the weakest members of society. Other measures designed to help workers—stringent safety requirements on the job, for example—may benefit some employees but harm others, causing unemployment, decreased wages, and increased prices. Welfare statutes intended to benefit the poor often redistribute resources to social workers, lawyers, and others in the bureaucracy. Programs seemingly meant to help family farmers in practice benefit huge agricultural corporations. Agencies entrusted with supplementing the enforcement efforts of private black plaintiffs sometimes end up taking the side of white defendants and attacking affirmative action. Most generally, and probably most important, we have seen that the marketplace is extremely adept at frustrating efforts to redistribute resources through regulation.

Undemocratic Processes and Outcomes

We have seen that some statutes attempt to respond to the undemocratic character of market ordering by counteracting coordination problems and vindicating collective values or aspirations. A principal goal of the New Deal period was to ensure that regulatory policy would be made through a democratic process that would reflect the public will.[69] But in the implementation process these aspirations are often defeated. Systems devised to promote democratic goals can be undermined by factional power or administrative self-interest. The result is a perversion of the democratic aspirations of regulatory reformers—perhaps the principal complaint of post-New Deal administrative law.

Examples are plentiful. They include the efforts of numerous independent regulatory commissions (the FCC, the ICC, the FTC, and the NRC) as well as of many executive agencies. The problems here include the secrecy of the process, the power of parochial interests, and the absence of accountability to the public. A characteristic response has been to promote "interest representation" in the administrative process, by way of ensuring that all affected groups are permitted to participate. There are, however, severe difficulties in deciding what interests are to be represented and which people should be permitted to speak on their behalf.[70] Concerns of this sort periodically produce an outpouring of writing on the crisis of legitimacy said to be produced by the growth of bureaucracy.[71] Other responses include an increase in the authority of Congress and the President over the administrative process, or deregulation and decentralization.

Linking Statutory Function to Statutory Failure

The difficulties discussed thus far reveal that New Deal constitutionalism and the rights revolution have contributed to a number of problems that the original Constitution sought to remedy. One purpose of the Constitution was to ensure both deliberation and accountability in government. Regulatory structures often fail to provide either. The problem of interest-group power—aggravated by modern institutions—was of course a central target of the system of checks and balances; and the system of federalism was designed to insure against the risks, realized under many current programs, of excessive uniformity and centralization. In these circumstances a major goal for modern public law is to create institutional arrangements to promote original constitutional goals in a different environment.

To move that task forward, it would be extremely valuable, if it were possible, to establish a tight connection between identifiable statutory functions and particular forms of statutory failure. The empirical work on the consequences of social and economic regulation remains, however, in a primitive state. Moreover, an assessment of those consequences must be based not only on the facts, but also on some understanding about the appropriate scope of regulatory controls in various areas. On the basis of existing information it is nevertheless possible to sketch general tendencies, suggesting the ways in which statutes falling in various categories are peculiarly susceptible to different pathologies.

(1) Social and economic regulation is affected, at the stage of both enactment and implementation, by collective action problems. In the now familiar typology,[72] statutes can be grouped into four categories: those that involve diffuse and numerous beneficiaries and well-organized regulated classes; those that involve well-organized beneficiaries and diffuse and numerous regulated classes; those that involve diffuse and numerous beneficiaries and regulated classes; and those that involve beneficiaries and regulated classes that are all well-organized.

Statutes falling in the first category tend to be inadequately enforced. Regulations protecting the environment, endangered species, listeners and viewers of radio and television, the poor, and members of racial minority groups are illustrations. The second category of statutes is a classic context for overzealous enforcement. The ICC and in some respects the FTC provide examples. Here the problem is that regulation can become a mechanism for arranging and enforcing a cartel at the expense of the public at large. For statutes falling in the third and fourth categories, the structure of the relevant parties does not skew implementation in any particular direction.

There are exceptions: sometimes regulatory statutes are preceded or followed by the creation of aggressive "public-interest" groups transforming diffuse interests into potent political forces. Other variables of course affect regulatory patterns. The typology does, however, have considerable explanatory power. In many cases inadequate protection and excessive controls can be explained by reference to problems of political organization at the stage of enactment and, especially, implementation.

(2) Statutes that are designed to promote public-spirited redistribution often have perverse or inadequate distributional consequences, as a result of poor design and implementation failure. Statutes falling in this category are frequently based on a weak understanding of the ways in which regulation interacts with the market, which is quite resourceful in nullifying or reducing the effects of redistributive legislation. Sensitivity to the likely operation of the market at the stage of drafting and implementation can reduce this problem.

In a similar vein, a large part of the resources devoted to the poor and the disabled is diverted to professional bureaucracies. To some degree this phenomenon is unavoidable. But the relatively little political power of the intended class of beneficiaries aggravates the problem.

(3) Statutes that amount to pure interest-group transfers are especially vulnerable to overextension. In the implementation process, well-organized groups are able to exert considerable influence. The experience of railroad regulation is perhaps the most prominent example; the same thing occurs with banking and agriculture controls.

(4) Statutes designed to reduce or eliminate the social subordination of disadvantaged groups are frequently subject to skewed redistribution and failure as a result of inadequate implementation. The very problems that make such statutes necessary in the first instance tend to undermine enforcement; market failure is matched by government failure. The fact that preferences and beliefs adapt to available opportunities—the cognitive and motivational distortions discussed

in chapters 1 and 2—adds to difficulties of political organization on the part of beneficiaries. For example, the statutes designed to reduce race and sex discrimination face severe barriers to aggressive implementation. Thus a recent General Counsel of the EEOC—having represented major corporations against the government in antidiscrimination suits—announced to his staff, upon confirmation by the Senate, that he would not bring suits involving equal pay, sexual harassment, and age discrimination, and that he would refuse to initiate class actions altogether.[73]

For various reasons, moreover, private actors face a set of barriers to initiating or becoming involved in enforcement proceedings. These include the stigma of being classified as a malcontent; the risk to future employment prospects; the humiliation of revisiting, in public, encounters with racism or sexism; the immense disruption of becoming involved in litigation in this area; and the personal, financial, and social costs of complaining about racist and sexist behavior by people in a position of authority.[74] These factors contribute heavily to underenforcement. Governmental efforts depend for their efficacy on one or more complainants. If complainants are reluctant to step forward, regulatory implementation will be severely undermined.

(5) Statutes that attempt to protect aspirations or noncommodity values, to shape preferences, and to protect future generations from irreversible losses are apt to suffer from inadequate implementation and from undemocratic processes and outcomes—unless a well-organized group is available to monitor the implementation process.[75] Here, as in the case of antisubordination legislation, the same factors that make the statute necessary tend to produce government failure. Consider in particular the history of federal efforts to promote aspirational and other goals through regulation of the broadcasting industry. Those efforts were largely unsuccessful in the 1960s and 1970s.[76] They ultimately disintegrated in the 1980s, with the repeal of the fairness doctrine and effective abdication to market forces. But the market will inevitably sacrifice the values that broadcasting regulation might achieve—promoting high-quality programming, bringing about a focus on public issues, allowing the expression of diverse views, and increasing local control and local participation. The current state of broadcasting regulation suffers as a result of its exclusive market orientation. All this is largely a result of the political power of the broadcasting industry, the diffuse character of the groups who

would benefit from regulation, and the relative powerlessness of those invoking interests in nonmarket values and future generations.

A similar failure can be seen in the pattern of enforcement of the Endangered Species Act, which, no doubt because of its weak political constituency, has been inadequately enforced and sometimes violated by those charged with implementing it.

(6) Statutes that respond to a short-term public outcry typically suffer from a failure of diagnosis or of coordination. They also tend to interfere excessively in the marketplace. Statutes protecting against cancer risks are a prime example; so too are some measures protecting the environment and the disabled—consider the automobile emissions program and the use of command-and-control regulation. Such statutes often become obsolete quite quickly. Then the problem for implementation is one of minimizing the damage. Special problems here include a misunderstanding of the complex systemic effects of regulation, a conception of regulatory statutes as involving rights to be vindicated rather than risks to be reduced, and an indifference to the inevitability of tradeoffs.

(7) Regulatory statutes fail quite generally as a result of the absence of political accountability or political deliberation, changed circumstances or obsolescence, a misunderstanding of systemic effects, and lack of coordination. The absence of political accountability is a particular problem. Statutory commands frequently become obsolete as a result of changing circumstances, and it is often difficult to coordinate disparate regulatory policies into an integrated whole.

All of these generalizations are of course subject to exceptions. Moreover, statutes typically involve compromise and logrolling, and regulatory failure of various kinds may be precisely what was intended by the enacting legislature. But if this is its intention, the legislature should be required to set out a clear statement to this effect; courts (and others) should not presume that failure is intended. In addition, the possibility that some kind of failure was intended is itself an indictment of existing institutional arrangements. That possibility need hardly be taken as a reason for general satisfaction with existing statutory regimes, which sometimes make things worse rather than better, and which in any case could easily be redesigned in such a way as to improve regulatory performance.

For the most part, problems in the modern regulatory state lie neither with intervention nor with the goals that underlie regulatory strategies. Instead, the problems are a product of poor diagnosis on the part of Congress, of interest-group power, of changing conditions, or of inadequate strategies for implementation; and none of these problems is irremediable.

Paradoxes of the Regulatory State—and Reform

An understanding of the mechanisms of regulatory failure leads fairly directly to suggestions for regulatory reform. I outline some general directions here.

Paradoxes

Any reform strategy must come to terms with what might be called paradoxes of the regulatory state:[77] approaches that turn out to be self-defeating in the sense that they bring about precisely the opposite of their intended purposes.[78] We have seen four major examples.

(1) To require the best available technology is to discourage technological development. By making it economically costly to bring about technological improvements, BAT strategies have, paradoxically, deterred research and innovation in pollution control.

(2) To regulate new risks in the interest of health and safety is to perpetuate old ones, and thus to reduce health and safety. A new-source strategy for pollution control will in some respects increase the very problem it is intended to solve.

(3) Efforts to redistribute resources through regulation end up harming the most vulnerable members of society. The minimum wage helps many workers, but it also freezes people out of the employment market altogether. Legal requirements of habitable housing and rent control have similarly harmful effects on those at the bottom of the ladder, by preventing them from obtaining housing at all.

(4) Strict regulatory controls produce underregulation, at least when the regulator has prosecutorial discretion. Ironically, stringent controls on toxic substances in the workplace and in the environment have resulted in extremely weak regulation. The reason is that government agencies are aware that once they regulate at all, they will, as a matter of logic, have to do so up to an irrational point, raising a threat to the survival of a whole industry. A statute that allows for balancing will often produce more, not less, regulation than one that focuses only on considerations of health.

These paradoxes are simple empirical truths; they are not claims about the appropriate scope of government regulation. And to make a full assessment of regulatory paradoxes, one would have to know the magnitude of the various effects. The focus on new risks might be on balance justified if the perpetuation of old risks turned out to be a minor problem. The minimum wage might be desirable if the unemployment effect for some were small in comparison to the raised income of others. But no approach to regulation can afford to ignore the existence of the paradoxes.

It would be a disaster if the existence of self-defeating regulatory strategies were taken as a reason for contentment with the status quo, or with a system that relies entirely on the market. On the contrary, an understanding of the paradoxes should make it possible to design promising strategies for reform. The goal is to learn from past mistakes, not to take them as a reason for satisfaction with the distinctly unsuccessful strategies that predated the New Deal reformation.

Structures

Most of the work of regulatory reform must come from Congress and the executive branch, and here structural changes could be extremely valuable. As we have seen, disparities in political power produce numerous failures at the stages of enactment and implementation. The New Deal attack on the original system of checks and balances, and the consequent faith in administrative autonomy, have led to increased risks of factionalism and self-representation—risks that often produce significant failures at the stage of implementation. One of the greatest lessons of the last half-century is the need to bring to bear some of the original constitutional understandings on the regulatory state. And while this project is a complex one, it may be useful to describe some general directions here.

Restructuring of the executive branch so as to permit the President to exercise a greater supervisory function, in the interest of coordination of regulatory policy, is an extremely desirable strategy. Not only does such an approach increase consistency and thus systemic rationality; it promotes democratic accountability as well. In this way increased presidential supervision might achieve some of the goals of the original constitutional effort to create a unitary executive. The independent agencies (including the FTC, the FCC, and the NRC) should also be brought under presidential supervision, in the interest of coordination and accountability. Through this device, one might work in the direction of a unitary policy in such areas as carcinogen regulation and disability policy.

No institution in the executive branch, moreover, is currently responsible for long-range research and thinking about regulatory problems. It would be highly desirable to create such an office under the President, particularly for exploring problems whose solutions require extensive planning, most notably the environment. Nor is there an office charged with acting as an initiator of as well as a brake on regulation. Some entity within the executive branch, building on the ombudsman device,[79] should be entrusted with the job of guarding against failure to implement regulatory programs. Such an entity would be especially desirable in overcoming the collective action and related problems that tend to defeat enforcement. The most natural place here is the Office of Management and Budget, which has already begun to oversee regulatory policy in the interest of precisely those considerations that brought about the framers' original decision to create a unitary executive branch.[80]

Reform of legislative processes is also critical. The decline of the party system, defects in the electoral process, the power of the media, and the increasing fragmentation of the Congress into many small subcommittees have increased the risk of legislative irrationality and myopia, in the form of erratic and ill-considered responses to short-term problems; they have also made coordination of regulatory policy far less likely. Possible initiatives here include the creation of a general committee within the Congress for overseeing the regulatory process; the development of a regulatory budget, taking account of the costs of regulatory programs; and the establishment of a permanent office, equipped with specialists and charged with assessing the costs and benefits of regulatory controls across agencies. Congress should also concentrate on establishing goals to be achieved through regulation, rather than on specifying the means for achieving those goals. Means-focused strategies suffer as a result of interest-group power; they are also poorly suited to the achievement of their own goals.

The New Deal attack on the federal system has diminished local self-government and local control, in a way that compromises some of the democratic goals of the original constitutional regime. It has also produced substantial inefficiencies, most notably through reliance on regulation that is ill-adapted to the vastly different conditions of various areas of the country. The problem of pollution control cannot sensibly be treated the same in New York as in Wyoming. In view of these differences, it is often simply irrational to have nationally uniform regulation. Greater options for state autonomy—introduced through legislation and administration and allowing different outcomes and different "mixes" for achieving the same outcomes—is in many contexts a desirable strategy.

Substance

There is enormous room for substantive reform as well. A central goal of any reform effort is to come to terms with the various paradoxes of regulation. A good first step here would be to adopt a presumption in favor of flexible, market-oriented, incentive-based, and decentralized regulatory strategies. Such strategies should be focused on ends—the number of lives saved, the amount of pollution reduced—rather than on the means of achieving those ends. Regulatory reform should also see a large shift from command-and-control regulation—embodied in design standards for occupational safety and rigid technological directives for pollution control equipment—to more flexible but equally protective performance standards. Emissions-trading in environmental law is a good example. Through such routes we should be able to obtain better pollution control at much lower cost.

Occupational safety and health law might also be reformed through greater reliance on employers' actual performance in reducing deaths and injury rather than on their compliance with rigid and uniform national design standards. Possible strategies here include (1) a tax or other penalties on employers for particular risks or dangerous conditions; (2) greater reliance on disclosure of risks rather than government specification of appropriate risk levels, at least where the risk is one that reasonable, informed people might run; and (3) active involvement of employees, through bargaining, in the process of monitoring safety in the workplace.[81] By combining aggressive risk disclosure policies with involvement of employees in establishing safety levels, one might achieve some of the advantages of the market while reducing the multiple dangers posed by reliance on markets alone.

In all areas of regulation, the old-new risk distinction should be sharply curtailed. The best way to do this is to ensure that old risks, in the workplace and the environment, are also subject to regulation—a particular imperative in the area of clean air and water. Pre-screening efforts, especially in the area of foods and drugs, should be made more flexible, with decreased delays; standards of evidence should be reduced before marketing and greater reporting and monitoring required after marketing; and conditional approval of new drugs should be made freer. In general, regulatory strategies should be candid about the need to balance costs and benefits. The rights-based approaches characteristic of contemporary regulation have been a recipe for underregulation; they are in any case misguided. This is so even if the willingness-to-pay criterion is rejected—as it often should be—and if an exceptionally high premium is placed on the benefits to be obtained through governmental controls.

Another promising route is the redesign of regulation to ensure a better "match" between the problem calling for governmental controls and the particular strategy chosen to resolve that problem. And in all cases, it is crucial to attend to the complex systemic effects of government regulation, the possibility that redistributive efforts will backfire, and the risk that any gains from regulation will have excessive costs or adverse side-effects. Through these various routes, it should be possible to respond to the failures of regulation and thus to learn from the past, while at the same time respecting both the aspirations of regulatory statutes and the goals of the original constitutional framework.

Reforms of this sort would ultimately produce a kind of American-style *perestroika*—a restructuring of institutional arrangements and substantive controls that is entirely unembarrassed by the use of government to reflect democratic aspirations, to promote individual autonomy and economic welfare, and to foster distributional equity, but that also insists on strategies that embody the flexibility, adaptability, productive potential, and decentralization characteristic of private markets.

CHAPTER

4

Courts, Interpretation, and Norms

Although much of the work of regulatory reform must come from nonjudicial institutions, it is inevitable that some role will remain for the courts, which are, after all, entrusted with the task of interpreting regulatory statutes. Statutory construction has sometimes served as a means of responding to regulatory malfunctions. Indeed, legislative reform must overcome an enormous burden of inertia. It is through interpretation, in the courts and the executive branch, that regulatory improvements, interstitial to be sure, can be brought about most easily. If those charged with interpretation had a solid understanding of the functions and failures of regulation, significant gains should be expected. For this reason, it will be useful to explore, in some detail, how the courts—usually thought to be charged above all with assessing the "meaning" of statutes—might undertake this role.

In the process I will be challenging a number of widely accepted propositions about statutory construction: (1) that courts must adhere to the original meaning of the statute, or the original intent of the enacting legislature; (2) that courts are to be faithful agents of the enacting Congress; (3) that statutory meaning is to remain constant over time; (4) that controversial views about public policy are not and should not be part of statutory construction; (5) that statutory meaning is reducible to legislative intent; and (6) that canons of construction, or background interpretive norms, are an outmoded and unhelpful guide to the courts. All of these aspects of the conventional wisdom, I suggest, are inconsistent with actual judicial behavior, and all of them provide at best incomplete and often perverse principles for statutory construction.

Flawed Approaches to Statutory Interpretation

How are courts to ascertain the meaning of legislative commands? In the conventional account, the ordinary tools of construction are the language, structure, and history of the relevant act. The weight of each of these is sharply contested. In one view, for example, legislative history is entitled to little or no consideration, reflecting as it does the power of a few members of Congress, staff employees, or self-interested private groups rather than the considered view of the legislature.[1] Moreover, there is no consensus about the appropriate approach to any of these tools. It is disputed whether the language of a particular statute should be studied in isolation and independently of other statutes; whether statutory text should be controlling if it leads to absurd results; and whether statutory language should be tempered when new circumstances are inconsistent with the assumptions of the enacting legislature.

Disputes over questions of this sort have produced a range of approaches to statutory construction, all with support in the decided cases. Each of them, however, suffers from fatal flaws. My purpose here is to explain how these approaches fail, both as accounts of how courts in fact approach statutes and as normative theories of interpretation. My principal claim is that all of them ignore the inevitable use of interpretive principles in the process of construction.

Courts as Agents

The most prominent conception of the role of courts (and others, including regulatory agencies) in statutory construction is that they are agents or servants of the legislature. As agents, courts should say what the statute means, and in that process language, history, and structure are relevant; but background norms, policy considerations, or general principles are immaterial. Above all, those who accept the agency view would bar courts from undertaking value-laden inquiries into (for example) appropriate institutional arrangements, or statutory function and failure, as part of the process of interpretation. The judicial task is one of discerning and applying a judgment made by others, most notably the legislature.

The agency view is usually defended by a claim of legitimacy, and here it has a large element of truth. In a democratic system, one with an electorally accountable legislature and separated powers, it is usually thought impermissible for courts to invoke considerations that cannot be traced to an authoritative textual instrument. The claim of illegitimacy is buttressed by (or perhaps reducible to) a range of prudential considerations: the use of outside sources will tend to increase judicial discretion, decrease legislative attentiveness, produce uncertainty, and risk usurpation by judges of powers accorded to legislative and executive actors.[2] Justice Holmes provided a particularly crisp expression of the agency view; after describing a regulatory statute as "foolish," he added: "If my fellow citizens want to go to Hell I will help them. It's my job." [3]

The agency view has several manifestations. Much of the history of statutory construction consists of shifts among the various possible sources of the instructions of the courts' "principal," the legislature.

Textualism. It is sometimes suggested that the statutory language is the only legitimate basis for interpretation. The principal feature of the textualist creed is the belief that courts have no license to rely on outside sources. The language of the statute is the source of judicial power and the object of judicial concern.

Textualism appears to be enjoying a renaissance in a number of recent cases, and perhaps in the academy as well.[4] This phenomenon is probably attributable to dissatisfaction with alternative interpretive strategies that emphasize the need for courts to rely on "purpose" or to produce "reason" in regulatory regimes. As we will see, strategies of that sort were suggested by commentators who disregarded or downplayed the existence of dissensus about what reason required or about the purposes of statutory regimes, and who failed to come to terms with the existence of sharp, ideologically based disagreements on such questions. The resort to textualism in the law is partly a response to a fear that without firm linguistic anchors, legal interpretation must devolve into ideological disputes that cannot be mediated by judges or other participants in the legal culture. It is here that there is a commonality between those who believe that legal interpretation is inevitably indeterminate—because of ideological strife—and those who embrace textualism for essentially the same reason.

Textualism contains an important and often overlooked truth. The emphasis on statutory terms stems from a recognition of the democratic pedigree of those terms, which are the enactment of the representative legislature and hence the relevant law. The Constitution specifies that Congress is the legislator, and legislation, to qualify as law, must pass through constitutionally specified channels. Statutory terms—not legislative history, not legislative purpose, not legislative "intent"—have gone through the constitutionally specified procedures for the enactment of law. Largely for this reason, the words of a statute provide the foundation for interpretation, and those words, together with widely shared conventions about how they should be understood, often lead to uniquely right answers, or at least sharply constrain the territory of legitimate disagreement. Resort to the text also promotes goals associated with the rule of law: the statutory words are available to affected citizens, and it is in response to those words that they can most readily order their affairs. An emphasis on the primacy of the text also serves as a salutary warning about the risks of judicial use of statutory purpose and of legislative history, both of which are, as we will see, subject to interpretative abuse.

Some textualists emphasize the dictionary definition of statutory terms; others are more sensitive to particular settings. Whatever its precise form, however, the textualist approach is inadequate.[5] The basic problem is that words are not self-defining; their meaning depends on both *culture* and *context*. There is no such thing as a preinterpretive text, and words have no meaning before or without interpretation. Statutory terms are indeterminate standing by themselves. Moreover, they never stand by themselves. They derive their meaning from the context and their background in the relevant culture.

To say this is not to say that the words used in statutes could mean anything at all. (Confusion of these quite different points has become common in recent work in literary criticism and in law.) But it is to say that the significance of congressional enactments necessarily depends on background norms about how words should be understood, and those norms are rarely supplied by the legislature itself. Indeed, the legislature itself must operate within the prevailing interpretive culture; it has no power to change it, at least not in any fundamental way.

Some of the relevant norms are so widely shared—for example, that Congress is speaking in English, that it is not joking or attempting to mislead, or that courts should not decide cases simply according to their predilections—that they are invisible. But in easy as well as hard cases, courts must resort to background assumptions if interpretation is to proceed. For example, the question whether the enactment of federal environmental statutes preempts all of state tort law is an easy one—it does not—not because of the statutory text itself, but because of universally shared understandings about the limited preemptive effect of federal enactments. Moreover, words have meanings only in and as a result of their contexts. They cannot be understood, and they never exist, in the abstract.

Consider, for example, the constitutional provision saying that only those over thirty-five may run for President.[6] Suppose that a thirty-year-old of great experience and maturity seeks to run for President in the face of this provision. Sometimes courts resort to statutory purpose to interpret statutory provisions in ways that diverge from their literal text, especially when circumstances have changed. The requirement that candidates for the presidency must be thirty-five or over might be a plausible candidate for this strategy. When the Constitution was written, social norms were different; young people could not vote; and there was a greater hierarchy between the young and the old. Why would it be frivolous to argue that the provision should be interpreted to permit people to run for the presidency at thirty?

Such an argument would in fact be frivolous, but not because the text is self-construing. Instead, it is because the thirty-five-year requirement does not produce obviously absurd results, there is no readily available alternative interpretation that would better serve its basic purposes, and an interpretation that abandoned the thirty-five year touchstone would not easily be susceptible to judicial administration. Ideas of this sort occur to interpreters so quickly that they do not have time even to register; and it is such ideas—not textualism, or language by itself—that provide the background norms for interpretation of seemingly unambiguous language. We will see a number of cases in which the plain text does not control because it leads to absurd or bizarre results, and here the reason is that a sensible and administrable alternative is available.

So far, those who accept textualist approaches might be in agreement. Perhaps they would agree that the meaning of words is largely a function of context and of background norms about how texts should be approached. Indeed, we may define an easy case as one in which the context is unproblematic and there is a consensus about the governing norms. But the problem for textualism goes deeper. In many difficult cases, the source of the difficulty is that the particular kind of background norm and the nature of its application will be highly controversial—either because of a split within the interpretive culture or because of the context within which the dispute arises.

Suppose, for example, that the question is raised whether a federal statute protecting the environment or an endangered species, and authorizing plaintiffs to bring suit, should be understood to compel judges to issue an injunction whenever a violation is shown, and thus to displace the courts' traditional power to "balance the equities" before granting injunctive relief. This question has arisen frequently in recent years and is of considerable importance to regulatory policy.[7] The issue cannot be resolved without invoking some kind of background norm; the text itself says nothing about it. Thus it is that courts have invoked pre-New Deal principles of judicial equity to require an unambiguous statement from the legislature before finding that Congress has eliminated the judges' equitable discretion—principles that, as we will see, may well be anachronisms in the regulatory state.

To take another example: would a statute creating a regulatory agency to bar racial discrimination in employment implicitly authorize private suits by victims of discrimination against employers who allegedly have engaged in discrimination? If the statute and its history are silent on the question, the case cannot be decided without introducing background norms. Thus it should be unsurprising that judges skeptical about implied causes of action have relied, not on statutory text, but on an assumption, traceable to a particular understanding of separation of powers, that only the legislature may create such rights, and that statutory silence does not do so.[8] Without such an assumption, statutory silence on the existence of an implied cause of action has no meaning.

The need for interpretive norms is not limited to statutory silence. Such norms are ubiquitous in any legal system, and indeed in grammar itself; they are necessary to make reliance on text an intelligible concept. These considerations help account for the pervasive difficulties with textualist approaches to statutory construction: ambiguity, delegation of power, gaps, underinclusiveness, overinclusiveness, and changed circumstances.

Ambiguity and Vagueness constitute the most familiar problem for textualism. It is not clear, for example, whether the term "feasible" contemplates cost-benefit analysis; whether a statutory reference to "wages" is meant to include employer contributions to a pension program; whether regulatory power over the broadcasting industry includes cable television; or whether a prohibition of discrimination bars voluntary race-conscious measures designed to counteract the effects of past and present discrimination against blacks.[9] In all of these cases, moreover, it is uncertain whether the language should be taken to refer to the original meaning of the words for the enacting legislature (assuming that idea can be made intelligible in light of the problems of aggregating the views of numerous actors) or should instead take account of contemporary understandings of what the words mean. Indeed, it is not even clear what bearing the desires of the enacting legislature on that question should have for interpretation. By itself, textualism cannot answer these questions; it is simply incomplete.

Delegation, Gaps, and Implementing Rules. The incompleteness of textualism is conspicuous when Congress has delegated lawmaking power to the courts. A related problem occurs when Congress has left a gap; here there is no self-conscious delegation, but courts must nonetheless make law, going beyond the text in order to interpret it. The line between statutory interpretation and federal common law becomes thin.

The Sherman Antitrust Act is an example. The decision about what trade practices amount to "conspiracies in restraint of trade" cannot be made by using the text of the act. The legislative history is suggestive on the question, but the instructions it provides are unclear, and in any case it is not clear that they are binding. In these circumstances, the Court has inevitably taken the act as a delegation of gapfilling power to the judiciary.[10] The notion that the overriding purpose of the Sherman Act is to promote consumer welfare, defined in economic terms, has been largely accepted by the Court,[11] but this notion is best understood as the most sensible way of implementing an open-ended prohibition, rather than as an inevitable reflection of the text or original understanding of the text. Much of the law of antitrust consists of the judicial development of implementing rules.

Other examples are not difficult to find. The text of section 1983,[12] among the most important of civil rights statutes, is silent on many crucial questions, including the available defenses, the statute of limitations, burdens of pleading and persuasion, and exhaustion requirements. With respect to these questions, the judges must fill any gaps. The Court has sometimes indicated that gaps should be filled by reference to the common law of the time.[13] But more frequently, it has filled gaps in accordance with its own views about how best to implement the statute—an approach that is probably consistent with the drafters' own understanding about how courts would act.[14]

Judicial implementation of Title VII of the Civil Rights Act of 1964[15] can be viewed in similar terms. The statutory prohibition of "discrimination" is uninformative about the role of discriminatory effects, the appropriate burdens of proof and production, and the mechanisms for filtering out discriminatory treatment. Judicial answers to these questions sometimes purport to be relatively mechanical responses to congressional commands, but in fact they amount to judge-made implementing devices responsive to the judges' own, necessarily value-laden views about how the statute is best understood. In light of the existence of textual gaps on the relevant questions, this is inevitable. Much of the law of Title VII is a fully legitimate (because unavoidable) norm-ridden exercise of developing gap-filling rules.

When the language of a statute calls for implementing rules to which it does not speak, the problem for textualism is insoluble. Courts must look elsewhere. In such cases, those who accept the agency view tend to look to purpose, intent, and history, but those sources will sometimes leave gaps or themselves reveal a desire to delegate lawmaking power.

Overinclusiveness. Language that would in many settings be entirely unambiguous should not be the only basis for interpretation in some cases; here context is the central problem. The literal language of a statute—its dictionary definition or meaning in ordinary settings—will suggest an outcome that would make little or no sense. Suppose, for example, that a state law says that no vehicles are permitted in public parks, and that a city proposes to build in a park a monument with tanks used in World War II.[16] Here what appears to be the unambiguous language must yield, for the statute could not be understood to forbid such a monument, which causes none of the harms the statute could plausibly be thought to prevent.

The example is not fanciful. The Supreme Court recently said that a statute exempting state and local public housing agencies "from all taxation . . . imposed by the United States" should not be interpreted to include an exemption from federal estate tax.[17] The Court held that the exemption did not mean what it appeared to say in light of the contemporaneous understanding that an excise tax was not ordinarily comprehended within the category of taxation. Or would the legislature's ruling that husbands should inherit from their wives "under all circumstances" forbid a court from refusing to allow inheritance by a man who has killed his wife? Suppose the legislature has said that an employer may discharge an employee "for any reason." Is the employer thereby authorized to fire workers who have refused to commit crimes on his behalf? Finally, consider whether a statute preempting "any and all State laws" that "relate to any employee benefit plan" covered by federal pension law should be understood to preempt state domestic relations law.[18] These are examples of what might be described as the overinclusiveness of textualism: the possibility that statutory language, read woodenly and without regard to context, will reach situations that it ought not to cover.

Courts encounter the problem frequently.[19] A famous passage from Wittgenstein indicates the basic difficulty: "Someone says to me: 'Shew the children a game.' I teach them gaming with dice, and the other says 'I didn't mean that sort of game.' Must the exclusion of the game with dice have come before his mind when he gave me the order?"[20] The example shows that sometimes the best interpretation of a textual command runs counter to its apparent literal meaning—even in cases in which the author did not have in mind the particular case at issue and did not make a judgment about how that case should be resolved. Here the exclusion of the absurd outcome should be seen not as amendment or usurpation, but as permissible, indeed conventional interpretation.

It is tempting to respond that if overinclusiveness is the problem, Congress should supply the solution. Suppose, however, that courts did decide to interpret statutes in accordance with their literal meaning even in cases of unintended or absurd applications. If Congress failed to amend the relevant statutes in response (because of other pressing business, for example), the result would be irrational law. Little can be said for that, certainly if the irrationality is unintended. If Congress did amend the statutes, it is unclear how much would be gained; the "literalism" approach would force the legislature to spend its limited time correcting, after the fact, mechanical judicial interpretations. Perhaps it might be thought that literalism would force Congress to be more careful with its words during the process of initial enactment. But the problem here is often that the particular case cannot easily be anticipated beforehand, and in any event there is little evidence that Congress responds to different interpretive approaches from the courts.

Underinclusiveness. Although it arises less frequently, there is also a possibility that textualism will be underinclusive. This problem occurs when statutory terms, regarded outside of their context, do not regulate conduct that the statute, most plausibly read, should be understood to control. A particular difficulty here is that a statute may be evaded by private ingenuity. The literal language of the statute does not cover the situation, but because the private conduct causes all of the harms that the statute was designed to prevent, courts sometimes hold a statute applicable notwithstanding its precise words.

For example, in the case of *Helvering v. Gregory*,[21] the relevant statute said that financial gains would not be "recognized" for purpose of the internal revenue code—and thereby subject to taxation—if they were "distributed, in pursuance of a plan of reorganization." A reorganization was defined as "a transfer by a corporation of . . . a part of its assets to another corporation," so long as "the transferor or its stockholders or both are in control of the corporation to which the assets are transferred." In *Gregory*, the taxpayer developed a plan by which to avoid taxation of her large profit on the shares of a company that she owned. The plan involved another corporation, created only to avoid taxation, to which the shares of the existing company were transferred. Three days after its creation, the new company was terminated, and the taxpayer received from the new company, as a liquidated dividend, the shares in the existing company, which she promptly sold. Read literally, this transaction was a "reorganization," and therefore the profits were exempt from taxation.

Judge Hand responded:

> The meaning of a sentence may be more than that of the separate words . . . The purpose of the section is plain enough; men engaged in enterprises . . . might wish to consolidate, or divide, or add to, or subtract from, their holdings. Such transactions were not to be considered as "realizing" any profit, because the collective interests still remained in solution. But the underlying presupposition is plain that the readjustment shall be undertaken for reasons germane to the conduct of the venture in hand, not as an ephemeral incident, egregious to its prosecution. To dodge the shareholders' taxes is not one of the transactions contemplated as corporate "reorganizations."

The *Gregory* case reveals that reliance on statutory text without regard to context might lead to an unduly narrow understanding of the statute. The problem of evasion should not be an excuse for judicial stretching of statutes (an ill-defined conception in this setting);

the legislature should normally provide the remedy. A statute's purposes are normally defined by its words and have no life apart from them. But the problem has called forth a judicial response in a number of areas, most notably taxation.[22] Consider in this regard Holmes's suggestion that courts are "apt to err by sticking too close to the words of a law where those words import a policy that goes beyond them."[23]

Changed Circumstances. The discussion thus far has assumed that circumstances have not changed significantly since the statute was enacted. But the difficulties of textualism become all the more intractable when time has affected the assumptions under which the statute was originally written. For example, would the statute forbidding vehicles in the park apply to a new and entirely unanticipated mode of transportation, one that is utterly silent and creates no pollution? Or consider the Delaney Clause, which forbids the use as food additives of substances that "cause" cancer; the Clause was originally enacted at a time when carcinogenic substances were difficult to detect and all detectable carcinogens were extremely dangerous. Currently, carcinogens are detectable at exceptionally low levels, and many of them pose trivial risks. In such circumstances, might the word "cause" allow the government to exempt from regulation carcinogens that pose trivial risks? To take another example, would a public policy exception to the charitable deduction in the Internal Revenue Code require the government to deny the deduction to schools that engage in racial discrimination, even if those who enacted the Code believed that such discrimination was perfectly consistent with public policy?[24] In short, it is by no means obvious that the statutory text should be understood in accordance with its original meaning, even if that concept were unproblematic. Indeed, I will be offering reasons to suggest that it should not be.

All this suggests two principal points. First, and most fundamentally, there is no such thing as an acontextual or acultural text that can be used as the exclusive guide to interpretation. In easy cases, background norms drawn from the legal culture—on which there is wide or universal consensus—and context are part of the process of ascertaining statutory meaning. Precisely because the norms are so widely shared, they appear invisible and are not an object of controversy. It is only in these cases (and only in this sense) that meaning can ever be said to be "plain." In other cases, usually treated as hard ones, courts must resort to a highly visible or a contestable background norm, or some gap-filling device, in order to resolve an interpretive dispute. It is in these settings, and in this sense, that textualism is inevitably incomplete.

Second, it is by no means obvious that courts should rely on the text or on the plain meaning of words even in cases in which such reliance is possible and leads to determinate results. Although textualism properly draws on the democratic primacy of the legislature, in some cases legislative instructions, taken in context, are unclear and the claim of command is a myth. An interpretive strategy that relies exclusively on the ordinary meaning of words is precisely that—an interpretive strategy that reflects a choice among competing possibilities—and in many cases it will produce irrationality, absurdity, or an inferior system of law. Here textualism is not incomplete but pernicious.

In cases of overinclusiveness, underinclusiveness, changed circumstances, and divergence between ordinary meaning and contextual or legislatively intended meaning, the best defense of textualism—calling for disregard of the unintended, irrational, or unjust outcomes produced by literalism—is one that treats it as a fighting faith, or an inference from the system of separation of powers rather than a necessary view about interpretation. Reliance on ordinary meaning and indifference to context, irrationality, and injustice will thus discipline the judges, limit their discretion, hold them to Congress' actual words, and warn the lawmakers to be clear about their language. In short, the dangers of what is plausibly an increase in judicial discretion are greater than the dangers of occasional injustice or irrationality.

It is by no means clear, however, that a system of textualism, so defined, will lead to a superior system of law, and considerable reason to suspect otherwise. In this sense too textualism is an inadequate guide to statutory meaning, and it often serves to disguise the actual basis for decision, which in difficult cases does not turn on text at all.[25] The most attractive form of textualism emphasizes not literalism but the meaning of words in context and read against shared interpretive norms; but even this version is inadequate in light of the need for contestable norms in hard cases and the interpretive difficulties produced by unintended irrationality and injustice.

Structural Approaches. Sometimes courts attempt to respond to the difficulties in textual approaches by reference to the structure of the statute. An interpretation of the disputed provision that fits awkwardly with another provision or makes it redundant or confusing should be rejected; an interpretation that makes sense of the statute as a whole should be adopted.

Structural argument has proved helpful in many cases,[26] and it is entirely unobjectionable. On the contrary, structural approaches provide significant interpretive guidance. Such approaches promote fidelity to congressional instructions, give a sense of context, and at the same time aid in making sense of complex regulatory enactments. But they suffer from two problems. First, they depend on an assumption that statutes are in fact internally consistent and coherent; this assumption is one that recent theories of legislation—pointing to the influence of interest groups, compromise, and irrationality—have questioned. If the assumption is false, the courts' treatment of statutes as internally consistent wholes must be justified as a way of making sense of enactments, not as an accurate way of implementing legislative instructions.

Second, structural approaches offer only partial help; they should be seen as limited supplements to textualism. In many cases, an examination of structure will leave considerable gaps or ambiguities. Here it will be necessary to look elsewhere.

Purposive Interpretation. In cases in which textual and structural approaches are inadequate, a natural and time-honored response is to resort to the "purpose" of the statute. This response was especially influential among academic commentators in the 1950s and 1960s, as a reaction against what appeared to be a judicial tendency to rely on statutory text in an unduly mechanical way.[27] The attack on textualism was a natural outgrowth of legal realism, a movement especially hostile to approaches that substituted mechanical rules for more functional and purposive inquiries. The resort to purpose was an effort to retain the agency theory of the judicial role while at the same time acknowledging the inadequacy of textualism.

Thus, for example, if a statute forbids vehicles in a public park, and someone tries to build a war memorial or to bring a bicycle into the park, the question whether the memorial or the bicycle is a "vehicle" within the meaning of the statute might be answered by asking if either of them creates harms that undermine the purposes for which the statute was enacted. Since the monument does not, the case is an easy one, and the statutory proscription does not apply. Moreover, if the background and history show that the legislature was concerned about noise and pollution, it will be plausible to suggest that bicycles do not fall within statutory prohibition. Characterization of statutory purpose is thus crucial in the face of ambiguity, and sometimes reliance on purpose will be helpful in solving interpretive problems. Exploration of purpose is a valuable way of providing a context within which to understand statutory terms.

Purposive interpretation is, however, far from a complete solution to the problem of statutory construction. The effort to describe the purpose of the statute will sometimes recall all of the problems of textualism in slightly different guise. First, the purpose will often be ambiguous or vague. Are the antitrust laws designed to promote consumer welfare in the economic sense, or do they attempt to protect small business? Is a statute forbidding racial discrimination intended to proscribe all distinctions on the basis of race, or only those distinctions that burden members of minority groups? Often such questions will not have been answered or even anticipated by the legislature itself.

All of these problems would be formidable even if the legislature consisted of one or a few people. But in the face of multimember institutions the problem turns far more troublesome, and the task of describing legislative "purpose" becomes as much creation as discovery. Collective action problems and difficulties of aggregating legislative purposes and preferences make it hard to speak coherently of a unitary legislative "purpose." There will be not one but many purposes in any statute; those purposes will sometimes conflict with one another, and they will have been compromised and traded off in complex ways. A statute designed to protect the environment might also be intended to protect Eastern coal producers; a statute designed to protect workers might also be intended to help union at the expense of nonunion employment. A judicial emphasis on one purpose at the expense of another will produce interpretive blunders. Those who emphasize the ambiguity and multiplicity of statutory purpose often stress as well the intractability of the ideological disputes that sometimes lie beneath interpretive questions. Here as well textualism provides a natural, albeit unsuccessful, refuge from purposive approaches.

Second, reliance on purpose may lead to overinclusiveness. Sometimes courts take the purpose of the statute out of context and use it to prevent behavior that, under the most plausible reading, the statute should not reach. An example would be to understand the statute forbidding vehicles in the public parks as designed also to prevent noise and thus to interpret it to bar the use of radios in the parks—

an absurd example, to be sure, but one that has arguable parallels in actual decisions.[28]

Finally, reliance on purpose may lead to underinclusiveness. The problem here lies in the unduly narrow categorization of statutory purpose, and thus a decision to prevent the statute from reaching a situation that should be understood as falling within its scope. Sometimes this leads to violation of the text. Consider, for example, a decision to exempt quiet cars equipped with unusually good antipollution devices from the reach of the statute forbidding vehicles in the parks—an example also having analogues in actual cases.[29] Judicial extrapolation of purposes, especially if done without close attention to statutory language and context, carries with it significant dangers of error.

Dissatisfaction with purposive interpretation is almost always a product of one or more of these three concerns. The difficulty is not simply a matter of mistake, though sometimes this is indeed the problem. In many cases reliance on purpose leads to conundrums that are conceptual rather than practical. When purpose cannot be discovered on the basis of an inquiry into the statute and its background, the decision must depend on something other than purpose; a more creative and value-laden judgment is required.

As with textualism, we have assumed thus far that the situation at the time of interpretation is the same as the situation when the statute was enacted. But it is common for things to change in significant ways since enactment, and here derivation of and reliance on the statutory purpose becomes even trickier. Assume, for example, that Congress enacts a statute imposing significant procedural requirements on regulatory agencies for adjudicating, but lenient requirements on agencies for rulemaking. Assume also that Congress thought that almost all important administrative business would be done through adjudication, but thirty years after enactment that assumption no longer holds, as agencies engage in extensive rulemaking and do most of their significant work in that way. Is it so clear that judicial bending of ambiguous provisions in the statute to impose greater procedural requirements in rulemaking is unfaithful to the purpose of the law?[30] Indeed, is it clear that such an interpretation is "bending" at all?

Suppose that Congress enacted a statute regulating banking with the understanding that the banking and securities businesses could be quite discrete and that banks would face little competition—but the rise of the money market fund has forced banks to compete in an integrated and competitive national market. In such circumstances, how should the Court decide whether a bank holding company can provide securities brokerage services in the face of statutory provisions containing various ambiguous restrictions on the combination of securities and banking business?[31]

The problem is that mechanical transplantation of statutory purposes to new settings is unlikely to produce sensible results; this is true from the standpoint of the enacting legislature. A usual understanding is that when a statute is ambiguous, interpreters should attempt to go back to the beliefs and hopes of the enacting legislature to determine how it would decide the question had it been presented. Judges should imaginatively reconstruct the original legislature, and the forces imposed on it, to see how it would deal with the new situation.[32] But in the face of changed circumstances, perhaps the better route would be to imagine the enacting legislature brought forward into the present and then to ask how it would decide the question in light of new developments of law, fact, and policy. This is the import of Justice Holmes's comment: "When we are dealing with words that also are a constituent act, like the Constitution of the United States, we must realize that they have called into life a being the development of which could not have been foreseen completely by the most gifted of its begetters . . . The case before us must be considered in the light of our whole experience and not merely in that of what was said a hundred years ago." [33] The comment applies not merely to the Constitution, but to the interpretation of all texts that operate in the face of changed circumstances.

The difference between backward-looking and forward-looking interpretation is a significant one. Consider, for example, *Bob Jones University v. United States*,[34] in which the Court was asked to decide whether a public policy exception to the charitable deduction required the Internal Revenue Service to deny that deduction to schools that discriminated on the basis of race. There is no doubt that if that question had been put to the Congress that initially enacted the relevant provision of the Code, it would have answered that there was no such requirement. Institutions that discriminated on the basis of race were common at that time, and they were not thought to violate public policy. But if the enacting Congress were brought forward to the present, and informed of changing developments of law and policy, it would in all likelihood have concluded that the deduction was impermissible. Perhaps the public policy exception should be taken to embody a general principle capable of change over time.

When circumstances have dramatically changed, backward-looking interpretation might produce absurd results, and often it is fully plausible that the enacting legislature itself intended the meaning of the statute not to be controlled by its original understanding. More likely, the legislature had no considered view on the question of backward-looking or forward-looking interpretation. In these circumstances, reliance on purpose will lead to intractable problems. Something other than purpose must be the basis for decision.

Nor is it sufficient to say that the legislature rather than the courts should respond to changed circumstances. Often it is unrealistic to expect a legislative response. Much more important, the issue for interpretation is the meaning of the statute in the new circumstances.[35] Meaning does not remain static across changes in law, policy, and fact. Interpretation that brings the legislature into the present will, however, inevitably involve a large measure of discretion; the characterization of purpose will inevitably have elements of creation as well as of discovery.[36]

For all of these reasons, purposive interpretation is far from a panacea. Although it is frequently helpful in providing a context within which to understand statutory terms, the effort to characterize legislative purpose often produces serious problems, whether or not circumstances have changed.

Legislative Intent and History. It is often suggested that in hard cases the meaning of the statute should be derived by ascertaining the intent of those who enacted it. This approach is similar to purposive interpretation, but here the goal is not to look at a general legislative aim or purpose, but instead to see more particularly how the enacting legislature wanted the question to be resolved. For example, the purpose of the statute prohibiting vehicles in the park may be to reduce noise and pollution; the legislative intent depends on whether members of the legislature saw (say) bicycles as "vehicles." For those who emphasize legislative intent, the legislative history is a central object of concern.

In recent years the Supreme Court has shown some internal division about both legislative intent and legislative history. Often it has suggested that the question for interpretation is one of congressional intent,[37] and in general, legislative history is treated as a key to the identification of intent. But some justices, most notably Justice Antonin Scalia, have expressed considerable doubt about legislative intent and legislative history in general.[38] In Justice Scalia's view, interpretation involves meaning, rather than intention. Legislative history is frequently written by well-organized private groups, and much of it, especially floor debates, is uninformative about congressional will.[39] Because the history does not reflect a considered legislative judgment about statutory meaning, judicial reliance on history tends to increase the power of interest groups over the interpretive process, and to do so at the expense of Congress itself. Above all, Justice Scalia contends, the legislative history was never enacted and is therefore not law.

Concerns of this sort are both legitimate and well taken. Usually the legislative history should not be permitted to defeat the statutory words as they are ordinarily understood in their context. This is so both because attention to language promotes the rule of law and because of constitutional and democratic considerations—the law rather than the intent was enacted. Moreover, such an approach is likely both to discipline Congress and to minimize judicial discretion. But Justice Scalia overstates his point. Frequently, the legislative history will reveal what some or many members of the Congress thought about the meaning of an ambiguous term, and it is important for the court to acquire that information. Rarely will the history simply reflect the views of self-interested private groups. Moreover, one cannot get a sense of the context and purpose of a statutory enactment without a reading of the legislative history; and as we have seen, context and purpose can provide significant interpretive help.

Finally, and most fundamentally, it is not clear where judges are to look if they fail to look at the legislative history. Without reference to the history, interpretation can become less bounded. Those who reject intent and history tend to be textualists, largely by default; but textualism is at best incomplete and sometimes perverse. And one can say all this without denying that Justice Scalia is correct in cautioning courts not to accord weight to legislative history at the expense of statutory language, and in recognizing the risk that parts of the history may have been composed by one or another side. In short, except in cases of unintended irrationality or injustice, courts should not permit history to overcome otherwise clear statutory language; but they would also be mistaken to ignore it.

For present purposes, the more fundamental point is that judicial reliance on legislative intent, whether or not derived on the basis of legislative history, suffers from a wide range of difficulties. First, legislative intent, like legislative purpose, is often a fiction in hard cases. The difficulties of aggregating the "intentions" of a legislative body, many of whose members would have resolved the issues in different ways or never thought about the question at all, are intractable. Frequently, intent is a myth—made rather than discovered. With or without these problems, there are risks of ambiguity, overinclusiveness, and underinclusiveness in relying on legislative intent, just as in relying on text and purpose.

These problems aside, it is far from clear that in all cases the lawmakers would want courts to decide cases of statutory construction by asking how the legislature intended the problem to be resolved. Congress may have sought to enact a general principle that is capable of change and growth over time. More realistically, the legislature will often have no considered view on the question whether its original intent is controlling. Issues of this sort suggest the flaws in the widely held idea that the original intentions of the legislature exhaust the meaning of a statute. In many circumstances Congress enacts a provision whose meaning is not solely a matter of original understanding, but partly a function of contemporary formulations of law, fact, and policy.

Consider, for example, the Immigration and Nationality Act, which excludes from the country aliens "afflicted with psychopathic personality, epilepsy, or a mental defect." [40] The Congress that enacted this provision believed that the phrase "psychopathic personality" included gays and lesbians. As Alexander Aleinikoff has argued,[41] however, contemporary medical (and ethical) views make the conclusion that gays and lesbians are not psychopathic probably irresistible. If this is so, courts might well conclude that what is controlling is the contemporary meaning of the statute, not what the statute's authors thought that it meant. The words were enacted; the original understanding was not. The problem is not unusual. The *Bob Jones* case raises the same issue; it comes up in many other contexts.

In the end, Congress enacts laws, not its own views about what those laws mean. Words have passed through the constitutionally specified mechanisms for enactment of laws; intentions have not, and they are therefore not binding. The role of the court is to decide on the meaning of the enacted words.[42] On that question, the intentions of a group or majority of lawmakers are sometimes relevant and helpful: if the legislators understood a statutory word as a term of art, that understanding should ordinarily prevail; courts should not indulge the usual meaning if it would produce unintended injustice or absurdity; legislative intentions, if truly ascertainable, should ordinarily be used to resolve ambiguities. But subjective intentions are not law, and are not controlling. For all these reasons, the notion of legislative intent is at best an incomplete guide to statutory construction.

Legal Process. Some enthusiastic supporters of purposive interpretation readily acknowledge that in some cases a reliance on purpose will be inadequate. Thus the celebrated treatment by Henry Hart and Albert Sacks in *The Legal Process* suggests that in solving hard cases the court "should assume, unless the contrary unmistakably appears, that the legislature was made up of reasonable persons pursuing reasonable purposes reasonably."[43] In a similar vein, Karl Llewellyn counselled courts to "strive to make sense *as a whole* out of our law *as a whole*."[44] Ernst Freund suggested that "in cases of genuine ambiguity courts should use the power of interpretation consciously and deliberately to promote sound law and sound principles of legislation."[45] Max Radin advised courts to ask: "Will the inclusion of this particular determinate in the statutory determinable lead to a desirable result?"[46]

Legal process approaches stand poised somewhere between agency theories of the judicial role and understandings of an altogether different sort. One group, particularly including Hart and Sacks, wishes to implement legislative commands by counseling courts to replicate legislative judgments on the point. Another seeks "reason" or "rationality" in statutes, quite apart from any actual or hypothetical judgment by the legislature.

On the agency view, the first problem with approaches of this sort is that they seem to be based on poor understandings about the legislative process. Hart and Sacks, for example, underplayed the role of interest groups in determining the content of statutes. The view that courts should treat statutes as if they promoted reasonable purposes in a reasonable way is a highly plausible one. Indeed, it will play a central role in the next chapter. But this claim is normative, not descriptive. The descriptive proposition is far from self-evident in view of the multiple pressures and purposes, many of them far from reasonable, that account for statutes, and the difficulties of aggregating preferences and beliefs in a multimember body. If taken seriously, the task of imposing reason on regulatory legislation often flies in the face of the legislation itself, and takes courts far from their traditional role as faithful agents of the legislature.

Much more fundamentally, the suggestion that courts should attempt to "make sense" of regulatory statutes, to treat them as would "reasonable people acting reasonably," or "to promote sound law and sound principles of legislation" is a conspicuous outgrowth of 1950s jurisprudence, when the "end of ideology" thesis played such a large role in political science and the law schools.[47] Advice of this sort is useful only when there is a consensus about what regulatory strategy makes sense or is reasonable. But in genuine interpretive disputes, such guidance is too open-ended to be helpful. Suppose that the question is whether the Occupational Safety and Health Act requires the agency to undertake cost-benefit analysis; whether the Civil Rights Act of 1964 outlaws race-conscious programs designed to increase the representation of blacks and women; and whether there is a private right of action to bring suit against polluters under the federal environmental laws. It is almost surely desirable for courts to interpret statutes so that they are reasonable and make sense; but without much more, these concepts are too contestable to be useful in hard cases. A perception of this point has led many to return to the text—an understandable but unsuccessful strategy.

Perhaps surprisingly, the same fundamental problems underlie the influential treatment of the subject by Ronald Dworkin.[48] Dworkin argues that courts should interpret statutes in accordance with the best principle that can be brought forward in support of what the legislature "has done." In Dworkin's view, the judge should see himself as "a partner continuing to develop, in what he believes is the best way, the statutory scheme Congress began." Thus the judge should ask "what coherent system of political convictions would best justify what [the legislature] has done," finding and applying to disputed issues of interpretation "the best justification . . . of a past legislative event."

This position is a clear heir to the legal process position—above all, in its emphasis on the use of judicial interpretation to produce reasonable results, to guard against arbitrariness, and to produce coherence in the legal system. In a number of respects, moreover, Dworkin's approach fits congenially with what I will be suggesting here. These include its insistence on judicial efforts to promote a principled rather than ad hoc set of legal requirements, and to foster what Dworkin calls "integrity" even in the face of legislative intent or the actual character of the legislative process.

Dworkin's approach is marred, however, by the open-ended and even banal character of its guiding interpretive principle—a failing that provides the final link between Dworkin's effort and that of the legal process school. The dangers of judicial discretion in searching for and giving content to "the best principle," and the relationship between any such principle and the legal culture as a whole, are largely unaddressed. The characteristics of the modern regulatory state are entirely invisible in Dworkin's treatment. There is no effort here to explore the substantive functions and failures of statutory regimes, or discussion of how the legal culture or the modern regulatory state might discipline the inquiry into interpretive principles. There is little exploration of the conspicuous dangers in permitting judges to discern "the best principle"—dangers aggravated by the largely untethered nature of Dworkin's effort to find the principle that best justifies what the legislature has done.

In Dworkin's account, far too sharp a dichotomy is drawn between "the best principle"—found through tools (to what extent?) external to the disputed provision or the prevailing legal culture—and "what the legislature has done," with the latter sometimes treated as if it were a kind of brute fact. His suggestion that courts should make the statute "the best that it can be" is quite close to Llewellyn's claim that courts should "make sense" of statutes, or Freund's argument that courts should promote "sound principles of legislation." In these respects, Dworkin's position is anachronistic, focusing in common law fashion on the judicial role in establishing "principle" and failing to come to terms with the distinctive purposes and pathologies of regulatory statutes. In these circumstances, an emphasis on text, history, or intention seems a most appealing refuge. In particular, reliance on text seems to have a far better democratic pedigree and to contain far more promise for limiting judicial discretion.

Similar problems beset Richard Posner's recent suggestion that "the judge's job is not to keep a statute up to date in the sense of making it reflect contemporary values, but to imagine as best he can how the legislators who enacted the statute would have wanted it applied to situations they did not foresee." [49] In hard cases this advice too is open-ended, and perhaps contradictory. Contemporary values may well be relevant to the legislature's own understanding of how statutes should apply to situations that it did not foresee. Furthermore, an entirely backward-looking approach of this sort may well lead to a less sensible system of law than would alternative approaches, as Posner himself seems to hint.[50] The final problem is that background norms of interpretation play an inevitable part in the process of statutory construction and cannot readily be captured in the notion of imaginative reconstruction.

The Traditional Sources and the Failure of the Agency View. With respect to the traditional tools of statutory construction, the discussion thus far suggests several conclusions. The text alone, in concert with shared background assumptions, is usually sufficient to resolve interpretive disputes. But sometimes it is ambiguous or reveals a delegation or gap. Moreover, the ordinary meaning of the words should not be decisive if the statutory structure or purpose (when subject to an uncontroversial characterization) suggests an alternative meaning, or if a literal interpretation would produce a conspicuously unjust or irrational application that was not clearly sought by the legislature. The legislative intent, as reflected in the legislative history, is admissible to resolve ambiguities; but usually it should not be permitted to overcome the ordinary meaning of the statutory words if that meaning is otherwise clear—except where literalism would produce unintended irrationality or injustice. In some cases, however, all of these sources of meaning will leave serious gaps or ambiguities.

As complete theories of statutory construction, then, the most prominent examples of the agency view of the judicial role appear to fail; it is time to see what conclusions emerge from that failure. Notably, the agency view amounts to a formalist approach to statutory construction—formalist because it sees the legal process as an entirely autonomous one, free from value-laden inquiries into (for example) appropriate institutional arrangements, or statutory function and failure, as part of the process of interpretation.

The agency view, and formalism itself, contain some important truths. It would be improper for courts to interpret statutes to mean whatever the judges think would be best. No one could defend an approach to statutory construction that would license judges to say that a statute means whatever they think a good statute would say. This basic understanding derives from the lawmaking primacy of the legislature—a product of the legislature's superior democratic pedigree[51] and its correlative power to do as it chooses, at least where there is no constitutional doubt. The Constitution itself accords to

Congress, and no one else, the power to make law. It follows that where there is neither interpretive doubt nor constitutional objection, it is the judgment of the electorally accountable branch, and not of the judges, that will prevail. Formalism in this sense, embodying a (political and value-laden) distinction between law and politics, is entirely unobjectionable.

But the broadest versions of the formalist position, and the agency view of statutory construction, are subject to two sorts of objections. First, the agency conception of "meaning" is far too crude. As we have seen, language is not self-interpreting, and sometimes it delegates, self-consciously or otherwise, gap-filling power to the courts. Courts cannot simply be agents. It is important to emphasize that this is a conceptual or logical claim, not a proposition about the appropriate distribution of powers among administrators, courts, and legislatures. It depends not at all on a belief in judicial activism, or on enthusiasm for the wisdom and decency of the judges. To recognize the need for interpretive norms is not to confer on courts power that they do not already, and necessarily, have.

Suppose this much were acknowledged, and it were suggested that courts should rely on the agency view as much as possible. Although this is a highly ambiguous concept, it can be taken to argue in favor of adherence to statutory meaning (perhaps text, perhaps text as informed by context, original meaning, or original intent) to the extent it is fairly ascertainable for judges using conventional or uncontested background norms. In such cases it is not, by hypothesis, necessary to introduce controversial norms in order to decide on what words mean, to fill gaps, or to resolve cases otherwise in equipoise; the usual or original understanding is sufficient. In general this approach is unobjectionable, but it will produce some serious anomalies. Examples here might include a statute allowing discharge by an employer of an employee for any reason, invoked in the case of an employee's discharge for refusal to commit a crime on the employer's behalf; or the words "cause cancer" in the Delaney Clause, invoked to require the FDA to regulate minimal risks, with attendant costs to health itself.

As these examples suggest, the second problem for the agency view is that its claim about legitimacy relies on question-begging and probably indefensible premises. That claim must be defended by a set of institutional and substantive arguments, and those arguments are hard to supply. The claim must be that a formalist approach to con-

struction—again, to the limited extent that it is possible—is constitutionally mandated, or that it will lead on balance to the best or most
sensible system of law. This claim must be understood as a belief that
the ordinary or original meaning of words must control, even if it
would lead to results that are unintended, or absurd or unjust, or
both. But it is far more likely that the occasional introduction of other
considerations will accomplish that goal.

Assume, for example, that statutory language, while ambiguous, is
most naturally read to lead in a direction that is, by general consensus, irrational; that a statute might be understood as giving open-
ended authority to a bureaucracy; that the most obvious reading of a
statute provides bizarre results in light of changes in the fifty years
since its enactment; or that an appropriations measure appears to
intrude on a carefully elaborated and sensible compromise in the environmental field. We will encounter many such cases below. In all of
these settings, invocation of nonformal considerations will lead to
better outcomes. In such cases, courts that act as something other
than mere agents and invoke contestable background norms will produce a more sensible system of law. Indeed, sometimes such a role
will be consistent with the best reading of Congress' interpretive instructions or is the best understanding to attribute to Congress when
it has made no considered judgment on the point. Interpreters should
be authorized to depart from the original meaning and to press the
usual meaning of words in particular directions if the context suggests
that this strategy would lead to superior outcomes.[52] And in view of
the long history of a role of this sort, it could not plausibly be thought
unconstitutional.

Of course there are risks in admitting power of this sort, largely in
the form of an increase in judicial discretion. Such discretion will not
always be exercised wisely, and the test for superior outcomes will
necessarily call into play controversial judgments of value and policy.
No decisive argument is available to demonstrate why and to what
extent the recognition of such authority will make matters better
rather than worse. But it is possible to point to institutional characteristics on the part of the judiciary that occasionally justify an aggressive role in interpretation.

Above all, the focus on the particular circumstances enables judges
to deal with applications that any legislature, no matter how far-
sighted, could not conceivably have envisaged. Broad statutory terms
may be perfectly sensible and comprehensible in the abstract, but dif-

ficulties emerge as those terms are applied in particular settings. Mechanical application of those terms in such settings is unlikely to produce sound results, even from the standpoint of the enacting legislature. In this respect, judicial decision of individual cases, allowing an emphasis on the particular context, contains significant advantages for interpretation. Consider here an attempt to inherit, under a generally worded spousal inheritance statute, by someone who has murdered his spouse.

Judicial independence is an important ingredient here as well. Because of their deliberative capacities, courts have significant advantages over a sometimes interest-driven legislature that is frequently responsive to momentary demands—a point confirmed by work in the public choice tradition. Considerations of this sort were emphasized by Alexander Hamilton in *The Federalist,* quite outside of the context of constitutional review.[53] The reservation of judicial authority to push ambiguous statutes in particular directions seems more rather than less likely to yield a coherent, rational, and just system of law. That position is consistent with historical practice as well.[54]

In cases in which the text, accompanied by conventional interpretive norms, is clear, it would of course be possible to use contestable principles modestly or quite aggressively. One might, for example, invoke the federalism principle so as to construe federal statutes extremely narrowly, preventing preemption unless there has been an exceptionally clear statement from Congress. Indeed, courts have occasionally used interpretive norms so as to construe statutes in ways that are plainly inconsistent with the outcome that would be reached through reliance on text, purpose, and ordinary understandings of linguistic commands. Judges and others who reject the formalist position can therefore be placed on a continuum from those who invoke contested background norms quite rarely, and almost always rely on the ordinary meaning of words, to those who use such sources to push statutes in particular directions in the absence of an absolutely unambiguous statement from Congress.

As a general rule, courts ought to be relatively modest with contestable background norms. The usual and indeed original meaning of words should ordinarily govern. Any other approach would lead to judicial abuses, and for reasons that go to the basic premise of democratic primacy. As we will see, however, courts should sometimes be more inventive in statutory interpretation. Here the problem with the agency theory is not so much that it is incomplete, but instead that it represents a choice among alternatives, and a pernicious one. There are cases in which the language of a statute will produce absurdity, in which constitutional considerations counsel courts to interpret statutes aggressively, in which changed circumstances call for innovation, and in which attention to interest-group power and statutory failure will justify a more creative role for the courts. In the abstract, it is difficult to decide to what extent departures from the agency model are appropriate. Chapters 5 and 6 deal more concretely with the problem.

Extratextual Norms

It is perhaps in response to the inadequacy of the agency theories that courts and commentators have sometimes developed approaches that rely on extratextual norms. Three such approaches have been of special importance in the last generation. The first invokes the difficulties in aggregating diverse legislative views and suggests that statutes represent "deals" among self-interested actors; the second invokes a background rule in favor of private autonomy; the third calls for a rule of deference to regulatory agencies. But these approaches also suffer from significant flaws.

"Deals." Both purposive interpretation and legal process approaches have been rejected by commentators finding guidance in welfare economics and modern public choice theory. On this view the legislative process is a series of interest-group struggles, and courts should develop interpretive principles from that foundation. The underlying conception of politics is that of interest-group pluralism, which sees politics as a battle for scarce resources among self-interested private groups. This view is often accompanied by a reference to the difficulties in aggregating the preferences and beliefs of numerous legislators. Collective action problems, strategic and manipulative behavior, and cycling make it difficult to think that legislative votes can be aggregated into a coherent or unitary statutory "purpose." [55] Courts ought, in this view, to enforce the unprincipled "deal" reflected in law.

Some of those who urge this view find its foundations in the thought of the framers of the American Constitution. [56] Consequently they suggest that courts charged with interpreting statutes should avoid reliance on unitary or public-regarding purposes, and instead enforce the statute according to its terms, which reveal the relevant deal. Courts should not see legislators as reasonable people acting reasonably; instead, statutes are often the disorderly outcomes of multiple pressures imposed on multiple actors. The contrast with the legal process school in particular could not be sharper.

Consider, for example, how an advocate of the deals approach might approach the question whether a federal statute banning racial discrimination in employment implicitly authorizes victims of discrimination to bring private suits against employers. If the statute does not expressly provide for private suits, the victims have not obtained that right as part of the statutory deal, and the right should be denied. By contrast, a court that saw the legislature as reasonable people acting reasonably, or that treated legislation as public-spirited, might well recognize private suits as a way of enforcing the statutory mandate.[57]

Advocates of the deals approach are correct to emphasize legislative compromise, and they have also performed a valuable role in suggesting that legislative purposes are often multiple and even conflicting. An interpreter's emphasis on a unitary purpose may be untrue to the enactment. Where there is an unambiguous deal, courts should be faithful to it. As a theory of statutory interpretation, however, this approach suffers from many of the failings of textualism.

The first problem is one of indeterminacy. In many cases the terms of any deal will be hopelessly unclear in the absence of background understandings that a system of interpretation—one that has nothing to do with deals—alone can supply. For example, an approach that sees statutes as deals is in fact unhelpful in cases involving implied causes of action. If a statute is treated as a deal between industries seeking protection against too much regulation on the one hand, and civil rights groups attempting to prevent discrimination on the other, what result is appropriate? The answer would be obvious if there were a background norm to the effect that regulatory statutes generally create private rights of action. In that case, the failure of industry to obtain a prohibition on such rights would suggest that the "deal" authorized them. The result would also be clear if the background norm forbade private rights without explicit legislative authorization: the deal did not include them. But the claim that statutes should be understood as deals provides no help in deciding on the relevant background norm against which the deal must be read. In the end, advocates of the deals approach—like most formalists—rely on an unarticulated substantive background norm; and it is that norm, on which the deals approach is utterly unhelpful and indeed silent, that is the true basis for decision.

Suppose that the problem of indeterminacy could nevertheless be overcome, and that in a certain category of cases a clear answer would emerge if statutes were treated as deals among self-interested actors. Suppose too that legislative preferences frequently cannot be aggregated into a coherent whole. The question remains whether courts should treat statutes as unprincipled deals. The argument in favor would have to claim that the legal system that would emerge is constitutionally compelled or would be preferable to the alternatives. Such an argument would stress the dangers of judicial discretion, the claim that statutes are in fact deals, the likelihood that a system of deals will be responsive to constituent demands for law, and the value of obtaining deals in the first place.[58]

Often, however, efforts to understand statutes as deals depend on artificial premises. Undoubtedly the deals idea has considerable explanatory power, but the empirical work points in two directions here.[59] Numerous people help produce statutes, and it is not easy to see how the multiple forces can meaningfully produce a deal. There is evidence in addition that public officials respond not merely to electoral self-interest—indeterminate as it is in many cases—or the exercise of political power by relevant groups, but rely instead on their own conception of the public interest. Many statutes cannot be explained in terms of interest-group pluralism. The claim of realism is therefore greatly overstated.

Even if statutes were deals, the argument that courts should treat them as such tends to break down if pluralist conceptions of politics cannot be defended. It is notable in this regard that far from having a good constitutional pedigree, the pluralist formulation runs afoul of the fundamental constitutional norm against naked interest-group transfers. That norm proscribes legislative efforts to transfer resources from one group to another simply because of political power. The norm has firm roots in both Madisonian republicanism—designed to ensure a measure of deliberation in government—and in current law under a number of constitutional provisions, including the equal protection, due process, eminent domain, and contracts clauses.[60]

To be sure, courts invalidate statutes as naked interest-group transfers quite infrequently, almost always finding a public-regarding justification for legislation. But judicial deference here is largely a product of the institutional position of the judiciary, which leads courts to give legislatures the benefit of every doubt. The infrequent enforcement of the norm against naked preferences should not be taken to deny its constitutional status, which can be vindicated by courts much less intrusively, and to that extent more justifiably, through statutory construction. An effort to treat statutes as mere deals would thus be inconsistent with the basic constitutional background.

The problems of the deals approach are not limited to indeterminacy, overstated realism, and lack of fit with the constitutional structure. That approach is difficult to defend on independent grounds. Interest-group pluralism is sometimes justified on the ground that it accurately aggregates citizen preferences, but in fact it is unlikely to perform that function. Pluralist systems instead reflect collective action problems, strategic behavior, cycling problems, the power of various groups over the agenda, and a host of other undesirable effects. Even if accurate preference aggregation could be achieved through politics, it is far from clear that the system would warrant support. Politics performs a number of functions that cannot be captured in the notion of aggregation of private preferences. As we have seen, aspirations, altruistic preferences, the interests of future generations, adaptive preferences, social subordination, and other matters have called forth statutory regimes protecting a range of values that will be ignored in a pluralist system.

Finally, courts that treat statutes as deals will tend to produce incoherence and irrationality in the law. Consider, for example, the question whether federal statutes regulating nuclear power plants preempt state tort law. In the absence of explicit legislative guidance, it would be far better for courts to attempt to fit state and federal law together, to the extent that they are able to do so, rather than to see if the constellation of interest groups compels a decision one way or the other.

A legal system that sees statutes as interest-group deals will therefore suffer from a wide range of problems. By contrast, a regime in which interpreters treat statutes as public-regarding is more likely to push statutes in public-regarding directions. Such a system would attempt to limit the reach of interest-group transfers and diminish the power of self-interested private groups. Where there is ambiguity in the statute, it would attempt to compensate for failures in legislative deliberation and to minimize the problems that arise from disparities in influence over political processes. A court should of course respect any deal that is unambiguously reflected in law. But a legal order that is alert to the risks of deals and that attempts to make sense of enactments will be far superior. The multiple failings of interest-group pluralism confirm the point.

Private Ordering. Sometimes it is suggested that courts should resolve interpretive doubts with a presumption in favor of private ordering. On this view, the constitutional system leaves citizens free to conduct their affairs without governmental interference, and that basic principle requires courts to interpret statutes to extend only as far as their explicit language and history require.[61] Under this view, for example, implied causes of action should be denied, not because statutes are deals, but because courts should not interpret statutes to intrude on private autonomy except to the extent that they are compelled to do so. On the same model, a statute providing for workers' compensation benefits would not prevent employers from discharging employees who file benefit claims, because employers may generally fire employees for whatever reason they choose, and the legislature has not specifically deprived employers of that right.

An interpretive principle of this sort would have enormous consequences for statutory interpretation, limiting statutes in all areas of social and economic regulation. Statutes regulating pollution, discrimination, securities fraud, and deceptive trade practices would be read as narrowly as possible. All gaps and ambiguities would be interpreted against application of the statute.

The presumption in favor of private ordering is nothing new. It is merely the most recent incarnation of the view that statutes in derogation of the common law should be narrowly construed. As we have seen, courts in the early part of this century attempted to limit the reach of regulatory statutes by reference to baselines rooted in laissez-faire and the common law. In some legal systems, and in some contexts, such a presumption would be desirable; and when Congress has neither legislated nor left a gap for interpreters to fill, no law constrains private behavior.

But in the wake of the New Deal attack on the common law and the subsequent rights revolution, a presumption in favor of private ordering can no longer be sustained. That presumption is no longer the appropriate background rule under a number of statutory regimes. This is so partly because the post-New Deal system is generally superior to its common law predecessor, recognizing as it does that modern regulation often promotes both economic welfare and distributive justice. But the more fundamental problem with a presumption in favor of private ordering is its inconsistency with the values that underlie modern government. Such a presumption would invoke understandings repudiated by the democratic branches of government in order—ironically—to discern the reach of statutes enacted and administered by those very branches. It would be exceptionally presumptuous for courts to invoke laissez-faire principles in support of such a judicial role. Gaps should not be filled in, and ambiguities should not be resolved, by reference to values that counter those of the enacting Congress in particular and the modern regulatory state in general.

Deference to Agency Interpretations. An alternative view, finding considerable support in recent cases, has it that courts should defer to agency interpretations of law whenever the statute is ambiguous. Because of their superior accountability and expertise, it is said, agencies should be given the benefit of every doubt. This view has firm roots in the New Deal period, with its enthusiasm for administrative autonomy; and it places a strong emphasis on the displacement of judicial lawmaking brought about by the creation of regulatory schemes. Thus it is that in the exceptionally important *Chevron* case, the Supreme Court said that courts should defer to agency interpretations of law unless Congress had "directly spoken to the precise question at issue." [62]

Even if read for all it is worth, the *Chevron* position would not resolve all disputed statutory questions. It would remain necessary to decide when statutes are ambiguous, and on that question courts have to rely on some methodology that is independent of the rule of deference. But a rule of deference would have significant consequences, since it would remit all disputed cases to regulatory agencies for administrative resolution. Moreover, such a rule has considerable appeal. The *Chevron* approach might enable agencies to apply their expertise to complex regulatory problems; take the harsh edges off laws; allow coordination and consistency in the regulatory process; counteract obsolescence; and promote accountability by taking account of the views of different administrations. [63] The approach is especially desirable when Congress has delegated law-interpreting power to the agency or when the question involves the agency's factfinding and policymaking competence, as in cases of mixed issues of law and fact.

For several reasons, however, a general rule of judicial deference to all agency interpretations of law would be unsound. Under the constitutional system, it is ordinarily for courts to say what the law is, and the case for deference to agency interpretations of law must therefore depend in the first instance on the law in the form of congressional instruction.[64] If Congress has told courts to defer to agency interpretations, courts should do so. But many of the recent regulatory statutes were born out of legislative distrust for agency discretion; these statutes hardly call for deference to agency interpretations. As we have seen, they represent an effort to limit administrative authority through clear legislative specifications. A rule of deference in the face of ambiguity would be inconsistent with an appreciation, endorsed by Congress, of the considerable risks posed by administrative discretion. An ambiguity is not a delegation of law-interpreting power. *Chevron* elides the two.

Furthermore, the notion that administrators may interpret statutes they administer is inconsistent with separation-of-powers principles that date back to the early days of the American republic[65] and that retain considerable vitality today. The basic case for judicial review depends on the proposition that foxes should not guard henhouses. It would be most peculiar, for example, to argue that courts should defer to congressional or state interpretations of constitutional provisions whenever there is ambiguity in the constitutional text; such a rule would wreak havoc with existing law and indeed with constitutionalism itself. Institutions limited by a legal restriction are not to be permitted to determine the nature of the limitation, or to decide on its scope. The relation of the Constitution to Congress parallels the relation of regulatory statutes to agencies. In both contexts, an independent arbiter should determine the nature of the limitation.

This basic principle assumes special importance in light of the awkward constitutional position of the administrative agency. Broad delegations of power to regulatory agencies, questionable in light of the grant of legislative power to Congress in Article I of the Constitution, have been allowed largely on the assumption that courts would be available to ensure agency fidelity to whatever statutory directives have been issued. If agencies are able to interpret ambiguities in these directives, the delegation problem increases dramatically. A firm judicial hand in the interpretation of statutes is thus desirable. The point can be made more vivid by imagining cases involving the question whether agency action is reviewable; whether agencies may issue fines; whether agency authority extends to a new or unforeseen area. It would be odd to say that the agency is permitted to decide the meaning of laws whose scope is directly relevant to the agency's self-interest. In short, a general rule of deference to agency interpretations of law would be inconsistent with the best reading of Congress' interpretive instructions, with the constitutional backdrop, and with the goal of promoting sound regulatory policy.[66]

Indeterminacy and Conventionalism

If the agency view is inevitably incomplete, and if some of the most prominent supplemental norms are hard to defend, the question becomes whether it is impossible to generate an approach to statutory construction that (1) adequately describes actual practice and (2) would be worthy of adoption. Some observers suggest that the interpretation of statutes produces "indeterminacy" in most or all cases.[67] Others, most notably Stanley Fish, style themselves conventionalists, and contend that it is not possible to theorize about interpretation, but only to "do" it, within the context of interpretive conventions so widely shared that they inevitably grip and constrain interpreters.

Those who accept conventionalism and those who believe that statutory interpretation produces indeterminacy disagree in an important way. For conventionalists, meaning is hardly open-ended. On the contrary, the conventionalist claim is that interpretive assumptions are so ingrained and pervasive that meaning is almost always determinate, and indeed the dichotomy between "subjective" and "objective" interpretation collapses. But the two positions have a large commonality. Both of them reject the possibility of criteria with which to distinguish between good and bad interpretations; in both accounts, words have the meaning that they do because people in a position of authority so interpret them. In this respect the indeterminacy thesis and conventionalism are at one; and it is here that both positions seem inadequate.

Indeterminacy. It is not always clear whether the claim of indeterminacy is intended to be normative or positive. On one view, for example, there are no correct answers to questions of statutory interpretation, but instead merely subjective (and perhaps arbitrary) opinions. On a quite different view, judicial decisions cannot be predicted in advance, even if there are criteria by which reasonable people might mediate among competing views.

Whether normative or positive, the suggestion that statutory meaning is indeterminate is widely overstated. Claims about the inevitable indeterminacy of interpretation usually suffer from a failure to take account of the contextual character of linguistic commands. When taken in their setting—in their culture and context—statutes are usually susceptible to only one plausible meaning. Judicial interpretation of statutes is frequently quite predictable, largely because background norms are uncontested among the judges. Even where background norms are disputed, it is often possible to know how the case will come out, because the governing norms are entirely predictable. For this reason, the claim of indeterminacy, if taken as a positive one, is implausible.

Moreover, it is possible to show as well, and by reference to reasons, that some interpretations are correct. To say that a value judgment is implicated in the choice of interpretive strategies or background norms is hardly to say that the choice among them is arbitrary or whimsical. The existence of subjectivity is a reason for a conclusion of arbitrariness only for the most incorrigible of positivists. Moreover, the fact that someone might argue that a statute means something other than what it appears to say, or characterize the legislative purpose in a counterintuitive way, does not mean that such arguments are convincing or even plausible. It should be a familiar point that the existence of hard cases does not show that all cases are hard; and as we will see, it is possible to develop criteria by which to deal with hard cases.

Conventionalism. It is correct and salutary to emphasize, as conventionalists do, that interpretive assumptions are always in force, and that texts are without inherent or necessary meanings in the strong sense that those meanings hold across different contexts and cultures. Moreover, some words simply mean what they mean; they are not a subject of reflection and criticism to someone who speaks the language. But these claims—attacks on implausible versions of textualism or formalism—provide no real help in the descriptive or normative tasks of interpretation. They do not explain how conflicts within a group of interpreters should be or are resolved. Above all, they do not suggest that participants in or observers of the legal culture should rest content with existing interpretive strategies, and that it is impossible to evaluate those strategies or proposed alternatives. Some such strategies are in fact a product of choice, and here choices turn on the reasons that can be offered in their behalf.

Consider, for example, the view that courts should defer to administrative interpretations of law, or narrowly construe measures interfering with state autonomy, or read ambiguous statutes to impose costs proportionate with their benefits, or interpret statutes generously to the Indian tribes. These principles play a large role in statutory construction, and they are contested within the courts. To say, with conventionalists, that texts simply mean what they mean, or what powerful or professional people think that they mean, is to give up on the important questions altogether.

Moreover, the conventionalist observation that interpretive norms themselves need interpretation hardly suggests that there are not criteria for assessing particular norms, or that people are unable to explain why such norms would make things worse rather than better. All of the norms mentioned above, for example, are subject to evaluation; and if universally accepted, they would have considerable importance.

In short, the conventionalist account is both too crude and too flat. It fails to account for the related phenomena of choice between interpretive strategies and of change over time. It treats interpreters as always the objects or recipients, and never the subjects or creators, of interpretive practice. In light of the omnipresence of choice, there is room for both theory and practice. The one informs the other, and this is so whether or not there are ultimate foundations (whatever such a thing might mean) with which to make assessments. There remains, then, a need to identify principles of interpretation, to explain how the process of construction takes place, and to provide help in the genuinely hard cases—large in number though not in proportion—in which there is interpretive doubt. As we will see, these principles are directly connected to an understanding and improvement of constitutional government after the rights revolution.

Criteria. It will be useful to see whether the criticisms of the extratextual norms discussed thus far might suggest some criteria by which to evaluate such norms. We have seen that a broad private autonomy principle is objectionable as a theory of the appropriate role of the state; as a guide to statutory construction, it fails above all because of its lack of fit with the modern regulatory structure and its underlying values. In contrast, the idea of agency deference has the virtue of attempting to respond to the practical operation of the regulatory state; it is unacceptable because of its inconsistency with congressional desires and the constitutional backdrop, and because of the likelihood that, if adopted, it would impair the performance of regulatory institutions. The "deals" approach properly attempts to bring to bear a realistic understanding of legislative processes. The understanding is too crude, however, and the deals approach would ultimately graft onto interpretation a conception of politics that would increase regulatory irrationality and injustice and that is in any case in severe tension with the constitutional framework.

If these criticisms are persuasive, they suggest that in order to be acceptable, interpretive norms must be consistent with the constitutional structure and with the fabric of modern public law; must improve rather than impair the operation of government institutions; and must reflect a conception of politics that is likely, if adopted, to combat pathologies in regulatory practice. Criteria of this sort are highly value-laden, but they suggest that it is possible both to criticize conventions and to mediate among different interpretive norms.

Interpretive Principles

The Unlikely Promise of Canons

If the traditional understandings of statutory construction are inadequate, how ought the problem to be approached? Some help might be found in an unlikely place. In interpreting statutes, courts have often relied on canons of construction. I will use the term "canons" to refer to all background principles of interpretation that are used in statutory construction.

We have seen, for example, that an important principle—prominent in the early period of administrative regulation—counseled courts to construe statutes narrowly when they were in derogation of the common law.[68] If, for example, it was unclear whether Congress intended to limit an employer's authority over employees as understood in common law, courts would interpret the statute so as not to intrude on that authority. Sometimes courts used this device quite aggressively, pushing a statute in a particular direction unless Congress provided unambiguous evidence of its intention to the contrary. This basic approach to regulatory statutes operated as the statutory analogue to the constitutional principle in *Lochner v. New York*,[69] in which the Court treated statutory measures as impermissible deviations from the neutral principles reflected in the common law. Both principles were rejected, and for the same reasons. They used a highly controversial set of regulatory ideas, embodied in nineteenth-century common law, as the baseline against which to decide the reach of a set of innovations developed by the democratic branches as a self-conscious rejection of the common law.

Legal realism provided some of the impetus behind the rejection of common law baselines. The realists, important contributors to the New Deal reformation, argued that governmental power lay behind common law rules, which could not, therefore, be treated as merely facilitative of private desires; those rules played a constitutive role as well.[70] The realists also attempted to discredit the canons of statutory construction. The most important example is Karl Llewellyn's celebrated effort to demonstrate that for each canon there is an equal canon pointing in the opposite direction.[71] The canon calling for adherence to the plain meaning of the text is countered by the principle that courts should vindicate the spirit of the law; the notion that statutes in derogation of the common law should be narrowly construed meets the principle that remedial statutes should be broadly construed; the idea that every word and clause should be given effect is countered by the principle that words and clauses may be rejected when they are repugnant to the rest of the statute. Llewellyn argued that dozens of canons of construction met counterparts that effectively nullified them.

In Llewellyn's view, an inspection of the decisions revealed that the canons of construction operated as mechanical, after-the-fact recitations disguising the reasons for decision. In the realist view, the real basis was frequently an illegitimate judicial policy preference. Even when it was not, the canons had the disadvantage of substituting unhelpful and mechanical rules for a more pragmatic and functional inquiry into statutory purposes and structure in the particular case. For the realists, the canons of construction were unhelpful, indeterminate, mutually contradictory, and at best meaningless boilerplate inserted into opinions in order to justify results reached on independent grounds.[72]

This view of the canons of construction has deeply penetrated modern legal culture. Almost no one has had a favorable word to say about them in many years.[73] For the most part, the canons are treated as anachronisms held over from the days of legal formalism.

Llewellyn's demonstration was persuasive insofar as it characterized the use of canons as a crude version of formalism. In fact, however, his claim of indeterminacy and mutual contradiction was greatly overstated, and some of the canons actually influenced judicial behavior, reflecting as they did background norms that helped give meaning to statutory words or to resolve hard cases. The notion that courts should narrowly construe statutes that stood in derogation of the common law is the most prominent example. As we have seen, Llewellyn was left in the end with hopelessly banal advice, suggesting that decisions depended on *"the sense of the situation as seen by the court"* and that "a court must strive to make sense *as a whole* out of our law *as a whole.*" [74] He failed to give substantive guidance about what "sense" might mean in different contexts, and he did not unpack the notion of "sense" and its possible relationship to canons of construction. Indeed, he did not recognize that quite particular, and defensible, conceptions of "sense," often forming the judge's initial, intuitive, or even considered approach to a dispute, might be reflected in canons of construction.

In a manner characteristic of legal realists, Llewellyn attempted to liberate legal fault from what he saw as flawed structures by denying the need for structures altogether, but inevitably structures will be present. His argument was also infected by a failure to appreciate the functions and failures of regulatory statutes. Because of this failure, it belongs in the same category as the common law understandings that, ironically, were his principal target.

The importance of Llewellyn's argument lay in its plea for particularism in statutory construction and in its persuasive if somewhat overstated claim that canons sometimes operated as a disguise for controversial substantive judgments, as unduly mechanical guides to interpretation, and as after-the-fact rationalizations. The canons sometimes did seem to offer contradictory guidance, or to be so abstract as to provide no help at all. And the use of canons—indeed the very term—is widely denigrated, largely because of their association with legal formalism and with approaches to interpretation that prevailed during the late nineteenth century.

But the canons of construction continue to be a prominent feature in the federal and state courts. The use of guides to interpretation—in the form of principles requiring a clear statement from Congress to reach certain results and background understandings—can be found in every area of modern law. And there is no sign that canons are decreasing in importance. Words cannot be interpreted without some sort of understanding about the background against which they are written. Moreover, some background principles seem to embody

plausible or even irresistible judgments about how words should ordinarily be understood, or how regulatory statutes should interact
with constitutional structure and substantive policy.

An analogy may be helpful here. The law of contracts is pervaded
by—indeed, it consists largely of—a set of principles filling in contractual gaps when the parties have been silent, or when the meaning
of their words is unclear.[75] It would be most peculiar to say that implied terms ("off the rack" provisions) are an illegitimate incursion
into the usual process of interpreting the parties' intent. Without implied terms of some sort, contracts simply would not be susceptible
to construction. Imagine, for example, that the parties have been silent on the time and place of performance, damages in the event of
breach, the consequences of dramatically changed circumstances, or
the consequences of a partial default. Implied terms are an unavoidable part of the process of construing contractual silences and terms,
and they provide the background against which people enter into
agreements.

To a large degree, interpretive principles serve the same function in
public law. They too help judges to construe both statements and
silences; they too should not be seen as the intrusion of controversial
judgments into ordinary interpretation. But there are differences as
well as similarities. In the law of contract, it is often said that implied
terms should attempt to "mimic the market" by doing what the parties would do if they had made provision on the subject.[76] In the law
of statutory construction, by contrast, the notion of mimicking the
market is far from a complete guide. Sometimes it will be unclear how
Congress would have resolved the question; sometimes the resolution
of the enacting Congress would have been different from that of the
current Congress, and it is not clear whose resolution should control;
sometimes courts properly call into play principles—many of them
constitutionally inspired—that push statutes away from the conclusion Congress would probably have reached if it had resolved the
matter.

The Functions of Interpretive Principles

Part of the problem in coming to terms with the canons, or background principles of interpretation, stems from the fact that they
serve a variety of different goals. Some of these functions are invisible:
the norms are so widely shared and so central to the very process of

communicating in English that they seem to be part of the words rather than the interpreter's tools. Some such "norms" are simply part of meaning and not subject to discussion; others are value-laden and can be evaluated. Still other norms look to values that are more conspicuously substantive or institutional; these norms often seem extratextual. Many interpretive norms serve multiple functions simultaneously, however, and the invisible norms serve institutional and substantive goals as well. But for the sake of exposition, we may group the functions of norms in four basic categories.

Syntactic Norms. Interpretive principles may orient the judicial reader to the text to help him ascertain its meaning in the particular case. This is the most uncontroversial function of the canons, though not all of them sensibly promote this goal. Most of these principles are so internalized that they are invisible and operate as an ordinary part of grammar or syntax itself. Some of them have been explicitly identified as guides to interpretation.

Thus, for example, the language of a particular provision will be taken in the context of the statute as a whole, and will not be interpreted so as to do violence to statutory structure.[77] This will be helpful in ascertaining the meaning of a term which, if understood in a different context, would be ambiguous or indeed have a clear meaning contrary to that indicated by the particular setting. The assumption that even apparently unambiguous statutory terms might have a counterintuitive meaning if other provisions of the statute so indicate is a sensible way of understanding statutory meaning in the particular case.

Suppose, for example, that the question is whether the term "feasible," a legal prerequisite for agency action under a regulatory statute, calls for a weighing of costs and benefits, or instead tells the agency to act unless the industry would be seriously jeopardized by the regulation. If the word "feasible" is used in the same sentence or provision as the term "cost-benefit analysis," then it is reasonable to assume that the word "feasible" itself does not call for cost-benefit balancing; otherwise the statute would be redundant or incoherent. The same considerations support the principle that statutory provisions should be read so as not to create an internal conflict.[78] Likewise, where there is a potential conflict, specific provisions should prevail over general terms in the same statute.[79]

Another syntactic principle is the controversial one of "expressio unius est exclusio alterius": to include one thing is to exclude another.

Courts sometimes use this principle when Congress has specified a list of actors entitled to something—say, the people authorized to obtain review of federal administrative action, or to obtain welfare benefits—in order to support the conclusion that those outside the specified categories are not entitled to the good in question.[80] In this view, the failure expressly to entitle the actors in question to the relevant good is an implicit decision to deny them that good, since Congress expressly singled out those people to whom it wanted the good to be granted.

If used mechanically, "expressio unius" will lead to incorrect results. The failure to refer explicitly to a particular group may reflect inadvertence, inability to reach consensus, or a decision to delegate the decision to the courts, rather than an implicit negative legislative decision on the subject. Congress could have explicitly solved the problem by specifying that the group in question may *not* receive the benefit, and the availability of that option weakens the inference that silence resolves the issue against the group.

Sometimes, however, the principle is a helpful way of discovering statutory meaning in a particular case. For example, in *Steelworkers v. Weber*,[81] the Court was asked to decide whether Congress had outlawed voluntary affirmative action by prohibiting "discrimination on the basis of race." In concluding that Congress had not done so, the Court relied on the provision saying that Congress did not intend to "compel" affirmative action, a provision whose enactment would be most puzzling if the basic antidiscrimination principle already invalidated affirmative action.

Similar considerations apply to the principle of "ejusdem generis," which suggests that where general words follow a specific enumeration, the general words should be limited to persons or things similar to those enumerated. This principle derives from an understanding that the general words are probably not intended to include matters entirely far afield from the specific enumeration. Indeed, the general words, if understood to be truly general, would make the specific enumeration redundant.

In some circumstances, the plain meaning approach to statutory construction—counseling courts to interpret the statute in accordance with its terms and to ignore considerations of history, structure, and policy in the face of clear text—is a similar effort to help orient the reader to make an accurate assessment of statutory meaning in the particular case.[82] The statutory language, if it is indeed plain, is the most accurate guide to the meaning of the statute. The plain meaning principle can therefore be understood as a means of avoiding reliance on factors that are likely to be misleading or not relevant. Meaning is a function of context, however, and insofar as the plain meaning approach argues in favor of disregarding context, it is misguided.

Interpretive Instructions. Interpretive principles may serve as guides to what might be called the interpretive instructions of the legislature. Such principles are designed to capture an actual or hypothetical legislative judgment about how statutes should be construed. They do not serve as guidance to meaning in the particular case, but instead attempt to incorporate explicit or implicit congressional desires with respect to the interpretive process.

The easiest cases here involve express legislative instructions about interpretation. Thus the first sections of the United States Code set out a series of guidelines for courts to follow in interpreting statutes.[83] The codes of other countries follow similar routes. Sometimes particular statutes provide guidance about interpretation—by, for example, calling for courts to interpret ambiguities in favor of those who rely on the statute. When the legislature has been explicit, there can be no objection to judicial use of the relevant instructions.

Some interpretive principles, however, are a product of an understanding of implicit rather than explicit legislative interpretive instructions. Here courts interpret statutes by concluding that Congress would prefer a particular interpretive strategy. For example, a familiar and often quite important principle is that appropriations measures should not lightly be taken to amend substantive statutes.[84] That principle is hard to defend as a means of ascertaining statutory meaning in particular cases. In truth, appropriations statutes are often designed to amend substantive statutes. But the principle becomes more plausible if it is understood as an effort to understand how Congress would want courts to interpret appropriations measures that it has enacted. Indeed, the rules of the House and Senate argue in favor of this idea, setting forth a general prohibition on substantive lawmaking through appropriations.[85]

Consider, in the same vein, the idea that statutes should be construed so as to avoid constitutional invalidity.[86] Although this principle does not attempt to discern statutory meaning in the particular case, it might be justified as an accurate reflection of how Congress would want courts to interpret statutes at the border of unconstitutionality. It is exceedingly reasonable to assume that Congress would prefer validation to invalidation.

Another example is the idea that judicial review of agency decisions will be presumed to be available.[87] Congress wants agencies to comply with its instructions, and in the absence of a clear statement to the contrary, courts should assume that litigants can enlist the judiciary to vindicate the claim that agencies have violated the law.

Improving Lawmaking. A third function of interpretive principles is to promote better lawmaking. Such principles might, for example, minimize judicial and administrative discretion, or push legislative processes in desirable directions. The effort is to improve lawmaking processes and the deliberation and accountability that are supposed to accompany them. In this respect, some interpretive principles fulfill goals associated with the separation of powers and with plausible assessments of comparative institutional competence. They are designed above all to channel certain decisions through certain institutions, or to improve the operation of those institutions.

The plain meaning principle, for example, might be an effort not to discover what Congress meant in the particular case, but instead to tell Congress to be careful with statutory language. The principle warns Congress that courts will not guess about the meaning of statutes or supply remedies for language that leads to absurd results. The hope—probably based on fictions—is that the principle will lead Congress to express itself clearly in the future.

Some principles designed to fulfill institutional goals require a "clear statement" before courts will interpret a statute to disrupt time-honored or constitutionally grounded understandings about proper arrangements. Clear statement principles, forcing Congress expressly to deliberate on an issue and unambiguously to set forth its will, are a common feature of statutory interpretation; they are a subset of the category of interpretive norms.

Presumptions in favor of state autonomy, of noninterference with presidential power in foreign affairs,[88] and of continued judicial power to balance the equities in deciding on remedies in environmental cases fulfill similar functions. All of these principles are designed to require a clear statement before courts will find congressional displacement of the usual allocation of institutional authority.

Similar considerations supply an additional defense for the principle that appropriations measures should not be construed to amend substantive statutes. That principle is designed in part to promote responsible lawmaking by ensuring that casual, ill-considered, or interest-driven measures do not overcome ordinary statutes. It is a familiar point that the deliberative process that often accompanies substantive statutes cannot work during appropriations decisions. The narrow construction of appropriations measures promotes the primacy of ordinary lawmaking, which has a broader constellation of interests and a higher degree of deliberation.

The principle that implied repeals will be disfavored can be justified on analogous grounds. So too can the idea that exemptions from taxation should be narrowly construed. The central notion here is that exemptions are frequently the result of lobbying efforts by well-organized private groups. A presumption against broad exemption raises the costs of inequity.

Similar goals are served by the assumption that where there is doubt, statutes should be construed so as to limit the discretion of regulatory agencies. We have seen that agency discretion has led to regulatory pathologies as a result of factionalism and self-interested representation; a principle in favor of narrowing discretion works against those risks. Also in this category—though existing quite awkwardly with the effort to limit administrative discretion—is the notion that courts should defer to interpretations of the law by regulatory agencies. This view, prominent in recent cases,[89] is often defended by reference to a judicial belief that when statutes have ambiguities or leave gaps, discretionary judgments should be made by the relatively more accountable agency rather than by courts. That substantive value judgment cannot be traced to Congress; it is a judicial construction (probably indefensible, at least if broadly understood)[90] designed to promote electoral accountability.

Substantive Purposes. Finally, interpretive principles may serve substantive purposes wholly apart from statutory meaning, interpretive instructions, or the lawmaking process. The category of substantive principles spans a wide range. Substantive principles may reflect an objectionable judicial value judgment, but they might derive instead from policies that have a firm constitutional pedigree or are otherwise easy to defend.

Some of the substantive interpretive principles may be treated as a form of "constitutional common law,"[91] in which courts, responding to policies having a kind of constitutional status, press statutes in particular directions. As we will see, some constitutional norms are unenforced, not because they do not have a solid constitutional foundation, but because the institutional position of the judiciary—which has a weak democratic pedigree—argues in favor of a deferential role. Statutory construction serves as a less intrusive way of vindicating the relevant norms.[92] Note, however, that in deploying constitutional norms to interpret statutes courts may be too aggressive, since they will not suffer the adverse reaction produced by a constitutional ruling, and congressional inertia may ensure against correctives for abuse.

Interpretive principles rooted in constitutional provisions help account for a large number of decisions. Consider, for example, the presumption that statutes enacted by Congress should not lightly be taken to preempt state law. In the wake of the New Deal, constitutional limits on federal power have rarely been enforced by the courts, but the ordinary assumption is that state law should remain intact unless Congress expressly decides otherwise. This assumption is traceable to central features of the constitutional structure, and it vindicates a constitutional norm, though one that perhaps coexists awkwardly with New Deal reforms and the rights revolution. Consider as well the rule of lenity in criminal law, which counsels courts narrowly to construe criminal statutes in the event of vagueness or ambiguity.[93] The principle is rooted in notions of due process, which require clear notice before the imposition of criminal liability.

A substantive principle no longer having constitutional foundations is that statutes in derogation of the common law should be narrowly construed. That notion used to fit comfortably with *Lochner* era understandings that treated the Constitution as immunizing the common law from democratic control, but it is hard to defend in the context of modern public law. The frequently invoked idea that "remedial statutes should be broadly construed" is another largely useless canon. All statutes are in a sense remedial; it would be odd to suggest that all statutes should be broadly construed. The principle is best defended as a corrective to the canon calling for narrow construction of statutes in derogation of the common law. The legal system would be better off without either canon.

One substantive principle without constitutional roots, but easily defended, argues that statutes and treaties should be construed favorably to Indian tribes.[94] There is no reason to think that this notion will tend accurately to capture statutory meaning in particular cases. It is instead a judge-made rule responding to inequitable treatment of Indians by the nation in the past, when property was usually taken from Indian tribes by brute force. In the face of that history, and obvious disparities in bargaining power, courts give Indian tribes the benefit of the doubt.

Other substantive canons counsel courts not to infer private causes of action from regulatory statutes; to assume that federal legislation applies only within the territorial jurisdiction of the United States; to assume that statutes do not apply retroactively; not to imply exemptions from taxation; to assume that criminal statutes require *mens rea;* to avoid irrationality; and to protect common law rights in the absence of a clear statement from Congress.[95]

An Alternative Method

The analysis so far suggests the ingredients of an approach to statutory construction with several components. Statutory text is the starting point, but it becomes intelligible only because of the context and background norms that give it content. Usually, the context is unproblematic, and the norms are so widely shared and uncontroversial that the text alone appears to be a sufficient basis for interpretation. In many cases, however, the text, in conjunction with such norms, will produce ambiguity, overinclusiveness, or underinclusiveness; in such cases courts must look elsewhere. Contextual considerations of various sorts—including the legislative history, the statutory purpose, and the practical reasonableness of one view or another—can in these circumstances provide considerable help. But the history might itself be ambiguous—or be the work of an unrepresentative, self-interested group—and the problem of characterizing purpose in a multimember body will, in many cases, lead to the familiar problems of ambiguity, gaps, overinclusiveness, and underinclusiveness.

In such cases, courts often must resort to conspicuous or contestable background norms of various sorts. Such norms are sometimes designed to orient judges to meaning in the particular cases, or to capture Congress' interpretive instructions; they may serve procedural or substantive policies. Sometimes they serve their intended purposes well, and those purposes are not terribly controversial. But sometimes the relevant purposes are disputable, and it is not always clear that they are in fact well-served by the particular principle. It is tempting to see background norms as a controversial intrusion of value judgments or policy concerns into the process of legal interpretation, but such a view would misconceive the nature of statutory construction.

The challenge is to identify norms on which people might be persuaded to agree. That task will be highly value-laden. It is impossible to select interpretive norms without making some assessment of their role in improving or impairing the operation of statutory law. The choice of norms will call for judgments of value and policy precisely to the (considerable) extent that formalist approaches to statutory construction are incomplete or unacceptable. It follows that the interpretive norms will be defensible only to the extent that good substantive and institutional arguments can be advanced on their behalf.

But if undertaken properly, the task of developing interpretive norms will not amount to an unanchored or entirely open-ended inquiry into the best outcomes in particular cases. Even when the traditional sources of interpretation leave gaps, courts should not resolve cases merely by deciding what result would in their view be best, all things considered. Instead the legal culture should be taken to impose a degree of constraint on the selection of the governing principle. For example, we have seen that a broad private autonomy norm is unacceptable largely because of its inconsistency with the fabric of the modern regulatory state; the same would be true for a norm in favor of (say) communism or fascism. Moreover, some interpretive principles—for example, the idea that statutes should be interpreted favorably to the Indian tribes or so as not to override state law—are so well-established that they have the status of precedents. Of course the decision to follow these constraints must itself be justified on normative grounds. But there are good institutional reasons to require courts to use principles that cohere both with the modern regulatory state and with existing interpretive norms—at least if the existing norms are not themselves anachronistic, and at least to the extent that the modern state and the existing norms are not themselves conspicuously irrational or unjust.

We are left, then, with the task of generating interpretive principles—a task that does not amount to an open-ended search for the right results in particular cases; that faces some serious constraints; but that has a significant normative or evaluative dimension. If it is properly executed, that task will significantly increase candor and clarity in interpretation, by making the relevant norms explicit and well-ordered rather than invisible and ad hoc; will make it easier to understand the actual dynamics of the interpretive process; will provide a clear and structured background against which Congress, administrators, and courts can do their work; will increase the likelihood of legislative or public correction of outmoded and unjustified norms; and will, in hard cases, give rationality and justice the benefit of the doubt, while furnishing relatively concrete guidance for unpacking these concepts.

CHAPTER

5

Interpretive Principles for
the Regulatory State

We have seen that interpretive principles perform a variety of functions in modern law; it remains to identify currently operative principles and to explain why interpreters should choose some background norms and not others in construing contemporary statutes. In light of the massive changes in the nature of the national government since the founding, it would be most surprising if existing principles were sufficient for statutory construction in the regulatory state.

Background norms vary from one country to another; the relevant principles diverge sharply in accordance with the assumptions that prevail in the nation's legal culture. It is in this light that one should understand disagreements about interpretive principles in various legal systems. Background norms also differ from one period to another within each particular country. In the United States, for example, the principles of the late nineteenth and early twentieth century reflected a belief in common law ordering that was largely repudiated in the 1930s. In the Warren Court period, the background norms were dramatically different from those that prevailed in the Burger Court and those that operate today.[1]

A large difficulty for statutory interpretation in the regulatory state is that despite the shift in the New Deal period, courts have sometimes continued to use norms that are a legacy of the common law or that misconceive the values, functions, and failures of the regulatory state. These norms seem to have taken on a life of their own, indeed they appear invisible to those who rely on them; they are often held unconsciously; their contested character or even their existence is not readily apparent to those who use them. But when the relevant norms are identified, it becomes clear that they sometimes conflict with the assumptions that underlie the modern regulatory state and indeed with the very statute whose interpretation is at issue. A similar problem is the use of principles that reflect a poor understanding of the operation of modern regulatory law, above all misconceptions of the probabilistic character of regulatory injuries and of the complex systemic effects of regulation.

In this chapter I attempt to carry out the task of outlining a series of interpretive principles that are designed to promote constitutional purposes and the basic goals of deliberative government in the post-New Deal period. All of the principles have some basis in current law, and many are constitutionally inspired. Some of the principles are responsive to concerns of institutional design. Many of them, moreover, are self-conscious attempts to respond to failures in existing statutory regimes, and they are sensitive to the diverse functions of social and economic regulation. My general goal is to show how background norms might vindicate underenforced constitutional norms, respond to changed circumstances within the constraints of text, and use notions of regulatory failure so as to achieve legislative goals.

In general, these principles should not be taken to justify interpretation that is entirely out of step with the agency conception of the judicial role, at least in cases where that conception leads—with the inevitable aid of generally shared background norms—to a clear result. Politically contestable background principles do not provide a license for courts to ignore the meaning of the statute if it is otherwise clear. Moreover, the principles are intended to be guides to interpretation, not substitutes for the more particularized inquiry that is called for by every disputed case of statutory meaning. Standing by themselves, the principles are useful but incomplete.

My discussion of background norms is directed in particular to courts seeking to discern statutory meaning, but its implications extend to other institutions, including regulatory agencies and Congress itself. In the first instance, agencies are charged with interpreting and enforcing their statutory mandate, and administrative practice is inevitably a product of background norms of interpretation. Moreover, understandings of the constitutional backdrop, of institutional practice, and of statutory function and failure influence legislative behavior at the drafting stage. The ultimate goal of a system of interpretive norms is to suggest ways in which national institutions might improve governmental performance—a goal far beyond the topic of statutory interpretation.

My principal focus here is on institutional and substantive norms; syntactic norms and norms that involve interpretive instructions will play little role. The first question, then, has to do with the field of application of institutional and substantive norms.

In easy cases there seems to be no need for such norms, and syntactic norms—most so widely shared that they need not be identified— appear sufficient to resolve the case. It would, however, be a mistake to characterize even easy cases in these terms; substantive and institutional norms are ubiquitous. Consider here the case of a federal environmental statute that is said to preempt all of state tort law. The reason that it does not do so is not syntax alone, but syntax along with, or inseparable from, a wide range of agreed-upon substantive and institutional understandings about the limited preemptive effect of federal enactments, the appropriate role of the judiciary, and so forth.

There are, in short, no cases that can be resolved without reference to substantive and institutional norms. But sometimes syntax or interpretive instructions, accompanied by other norms on which there is a wide consensus, are so clear that it would be wrong or unnecessary to introduce controversial substantive or institutional norms. This is a more precise formulation of the (generally correct) claim that the latter norms should not be permitted to override "the text."

As an example we might consider *Young v. Community Nutrition Institute*,[2] in which the Food and Drug Administration (FDA) was asked to promulgate regulations limiting the quantity of aflatoxin, a carcinogenic substance. The statutory language said: "Any poisonous or deleterious substance added to any food, except where such substance is required in the production thereof or cannot be avoided by good manufacturing practice, shall be deemed to be unsafe for purposes of [the basic prohibition of the Act]; but when each substance is so required or cannot be so avoided, the Secretary *shall promulgate regulations limiting the quantity therein and thereon to such extent as he finds necessary for the protection of public health,* and any quantity exceeding the limits so fixed shall also be deemed unsafe."

The most obvious reading of this language is that when dangerous substances are required in the production of food, the Secretary must promulgate regulations setting a tolerance level. The words "to such extent as he finds necessary" allow the Secretary discretion to decide on the tolerance level, but do not confer on him discretion not to promulgate regulations at all. Such a reading is supported by the fact that an interpretation that would confer discretion not to issue regulations would make the entire provision unnecessary. In *Young*, however, the Supreme Court invoked the principle calling for deference to agency interpretations of law in order to uphold the FDA's view that the statute allows the agency not to promulgate regulations. For the FDA, "to such extent as he finds necessary" modifies "shall promulgate" rather than "the quantity therein or thereon." Seeing the statutory language as ambiguous, the Court deferred to the agency's interpretation. The *Young* decision may be taken as an example of a case invoking a contestable institutional norm—deference to agency interpretations—in a context in which syntax alone, accompanied by agreed-upon background norms of other sorts, leads to a single answer. The Court's use of the deference norm was incorrect because there was no ambiguity in the statute.

In other settings, however, norms that go to syntax or to interpretive instructions, accompanied by generally held background understandings, will lead to indeterminacy. In such hard cases conspicuous or contestable institutional or substantive norms must be invoked to break ties, to resolve cases otherwise in equipoise, and to help decide what to do in the face of changed circumstances or apparently absurd results.

The Principles

The interpretive principles outlined below fall in three categories: constitutional norms, institutional understandings, and efforts to correct statutory failure.

Constitutional Norms

Statutory interpretation always takes place in the shadow of the Constitution, and the constitutional norms that deserve a prominent place in statutory interpretation span a wide range. Many of them have been mentioned in Chapter 4. A central point here is that federal courts underenforce many constitutional norms, and for good reasons. Constitutional law is an uneasy amalgam of substantive theory

and institutional constraint, and the constraints properly lead courts
to be reluctant to uphold constitutional principles with complete
vigor. There is a difference between what the Constitution actually
requires and what constitutional courts are willing to require the political branches of government to do.

It follows that some statutes should be understood as responses to
Congress' constitutional responsibilities even if courts would not require Congress to carry out those responsibilities in the first instance.
It also follows that relatively aggressive statutory construction provides a way for courts to vindicate norms that do in fact have constitutional status, and to do so in a less intrusive way than constitutional
adjudication.

Federalism. In the system of American public law, the basic assumption is that states have authority to regulate their own citizens
and territory. This assumption justifies an interpretive principle calling for a clear congressional statement in order to support federal
preemption of state law. A principle of this sort is of course no substitute for an inquiry into the relationship between state and federal law
in the particular context; but the principle will frequently be of considerable aid in disputed cases.

Political Deliberation. We have seen that the constitutional system
is designed to ensure a kind of deliberative democracy. The American
constitutional regime is built on hostility to measures that impose
burdens or grant benefits merely because of the political power of
private groups; some public value is required for governmental action. This norm, traceable to the origins of the Constitution and
firmly rooted in current law, has a number of implications for statutory interpretation. It suggests, for example, that statutes that embody mere interest-group deals should be narrowly construed. It also
suggests that courts should develop interpretive strategies to promote
deliberation in government—by, for example, remanding issues involving constitutionally sensitive interests or groups for reconsideration by the legislature or by regulatory agencies when deliberation
appears to have been absent. Much of American administrative law
is founded on this idea.[3]

Constitutional Invalidity and Doubts. The principle that statutes
should be construed so as to survive constitutional challenge is a natural outgrowth of the system of separation of powers. The principle
minimizes interbranch conflict—Congress itself would prefer validation to invalidation—and it promotes judicially underenforced con-

stitutional norms. The mild sort of "bending" that sometimes results is legitimate, for courts (and agencies) are not mere agents of the enacting legislature. Their obligation is to the legal system and the citizenry as a whole. If statutes can fairly be construed to be valid, courts should so construe them.

This basic idea provides support for the broader idea that courts should construe statutes so as to avoid constitutional doubts.[4] This latter principle calls for a more aggressive judicial posture in statutory construction, allowing judicial "bending" of a greater range of statutes. Judge Richard Posner has criticized that principle on the ground that it creates a kind of "penumbral Constitution,"[5] one that allows courts to press statutes in particular directions even though—and this is his central point—they would ultimately be found not to offend the Constitution.

But Judge Posner's objection becomes less forceful in light of the fact that constitutional norms are quite generally underenforced. The aggressive construction of questionable statutes, removing them from the terrain of constitutional doubt, can be understood as a less intrusive way of vindicating norms that do in fact have constitutional status; and this point applies even if courts would not invalidate those statutes if they were forced to decide the question. An approach of this sort ensures a greater degree of compliance with constitutional norms, taking account of judicial underenforcement and requiring congressional deliberation on troublesome issues.

Accountability. Some interpretive norms represent constitutionally inspired efforts to promote a sound allocation of institutional responsibility. We have seen, for example, that courts are reluctant to interpret statutes as intruding on the President's power in foreign affairs or as interfering with judicial power to "balance the equities" in cases involving possible injunctive relief.

Other strategies of interpretation can be similarly understood. In the period since the New Deal, courts have permitted Congress to delegate exceptionally broad policymaking authority to regulatory agencies. Such broad delegations were at one time thought to offend Article I of the Constitution, which vests legislative power in Congress.[6] In recent years courts have been reluctant to enforce the nondelegation doctrine. This reluctance is partly attributable to the difficulty of developing standards for distinguishing between prohibited and permissible delegations, partly a product of the intrusiveness of any such judicial role, and partly a result of frequently good reasons for the delegation of discretionary power to regulatory agencies. But through statutory construction courts are sometimes able to vindicate the constitutional principle against delegation of legislative power. They can do so, for example, by narrowly construing delegations of policymaking power.

The most celebrated example here is *Kent v. Dulles*,[7] in which the Supreme Court concluded that the Secretary of State may not deny a passport to a member of the Communist Party unless Congress has clearly authorized him to do so. A related issue was posed in the Supreme Court's decision in *Hampton v. Mow Sun Wong*,[8] in which the Court held—as a matter of constitutional law—that any decision to prevent aliens from serving as federal employees must be made by Congress or the President rather than by the Civil Service Commission. In other cases the Court (and individual justices) have suggested that the Constitution prevents certain disabilities from being visited on certain groups unless an accountable actor has so decided.[9] Decisions of this sort impose a clear statement principle to the effect that important decisions are to be made by accountable actors.

Nondelegation principles are also promoted by various doctrines dealing with the degree of judicial deference to agency interpretations. The idea that courts should interpret congressional enactments on their own, without deferring to agency constructions, is intended to avoid the delegation problem that would be raised by allowing administrators to interpret the scope of their own authority. The exceptionally important idea that a delegation of power to an administrator implicitly permits presidential supervision and control is a similar effort to promote political accountability.[10] This idea promotes the constitutionally grounded goals of a unitary executive branch: centralization, expedition, and accountability in law enforcement.

The Rule of Law. In interpreting statutes, courts indulge a clear statement principle in favor of the rule of law: a system in which legal rules exist, are clear, do not apply retroactively, operate in the world as they do in the books, and do not contradict each other.[11] The most celebrated aspect of this general idea is the rule of lenity; courts resolve ambiguities favorably to the criminal defendant. Courts also interpret statutes so as to minimize administrative discretion, to apply prospectively, and to require or permit rules: "The law in general . . . does not interpret a grant of discretion to eliminate *all* 'categorical rules.'"[12]

Disadvantaged Groups. Some of the most difficult questions in

contemporary constitutional law involve the extent of protection af-
forded to disadvantaged groups by the equal protection clause of the
fourteenth amendment. In one of its most important and controversial decisions since World War II, the Supreme Court held that to
make out a violation of the equal protection clause, blacks, women,
and others must show "discriminatory intent" on the part of the enacting legislature. The fact that a particular practice has a severe disproportionate adverse effect on blacks and women is insufficient.[13] As
a result, measures that continue to subordinate blacks and women—
for example, tests of physical ability or educational attainment, or
electoral systems that conspicuously produce only white officials—
survive constitutional scrutiny, and this is so even if they are hard to
justify on independent grounds.

The requirement that litigants must show discriminatory intent in
order to make out a constitutional claim has proved of enormous
importance, furnishing a severe barrier to constitutional complainants. The requirement is also controversial as a matter of substantive
constitutional theory.[14] Because the requirement is difficult (though
not impossible) to defend in substantive terms, it is probably best
understood as an outgrowth of institutional concerns. If courts held
that a disproportionate effect was sufficient to raise constitutional
doubts, a wide variety of seemingly neutral governmental policies
would be drawn into serious question—an outcome that might be
improper for institutional reasons having to do with the limited role
of the judiciary in American government.

Courts have also invoked institutional considerations to justify
modest use of the Constitution to protect certain groups, including
most notably the handicapped and gays and lesbians.[15] In this light,
statutes that provide protection in these settings might well be seen as
a response of the legislature to its (judicially unenforced) constitutional responsibilities. Hospitable construction of statutes designed to
protect disadvantaged groups provides a way for courts to protect the
constitutional norm of equal protection in a relatively unintrusive
manner.

Property and Contract Rights. In the aftermath of the New Deal,
courts have been reluctant to use the Constitution's explicit protection of property and contract in a way that would significantly interfere with social and economic regulation.[16] To a large degree, the
reluctance is a product of the Court's substantive belief that redistributive goals fall within the state's police power under these clauses—a

large shift from the beliefs of the founding generation. But part of the Court's reluctance is a result of its understanding that in the post-New Deal period interferences with private contract and private property have considerable popular support, and the judiciary ought therefore to intervene only in egregious cases.

The Court's unwillingness to provide more protection to rights of contract and property may or may not be justified.[17] But courts can vindicate those rights less intrusively through the narrow construction of regulatory statutes that raise serious constitutional doubts under the contracts and takings clause.

Hearing Rights. The Constitution is designed in large part to provide procedural safeguards, affording rights to a hearing and to judicial review in cases involving important rights.[18] The precise extent of these safeguards is sharply disputed. It is unclear, for example, whether Congress has the constitutional power to eliminate hearing rights for those seeking regulatory benefits, or to say that federal courts may not review certain statutory claims.

In this area statutory interpretation is often done conspicuously in the shadow of constitutional hearing rights. It is for this reason that courts frequently interpret narrowly statutory provisions purporting to eliminate rights to a hearing and to judicial review.[19] The ordinary presumption is that such rights are available so that the constitutional issue need not be resolved.

Welfare Rights. In the 1960s and 1970s a number of commentators urged the Supreme Court to give constitutional protection to the right to minimum levels of subsistence.[20] There are, however, formidable institutional objections to a judicial role of this sort. For the Supreme Court to undertake to protect welfare rights entirely on its own would raise extremely serious questions of democratic legitimacy and managerial competence. But perhaps a Court that saw substantive force in the claim for constitutional welfare rights would attempt to vindicate that claim not through the Constitution itself, but through aggressive statutory construction so as to ensure against irrational or arbitrary deprivations of benefits. Such an approach would tend to produce evenhandedness in the distribution of welfare in a democracy that has committed itself to a social safety net. Aggressive statutory construction, requiring a clear statement for selective exclusions, might produce many of the advantages of recognition of constitutional welfare rights without imposing nearly so severe a strain on the judiciary.

Institutional Concerns

A number of interpretive principles respond directly to institutional concerns having to do with the actual or appropriate functioning of governmental entities. Most of these principles are straightforward and can be discussed briefly.

Appropriations Statutes. As we have seen, courts construe appropriations provisions quite narrowly. For reasons explored above, that principle can be connected with judicial understandings about the character of the appropriations process, in which legislative deliberation is highly unlikely. Interest-group power is peculiarly likely to make its effects felt in this setting.

Presumption in Favor of Judicial Review. Courts presume that the legislature has not precluded judicial review of agency decisions. This assumption is partly attributable to a belief—vindicated by recent experience, as we saw in Chapter 2—that regulatory agencies are susceptible to factionalism and self-interested representation. Judicial review operates as a powerful ex ante deterrent against dangers of this sort; it is also an ex post corrective. If Congress is to eliminate judicial review, it must do so explicitly.

Exemptions from Taxation. Courts do not infer such exemptions. This principle is partly a result of a desire to protect the Treasury; partly a product of a view that exemptions from taxation frequently reflect the influence of well-organized private groups; and partly responsive to the fact that the Congress carefully monitors the revenue process and is in a good position to make exemptions when it wants to do so. An express exemption is required.

Presumption against Implied Repeals. Courts do not lightly assume that one statute has repealed another. This principle assumes that Congress, focusing as it usually does on a particular problem, should not be understood by that focus to have eliminated another program that was probably the product of sustained attention.

Administrative Discretion. Much of administrative law is a response to perceptions about likely institutional performance. Consider, for example, the idea that courts should defer to agency views of policy and fact in cases in which discretion has lawfully been conferred.[21] This idea is a response to the superior democratic accountability and fact-finding capacity of the agency, and a corresponding belief that courts ought to treat agency decisions with respect. Similarly, the rare judicial decisions finding agency action not to be subject to judicial review are based on perceptions that judicial intervention is likely to be counterproductive in the circumstances.[22]

Cautious Approach to Legislative History. Legislative history is sometimes written by one or another side in a dispute over the content of the law, and the history will sometimes reflect a view that could not prevail in the processes of congressional deliberation. Moreover, the history was never enacted, and it is thus not law. Courts should adopt a firm principle of the priority of statutory text to statutory history. This principle does not call on courts to disregard the history when the statute is ambiguous, but simply to give it limited weight in cases of conflict.

Respect for Precedent and Postenactment History. The view suggested here argues in favor of an interpretive principle calling for stare decisis (respect for precedent) in statutory interpretation, and for some deference to postenactment history showing support for a particular interpretation. Suppose, for example, that Congress has acquiesced in a judicial interpretation; that a judicial construction is long-standing; or that after enactment of the statute, Congress appears to have endorsed a judicial construction or to have interpreted the statute to mean one thing rather than another. Since statutory construction is not merely a matter of applying the view of the enacting legislature, postenactment events are an admissible part of interpretation even though they do not bear on original meaning. If a goal of interpretation is to promote stability and coordination in public law, subsequent events are quite relevant. On the other hand, a postenactment committee report has the usual dangers of legislative history and deserves some suspicion in light of its after-the-fact, possibly trumped-up character; and while relevant, it should not be permitted to countermand the statutory words.

Counteracting Statutory Failure

I have suggested that a number of interpretive principles in current law are intended to counteract failures in social and economic regulation. The account of statutory failure offered in Chapter 3 leads to a variety of interpretive strategies.

Where there is ambiguity, courts should construe regulatory statutes so that (1) politically unaccountable actors are prohibited from deciding important issues; (2) collective action problems do not subvert statutory programs; (3) various regulatory statutes are, to the extent possible, coordinated into a coherent whole; (4) obsolete statutes are kept consistent with changing developments of law, policy, and fact; (5) procedural qualifications of substantive rights are kept narrow; (6) the complex systemic effects of regulation are taken into account; and, most generally, (7) irrationality and injustice, measured against the statute's own purposes, are avoided. These principles apply across the universe of regulatory statutes, though their application will vary with the statutory function.

In cases of statutes designed to remedy market failures, courts should attempt to ensure that the costs are proportionate to the benefits and de minimis exceptions to regulatory requirements are permitted or required. In light of the conventional difficulties in the implementation process, courts should generously construe statutes designed to protect traditionally disadvantaged groups and noncommodity values. By contrast, statutes that embody interest-group transfers should be narrowly interpreted.

Some of these ideas have solid roots in existing law; some are based on contestable substantive ideas presented in Chapter 3; some are proposed for the first time here. Notwithstanding their number and variety, the principles are united by certain general goals. These include, above all, the effort to promote deliberation in government, to furnish surrogates for it when it is absent, to limit factionalism and self-interested representation, and to help bring about political equality.

Promoting Political Accountability. Courts should construe statutes so as to increase the likelihood that decisions will be made by officials who are politically accountable and highly visible. As we have seen, a number of cases growing out of constitutional concerns vindicate this basic principle. These cases reflect judicial reluctance to allow agencies to exercise discretionary power that has not been clearly delegated, and require accountable actors to make decisions involving important rights and politically weak groups.

An exemplary decision falling in this general category is *National Resources Defense Council v. Morton.*[23] In that case, the court was confronted with the question whether the National Environmental Policy Act created an obstacle to a proposed grant of leases for development of submerged lands off the coast of Louisiana. The proposal was justified as a means of promoting energy development, but the consequence of the leases would have been to create a wide range of environmental risks, including oil spills and damage to fish and wildlife, beaches, water areas, and historical sites. The court ruled that the Department of the Interior was required to discuss and consider, in its environmental impact statement, the alternative of imposing oil import quotas. This was so even though the Department had no legal authority to adopt or put into effect such quotas.

A salutary consequence of the decision was to ensure that in a huge and fragmented executive branch, a single document would be available for presidential and public review, taking account of all of the environmental costs and energy benefits of different courses of action. The court's decision promoted political accountability by supplying a partial corrective to the fragmented character of the executive branch of the federal government.

Other approaches to statutory construction can be similarly understood. The principle that administrative interpretations of statutes should be given deference by the courts is an example. Indeed, in the most important recent case involving that principle, the Supreme Court referred expressly to the superior position of the President in comparison to the judiciary.[24] For reasons discussed above, it would be a mistake to take such a position too far, but the principle is sound insofar as it recognizes that Congress may and sometimes does delegate to regulatory agencies and the President the power to fill statutory gaps.

Collective Action Problems. We have seen that regulatory statutes are often subverted in the implementation process, partly as a result of the diffused character of the class of regulatory beneficiaries. In a usual scenario, the beneficiaries of regulatory programs, though numerous and ordinarily disorganized, are able to mobilize to obtain protective legislation. As the statute is implemented, such groups tend to dissipate, and well-organized members of the regulated class are able to exert continuing pressure on the implementing agency. The result is that the regulatory program will be skewed. Government failure mimics market failure.

Many judicial decisions have been responsive to the possibility that collective action problems will undermine regulatory programs. The most conspicuous examples are decisions in the 1960s, 1970s, and 1980s aggressively construing regulatory statutes in order to protect the environment.[25] Many other illustrations can be found in judicial decisions from the late 1960s to the present, taking a careful look at administrative decisions that jeopardize the interests of regulatory beneficiaries.[26]

Cases responding to overzealous regulation—involving OSHA regulation, banking controls, and transportation regulation—may be a product of a similar concern.[27] Here the problem is that a collective action problem or structural infirmity inclines the agency toward excessive intrusion into the marketplace.

Consistency and Coherence. It should come as no surprise that the post-New Deal proliferation of regulatory programs has led to inconsistency and sometimes incoherence in the law. For example, we have seen that the standards for regulating carcinogens are notoriously variable, calling for excessive controls in some areas and unduly weak regulation in others.

The legal system might respond to such problems in various ways. First, one might conclude that in light of the nature of the legislative process, problems of this sort are no cause for alarm. Under this view, it should be unsurprising that at various times and in disparate areas, various constellations of interests succeed in the legislative process. For this reason each statute should be interpreted in isolation from all others. If the result is statutory incoherence, so be it. Incoherence is a price of pluralist politics.

A second response would be that the executive branch and Congress ought to take steps to bring about regulatory coherence. The budgetary process is a means of accomplishing this goal; decisions about appropriations might be a method of coordinating disparate regulatory programs. Congressional committees might be organized to increase statutory coherence. As we saw in Chapter 1, several presidents have moved in the direction of regulatory coordination.

A third approach would call on courts to employ clear statement principles of statutory construction so as to help bring about consistency and coordination in the law. A judicial role of this sort has clear precedent in the old idea that statutes governing the same subject matter should be construed together,[28] and in contemporary administrative law. The *Morton* decision, described above, should be understood as an effort to counteract the fragmented and uncoordinated character of federal environmental policy, by ensuring that environmental impact statements contain a full discussion of the repertoire of solutions available to national officials.

To take another example, in the *Bob Jones* case[29] the Supreme Court held that the Internal Revenue Service could not grant tax deductions to schools that discriminate on the basis of race. The source of the prohibition was a statute giving deductions to institutions serving charitable purposes, but with an implicit exception when public policy requires denial of the deduction. There is no doubt that when the statute was initially enacted, public policy did not prohibit deductions to institutions that discriminated on the basis of race. Racial discrimination in education was common at the time, and it could not plausibly be suggested that the enacting Congress thought that discriminatory schools violated public policy. The *Bob Jones* decision is best understood as an effort to ensure that the IRS takes account of the widespread social antagonism toward racial discrimination, as part of the general thrust of contemporary public policy.

Some cases limiting agency authority to impose significant costs for uncertain or speculative benefits can be understood in similar terms.[30] Decisions of this sort are justified as part of the integration of statutory systems into a coherent whole that could plausibly be understood as the outcome of deliberative processes.

Statutory Obsolescence. Sometimes statutory construction is informed by an effort to ensure integrity and coherence in the law by updating obsolete statutes—or, to put it less contentiously and indeed more accurately, by interpreting them in a way that takes account of changing conditions. Here the courts reject the idea that the meaning of a statute is exhausted by the original understanding of its authors. Moreover, there are good reasons to permit courts to go beyond the original understanding in dramatically changed circumstances, at least in three settings: when the statutory term is general and thus invites change over time ("public policy"); when the statutory text is ambiguous ("feasible"); and when changed circumstances make the original understanding irrational or incoherent, or introduce a problem of translation.[31]

The problem of statutory obsolescence has three principal manifestations. First, and most obviously, a statutory provision may no longer be consistent with widely held social norms. In such cases the question is whether the social change justifies a reading of the statute that does not accord with the desires of its authors—a question that the enacting legislature may well have intended courts (and agencies) to answer in the affirmative.

Second, the legal background may have changed dramatically as a result of legislative and judicial innovations. A statute enacted in (say) 1935 may have ignored environmental considerations that are widely recognized in statutes enacted after 1960. Here the question is whether the changed character of the legal background has consequences for interpretation of the 1935 statute.

Third, the factual assumptions underlying the original statute may no longer hold. As we have seen, those who enacted statutes regulating broadcasting assumed limited licensing because of the corresponding limitations of the spectrum. In the face of new technology and the rise of cable television, that assumption has become unrealistic. Here the interpretive problem is that legislative goals and expectations—if described narrowly—cannot be mechanically transplanted to a dramatically different factual setting, at least not without producing results that are perverse from the standpoint of a modern-day observer or of the enacting legislature itself. The Congress that enacted the Immigration and Nationality Act thought that gays and lesbians suffered from a "psychopathic personality" that would justify their exclusion from the country; that conclusion, admittedly one of value as well as of fact, has been repudiated by medical authorities.

All these problems present questions not only of statutory meaning, but also of interpretive instructions: how would Congress have wanted courts to approach its enactments in the face of obsolescence? There will rarely be a direct answer to this question. Here, as in constitutional law,[32] the problem of changed circumstances requires courts to decide whether statutes enact general concepts rather than particular conceptions, or whether the meaning of statutory terms should change when there have been changes in law, policy, and fact. I propose here that if the text is ambiguous, or has become ambiguous because of changes, courts should often decide both questions in the affirmative. An approach that calls on courts to interpret statutes in a way that takes account of changed circumstances is likely to be the more natural way of ascertaining meaning; produce greater coherence in the law; reduce the problem, pervasive in modern regulation, of rule by measures that are badly out of date; and lead to a legal system that is both more rational and more consistent with democratic norms.

It is tempting but inadequate to say that the legislature should respond to the problem of changed circumstances. The question is what the statute means in those circumstances, and that question is for the courts. Interpretation that takes account of changed circumstances does not "amend" the statute, but on the contrary is the best way of remaining faithful to it. Meaning does not remain constant throughout changes in law, fact, and policy. To say this is not at all to say that courts should be permitted to rewrite statutes when changed circumstances make rewriting seem like a good idea. The case for interpretation that takes account of changed circumstances must rest on the interaction of the statutory words and those changes; the changes must have created ambiguity or an alteration in meaning.

The most obvious examples are open-ended terms ("feasible" or "public policy") in the face of changed facts or values; here Congress has invited interpretation that changes over time. But consider as well the problem of interpreting the Delaney Clause. It will be remembered that the Clause contains a general prohibition on the use of carcinogens in food additives, which was enacted in a period when carcinogens could be detected only at high-risk levels. The enacting Congress assumed that carcinogenic substances were both rare and extremely dangerous—assumptions that were false by 1985. Should the statute be interpreted so as to permit de minimis exceptions in a time in which carcinogens can be detected at exceptionally low levels posing trivial risks to health? The FDA has said yes; the federal courts have said no. But it was simply wrong to suggest that the original congressional enactment necessarily resolved the question in the face of unanticipated scientific developments.

Courts have responded to all three kinds of obsolescence by construing regulatory statutes in a way that takes account of changed circumstances. An example of the first is *King v. Smith*,[33] in which the Supreme Court invalidated a state rule depriving women of welfare benefits whenever they lived with a man—even if cohabitation occurred as rarely as once a month. The Court emphasized that there had been a steady trend in the direction of eliminating moral requirements for welfare recipients. Moreover, the "man in the house" rule had been irrational, punitive, and both sexist and racist in operation. In fact, however, the Court was unable to point to any statutory provision that unambiguously invalidated the rule. The decision in *King v. Smith* amounted to an aggressive reading of the statute to conform to what the Court understood to be the current (and justified) national consensus.

Recent decisions requiring regulatory agencies to consider costs and benefits can be understood in similar terms.[34] The same conclusion may well apply to the courts' effort to read the Sherman Act as an effort to promote economic welfare (rather than, for example, to protect small business as such). An interpretive principle of that sort is the only administrable standard, and such a principle conforms best to contemporary understandings about the nature of a well-functioning antitrust law.[35]

The second form of obsolescence is reflected in judicial construction of statutes of the 1920s and 1930s so as to require old-line agencies to take account of environmental concerns.[36] Here the legal background has changed so dramatically that what might seem to be a straightforward interpretation of the old statutes would produce incoherence. The same point helps to explain the courts' narrow construction of provisions of the UCC that had not anticipated the consumer revolution in the law of products liability.[37] The Court's decision in the *Bob Jones* case can be understood in similar terms. Changing legislative and judicial developments had made racial discrimination inconsistent with public policy in the 1980s, even if there was no such inconsistency when the charitable deduction was first enacted.

For the third form of obsolescence, in the areas of banking, broadcasting, and carcinogen regulation, judicial interpretation has been a straightforward response to changed circumstances.[38] Here it is implausible to resolve statutory ambiguities by asking how Congress would have answered the question at the time of enactment. In light of the dramatically changed nature of the relevant markets, such an approach would be a recipe for absurdity, even from the perspective of the enacting Congress itself. Sometimes there is no alternative but to extrapolate purposes at a certain level of generality and to assess the changed circumstances in light of those purposes. Such an approach would of course be unacceptable if the statutory language forecloses it; but often changed circumstances will produce ambiguity.

Dean Calabresi has argued that courts should have the power to invalidate obsolete statutes, returning them to the legislature for reconsideration.[39] A judicial role of this sort would be extremely controversial, and properly so. The real problem posed by obsolescence or changed circumstances is that it makes interpretation in the ordinary sense far more difficult. Efforts to translate statutes into new settings cannot succeed simply by asking what the statute meant when it was enacted. A principle that calls for courts to exercise some creativity here provides a far less intrusive function for the courts; and it has unmistakable foundations in current law.

Narrow Construction of Procedural Qualifications. Sometimes courts are confronted with questions about the proper methods for enforcing a statutory mandate: for example, whether to imply a private right of action to enforce a regulatory statute; the appropriate procedures for adjusting or eliminating a substantive benefit, as in a claimed right to a hearing before the elimination of welfare benefits; and the availability of judicial review to test administrative enforcement or nonenforcement. We have seen that constitutional questions are often implicated here. But the constitutional issues might be avoided if courts adopted a clear statement principle to the effect that procedural qualifications of substantive rights will be narrowly construed. Such a principle might be grounded in the belief that the procedures are less likely to be the product of a deliberative process than was the substance, and that procedural qualifications might enable well-organized groups to defeat substantive programs. Under this view, numerous Supreme Court decisions can be placed in a single category—that of statutory construction. A central goal here is to ensure that procedural rights are available as a check, both ex ante and ex post, on factionalism and self-interested representation.

The background rule in favor of judicial review of agency decisions is the most conspicuous example here.[40] Suppose, for example, that the question is whether courts can review an alleged violation of a statute limiting the power of the Central Intelligence Agency to discharge its employees. If Congress has not expressly foreclosed review, the substantive limitation should be enforceable by the judiciary. All of these concerns have greatest weight in cases in which constitutional norms are at stake; they are weakest in cases involving ordinary economic legislation, in which thin procedures are more plausibly taken as the price of thick substantive rights.

Understanding Systemic Effects. In Chapter 2 we saw that regulation is frequently unsuccessful because of a failure to understand the complex systemic effects of governmental controls. A similar flaw has undermined interpretive efforts by the federal courts. Courts dealing with regulatory issues commonly act as if the decision will create only ex post winners and losers in the particular case. This misunderstanding leads to statutory construction that is uninformed by the real-world impact of regulation.

Consider, for example, the creation, by a district court, of the "prevention of significant deterioration" (PSD) program in *Sierra Club v. Ruckelshaus*.[41] In that case the court ruled, in the face of an ambiguous statute, that state implementation plans under the Clean Air Act must not merely comply with national air quality standards, but also prevent the degradation of air currently cleaner than required by those standards. The court's goal was to ensure that federal environmental policy would protect visibility in currently pristine areas.[42] While its decision has to some degree promoted that goal, it has also had unanticipated systemic effects—proving immensely expensive, delaying the highly desirable substitution of low-sulphur Western coal for high-sulphur Eastern coal, and protecting dirty existing plants against replacement with cleaner new ones.

All this has been a product of a decision that prevented companies from relocating West in order to comply with national environmental law. It is far from clear that the environment is better off as a result. The court that decided the *Sierra Club* case was unaware of these effects. Because the textual basis for the decision was quite thin, an understanding of the environmental and nonenvironmental costs associated with the PSD program might well have led to a more limited or even contrary ruling.

Similar examples are provided by the Supreme Court's OSHA decisions, taken up in more detail in Chapter 6, in which the Court appeared to assume that greater protection for workers would automatically follow from reading the OSHA statute to impose stringent limitations on toxic substances. Instead, stringent requirements tend to lead an agency not to regulate at all, thus producing, ironically, underregulation. The Court also ignores the risk that such requirements might impose costs that will ultimately be borne by workers themselves.

Avoiding Irrationality and Injustice. It is a familiar principle that statutes should be construed so as to avoid irrationality and injustice, even when the language of the statute seems to lead in that direction.[43] The principle is controversial because there is no obvious basis for deciding whether an outcome is irrational or unjust, and because it is arguable that both should be corrected by the legislature rather than the courts. The concrete focus of adjudication, however, has enormous advantages in revealing that statutory provisions have produced peculiar consequences in particular settings; and the judgment that the consequence is peculiar—and could not plausibly have been intended—is sometimes irresistible. The text will on occasion appear to compel results that the legislature could not have anticipated and resolved in enacting a broad standard. In such circumstances, what might seem to be aggressive construction is entirely legitimate. Here the emphasis of the legal process school on the need to construe statutes so that they are reasonable has continuing relevance and provides a fair degree of interpretive guidance.

In *Eisen v. Carlisle & Jacquelin*,[44] for example, the Court was asked to decide on the requirements for notifying class members in a class action in which the individual claims were extremely small. The plaintiffs alleged that the defendant violated the antitrust statutes in a way that injured huge numbers of people in minor ways. Individual damages were generally under $100, but the collective harm was in the many millions. The question in *Eisen* was whether the class representative had to provide notice to each member of the class. If individual notice was required, the class action could not go forward; the expense of providing notice dwarfed the plaintiff's resources.

The relevant part of Rule 23 required "the best notice practicable under the circumstances, including individual notice to all class members who can be identified through reasonable effort." A unanimous Supreme Court held that the language must be interpreted literally, so that identifiable class members had to be notified of the suit. By imposing the enormous costs of notice on the class representative, the result of *Eisen* has been effectively to bar the small claim class action in most settings.

In two respects the decision in *Eisen* appears exceedingly peculiar. First, the purpose of notice is to protect those who are to be notified. But in a case in which those notified do not have individually viable claims, it seems odd to suggest that notice is required in deference to their interests. Surely it would be preferable for them to have their legal rights vindicated without individual notice than not to have their rights vindicated at all. Realistically appraised, their interests argue against, not in favor of, individual notice.

Second, Rule 23, as interpreted in *Eisen,* calls for a balancing test with respect to the costs of identifying class members, but for an across-the-board requirement, entirely indifferent to cost, with respect to notification of those who can be identified. It is utterly irrational to allow balancing with respect to the costs of identifying class members, yet to impose a per se rule in favor of notice when the costs of identification are low and the costs of providing notice extremely high.

The source of the problem in *Eisen* was that the drafters of the notice provision of Rule 23 did not focus on the case of individually small but collectively large claims when they wrote the notice provision. In such cases the literal language, read acontextually, led to an absurd result. One of the central purposes of the class action provision is to permit the aggregation of small claims to ensure that rights that would otherwise not be litigable are in fact vindicated. The *Eisen* Court's reading of the notice provision defeated that purpose. In these circumstances, the literal language should have yielded. Other cases illustrate the same principle.[45]

Two interpretive principles would be especially useful in dealing with statutes designed to overcome market failures.

Proportionality. Statutes should be construed so that the aggregate social benefits are proportionate to the aggregate social costs. Implicit in some of the recent cases,[46] this principle is likely to produce sensible regulation and is therefore the appropriate understanding to attribute to Congress under normal circumstances. It recognizes that well-organized groups are sometimes able to obtain legislation that would not be the outcome of a well-functioning deliberative process; that a proportionality principle will work against underregulation as well as overregulation; that bureaucratic incentives can press agencies in the direction of overzealous enforcement; that the statutory text is sometimes an impulsive reaction to short-term problems; that temporary public concern can result in hasty drafting; and that Congress is not able to focus on all applications of statutory standards. In Chapter 3 we saw that statutory failure is often a product of excessive controls and inadequate implementation. Both can result from the failure to import a proportionality principle into social and economic regulation.

Important evidence of judicial support for this principle comes from the experience of OSHA in regulating toxic substances. The language of the statute provides that the Secretary must assure, "to the extent feasible," that "no employee will suffer material impairment of health" as a result of exposure to toxic substances.[47] If the words are taken outside of their context, they are most naturally read to require the Secretary to regulate even minor risks to the point where the industry would be endangered by the regulation. As the Supreme Court has interpreted this provision, however, the Secretary must show a "significant risk" before he may regulate. The "significant risk" requirement—an aggressive construction of the statute—provides a salutary check on extremely costly regulation that does little good.

The Court has also ruled, however, that the Secretary may not apply cost-benefit analysis.[48] Once he has shown a significant risk, he must regulate even when the industry would be jeopardized. The consequence of the preclusion of cost-benefit analysis has been a system that includes both too much and too little regulation. Because it is legally compelled to regulate to the point of feasibility, OSHA has been reluctant to regulate many substances at all.

It should not be surprising that the statutory scheme, as judicially interpreted, has produced a pattern of OSHA regulation that shows exceptionally severe and quite arguably perverse control of some substances, and little or no control of others.[49] Both over- and under-regulation are predictable consequences of a regulatory scheme that combines a draconian standard with prosecutorial discretion. Because of dangers of this sort, courts should generally assume that Congress intends agencies to impose regulation after some kind of balancing of costs and benefits. For example, in *National Resources Defense Council v. Thomas*[50] the court concluded that section 112 of the Clean Air Act, which requires emissions standards that provide "an ample margin of safety," permits the administrator to consider cost and technology, despite the statute's failure expressly to refer to those factors.

Of course a proportionality principle contains no uncontroversial metric with which to measure social costs and social benefits. If courts understand benefits and costs technically—as in the economic formulation—and make the assessment turn on private willingness to pay, they will be relying on a highly controversial approach that may well have been repudiated by the legislature that enacted the program in question. As we have seen, the very decision to create a regulatory system is often a rejection of the criterion of social choice based on private willingness to pay.

For these reasons, the proportionality principle is most useful for cases of economic regulation. It becomes workable on the assumption that in some cases it will be clear, by reference to a widely held social consensus, that social benefits are small in comparison to social costs. In such cases the proportionality principle can be administered by reference to widespread intuitions, and statutes should be construed so as not to permit or require the action at issue. Consider, for example, regulatory interventions costing millions or even billions of dollars, imposed for the sake of extremely doubtful gains in terms of safety and health. And although the calculus will be more complex, a proportionality principle should also be applied in cases involving other sorts of values, in order to reduce the various problems introduced by conceiving of collective benefits as "rights."

De Minimis Exceptions. It follows from the proportionality principle that regulatory statutes should ordinarily be understood to contain exceptions for de minimis risks or problems. Administrators should generally be authorized to refuse to impose costly regulations for highly speculative or minimal gains. Many courts have reached precisely this conclusion, holding that in the absence of a clear congressional statement administrators may make de minimis exceptions to regulatory controls.[51] Indeed, courts should probably require such exceptions in the absence of explicit statutory text or plausible substantive justifications to the contrary.

Disadvantaged Groups. For the same reason that statutory protection is often necessary, disadvantaged groups are especially at risk in the process of implementation. Where there is ambiguity, courts should resolve interpretive doubts in their favor. As we have seen, the problem of judicial underenforcement of constitutional norms is particularly relevant here; courts can vindicate those norms less intrusively through statutory construction. Disadvantaged groups are also peculiarly vulnerable in the implementation process. Aggressive construction in their favor can counteract statutory failure.

This idea has clear roots in existing law, though the basic principle has rarely been explicitly recognized. The most explicit example is the well-established idea that statutes should be interpreted favorably to Indian tribes. The Supreme Court's general hostility to the creation of implied rights of action finds a conspicuous exception in the civil rights laws. In a number of cases courts have allowed members of disadvantaged groups to bring suit directly against alleged discriminators, when government has failed to protect them.[52] The same category includes a number of decisions interpreting statutes protecting the disabled.[53] Responding to this rationale, many courts have also broadly construed statutes forbidding discrimination on the basis of race and sex,[54] though there are recent decisions to the contrary perhaps in response to a competing principle of employer autonomy.

Aspirations; Noncommodity Values. As we have seen, statutes are frequently designed to protect aspirations or noncommodity values that the marketplace undervalues. Those values—exemplified in laws regulating broadcasting and protecting the environment and endangered species—are often jeopardized in the postenactment political "market," for the same reason that they are threatened by the willingness-to-pay criterion of the economic marketplace. Ideas of this sort appear to underlie the many decisions interpreting the public interest standard of the Federal Communications Act so as to prod the FCC to promote diversity, local control, local participation, and high-quality programming, and to work against racism and sexism in broadcasting—even when the market for broadcasting fails to respect such norms. Similar attitudes help account for decisions that deal skeptically with efforts to deregulate broadcasting[55] and that require protection of the environment.[56] An approach of this sort would not be appropriate in the area of economic regulation, where noncommodity values are not at stake, but it plays an important role under some systems of regulation.

A revealing case here is *Syracuse Peace Council v. FCC.*[57] In that case the court faced an FCC decision to repeal the "fairness doctrine," which required licensees to (a) cover important issues of local controversy and (b) allow contrasting viewpoints on those issues. The FCC said that because the doctrine allowed public officials to judge editorial decisions and to control programming content, it was inconsistent with principles of free speech. In any case, the FCC said that the market would generate fair and diverse coverage of controversial questions.

The court upheld this decision, deferring to the agency on these "almost entirely predictive" judgments. But a principal source of those judgments was the National Association of Broadcasters—hardly an objective reporter of the facts. There was solid evidence that the fairness doctrine had often been responsible for coverage of and diversity on controversial issues. Finally, it was unclear why the FCC has not decided to take some middle ground—one that would, for example, retain the first part of the fairness doctrine.

Similarly doubtful is the Supreme Court's decision in *FCC v. WNCN Listeners Guild.*[58] There the Court upheld an FCC decision to abandon a policy calling for a hearing on "format changes" when (a) the changes produced a protest from the listening community, (b) there was no good substitute for the programming in the relevant area, (c) the original format was economically feasible, and (d) the segment of the public that preferred the original format was too small to be accommodated by available frequencies. The FCC said that the hearing requirement deterred experimentation and desirable changes, that government should not be evaluating programming, and that in any case the market would respond well to the desires of the public. The problem with this reasoning is that in the limited circumstances in which the previous policy called for a hearing, there were severe doubts about whether diversity would be provided.

More generally, the FCC was insufficiently responsive, in both *Syracuse* and *WNCN*, to the problems inherent in exclusive reliance on markets in broadcasting, even in a period with numerous outlets. The first problem is that because of the crucial importance of advertising for programming decisions, the link between listener or viewer desires and broadcasting performance is less tight than in ordinary markets. The purchaser of the product is in significant part the advertiser rather than the listening public; the public is often the product to be sold rather than the purchaser. There is a connection between the public's tastes and advertising decisions, but that connection is not always close, especially when advertisers have their own distinctive agendas.

The second problem is that even in places with a fair number of broadcasters, people with unusual tastes might be completely unaccommodated, even though it would be possible to provide services for them without high cost to others. Suppose that 85% of listeners in a certain community like popular music, but that 15% want classical music or news; suppose too that there are only five stations. It may well be that the market will provide five popular music stations, dividing the 85% majority. This is so even though a system of four such stations and one for the minority of 15% would be a significantly better way of satisfying public desires in view of the fact that the decrease from five to four would not really harm the 85% majority.

The third problem is that the voting public appears to want (a) to ensure more diversity in broadcasting than the market provides, (b) to promote high-quality or public affairs broadcasting notwithstanding consumption decisions, and (c) to counteract the sometimes harmful preference-shaping effects of broadcasting decisions through regulatory controls.[59] It may be that none of these three problems justified the fairness doctrine or the format principles.[60] But the FCC did not respond well to any of the problems, and it would undoubtedly be possible to design a system better than the status quo.

Narrow Construction of Statutes Embodying Interest-Group Transfers. Courts should narrowly construe statutes that serve no plausible public purpose and amount merely to interest-group transfers. This idea, traceable to a basic constitutional norm and following from the proportionality principle, helps to account for a number of decisions in the area of economic regulation, including banking and agriculture.[61] It also helps to explain the courts' approach to the

Robinson-Patman Act and likewise their effort to understand the Sherman Act as an attempt to promote consumer welfare rather than as protection of small business as such.[62] When the absence of a public purpose is palpable, this principle should be unexceptionable, and it is of considerable importance.

This principle must not, however, be confused with the unjustifiable idea that statutes in derogation of the common law should be narrowly construed; and it is not a license for grudging interpretation of statutes that promote noncommodity values or that embody public-spirited redistribution. As the experience of the early part of this century reveals, it is not for courts—in the process of statutory construction—to take a side of the regulatory debate that runs in the face of a legislative judgment. For this reason courts should attempt to discern a public-regarding purpose where it is plausible—without, however, blinding themselves to the reality that sometimes one cannot with a straight face maintain that such purposes are at work. Of course there will be some difficult line-drawing problems here.

Priority and Harmonization

It will not have escaped notice that the principles I have proposed will sometimes conflict with one another—a possibility that renders the basic approach vulnerable to a neorealist objection, that in practice it will provide contradictory guidance for the judiciary. Thus, for example, the principle in favor of state authority will sometimes collide with the principle favoring disadvantaged groups. The presumption against amendment through the appropriations process might contradict the principle in favor of generous construction of statutes protecting nonmarket values. The examples could easily be multiplied.

In cases of conflict, either the interpretive norms are indeterminate, or it will be necessary to develop principles of harmonization and priority. I will shortly be arguing that it is indeed possible to develop such principles, but to make this claim is not to say that the application of interpretive norms can be purely mechanical. Inevitably, statutory construction is an exercise of practical reason in which text, structure, history, and purpose interact with the background understandings in the legal culture. In light of the dependence of outcomes on particular contexts, a fully systematized or mechanical approach to statutory construction would be unworkable. But short of such an approach, it is possible to develop some guidelines.

Priority. The first task is to develop rules by which to rank or weigh interpretive norms. Although particular judges (and administrators) will rank such norms in various ways, it should ultimately be possible to achieve a more precise understanding of statutory construction—both as a descriptive and as a normative matter—through generating a hierarchy of interpretive principles. Here as well, the overriding goal is to promote the purposes of constitutional democracy while taking account of the changes introduced by the rise of the regulatory state.

In that hierarchy, the presumptions in favor of decisions by politically accountable actors and in favor of political deliberation should occupy the very highest place. The principle of political accountability has an unmistakable foundation in Article I of the Constitution, and it is an overriding structural commitment of the document. The principle has foundations as well in assessments of institutional performance. At the same time, it operates to counteract characteristic failures in the regulatory process. In this sense, the norm of political accountability draws on all three of the basic sources of interpretive principles.

The commitment to political deliberation belongs on the same plane, as a basic constitutional commitment. It is implicit in the systems of checks and balances and federalism, and it has roots in Madison's conception of political representation. The absence of deliberation has also contributed to regulatory failure. The belief in political deliberation and the belief in political accountability are thus closely allied in American constitutionalism.

Other interpretive principles traceable to constitutional norms also deserve great respect; they occupy the next highest position in the hierarchy. This category includes the norms in favor of state autonomy, against delegations of legislative authority, in favor of disadvantaged groups, and in favor of narrow construction of interest-group transfers. As we have seen, all of these principles have constitutional status; they are underenforced as a result of the institutional position of the judiciary. It is also possible to create a kind of hierarchy within constitutionally based interpretive principles. Thus, for example, the principle in favor of state autonomy occupies a lower place than the principle in favor of protection of disadvantaged groups. This is a natural inference from the fourteenth amendment and from various cases as well; the Constitution imposes a self-conscious limit on state authority when such groups are at risk.

Finally, interpretive principles without constitutional status occupy the lowest rung. These include the presumptions in favor of coordination and proportionality, in favor of taking account of systemic effects, against implied repeals, and against obsolescence. All these should play a less significant role in cases of conflict. These principles might themselves be placed in lexical order. For example, the principles calling for de minimis exceptions and proportionality, and for taking account of systemic effects, should occupy the highest position among nonconstitutional principles. To use, say, the principle calling for broad construction of statutes favoring aspirations and nonmarket values as a reason to abandon proportionality would ultimately sacrifice those very values—because of the likelihood that stringent regulation will produce regulatory irrationality and, ultimately, underregulation. Indeed, the background principles in favor of de minimis exceptions, accounting for systemic effects, and proportionality should ordinarily apply unless a constitutional principle trumps them.

Harmonization. Principles of harmonization are designed not to rank interpretive norms, but to reconcile them in cases of possible conflict. A principle of harmonization would call for courts to understand (for example) that the proportionality principle must be applied differently when nonmarket values are at stake. In such cases, it need not be controlling that the costs and benefits, understood in terms of dollars, are disproportionate. The cases reflect a similar understanding, for as we have seen courts have interpreted statutes quite generously when aspirations and noncommodity values are involved.

Another principle of harmonization would recognize that cases turn not simply on the applicability of interpretive norms, but also on the degree of their infringement. Thus, for instance, an enormous grant of discretionary lawmaking power to a regulatory agency would argue more strongly in favor of aggressive statutory construction than a minor grant of such power. To give another example: if the norm in favor of limited delegations conflicts with the norm in favor of coordination of regulatory policy, the degree of the infringement on both norms would be highly relevant to the decision.

We might illustrate principles of priority and harmonization with *Santa Clara Pueblo v. Martinez*,[63] in which the Supreme Court was asked to decide whether the Indian Civil Rights Act could be enforced in federal court by a tribal member whose rights had allegedly been violated. In concluding that it could not be, the Court relied not on the ambiguous text of the Act, but on background principles of tribal sovereignty. The Court said that in the absence of a clear legislative statement, a federal statute would not be construed so as to intrude on "tribal autonomy and self-governance." The Court thus resolved the case through reliance on an interpretive principle, and indeed it would probably have been impossible to decide *Martinez* without some such principle.

In the circumstances of *Martinez,* however, the notion of tribal autonomy was entitled to much less than usual weight. The plaintiff sought to invoke the Indian Civil Rights Act so as to vindicate principles of sex equality—embodied in an equal protection clause in the Act—against a tribal rule that gave rights of membership to children of fathers born off the reservation, but not to children of mothers born outside it. It is one thing to invoke Indian autonomy so as to limit federal intrusions into tribal self-determination on such matters as gambling and civil and criminal jurisdiction. It is quite another to invoke that principle as a reason to give a narrow construction to a federal statute providing Indian women with a right of nondiscrimination held by all American women. The principle in favor of tribal sovereignty should have been overcome by the nondiscrimination principle of the equal protection clause as incorporated in the Indian Civil Rights Act.

Fissures in the Interpretive Community

Outside of law, and to some extent within the legal academy, it has become fashionable to suggest that interpretive disputes are resolved on the basis of agreements within the community of interpreters.[64] The meaning of judicial precedents, constitutional provisions, and statutes is largely a function of interpretive principles that are widely shared in the relevant community.

To some degree, this view is compatible with the approach suggested here. It too suggests that there is no preinterpretive text; it too recognizes the need for background principles by which to give content to legal and other commands. But at least in law, and probably elsewhere, those who attempt to undertake or evaluate interpretive practices must do much more than simply invoke the existence of agreed-upon background principles within the community. The problem is that in hard cases and over time, the community will be badly divided. Different people will bring disparate background norms to bear on the question of meaning, and these norms will produce disagreements over the construction of statutes. In such cases the question is whether it is possible to develop criteria with which to evaluate the competing norms, whether cases turn on wholly subjective assessments by individual judges, or whether one must rest content with the assertion that legal terms have the meaning that they do because the people who wield authority are able to convert their positions into law.

In the area of statutory construction, it is possible to evaluate competing interpretive principles in three distinct ways. First, some of the relevant principles are constitutionally inspired—an outgrowth of a considered judgment about what the Constitution requires. To be sure, such judgments are not unanimously held and themselves require a theory of interpretation. But this does not undermine the basic point. The meaning of the Constitution is contested, but far from entirely open-ended within the legal culture; and constitutional principles help to discipline and inform the process of statutory construction. And some of the ideas developed here bear on the appropriate interpretation of the Constitution as well.

Second, some background norms are a product of engagement with contemporary institutional arrangements and with the functions of the modern regulatory state. The principles calling for narrow construction of appropriations statutes and for a cautious approach to legislative history are rooted in solid understandings about the operation of modern government. Similarly, it would be most inappropriate for courts (and others) to bring to bear interpretive principles that rest on a rejection of the values that animate modern regulation. The institutions and principles of statutory regimes thus provide a source of background norms and severely limit the field of legitimate disagreement.

Finally, some interpretive norms are an outgrowth of the failures of regulatory statutes and of the ways in which regulation produces irrationality. The principles calling for proportionality, for attention to systemic effects, for political accountability, for de minimis exceptions, for consistency and coherence in regulation, and for counteracting obsolescence are prominent examples here. These principles are not uncontestable in the abstract, and their application will itself bring about interpretive disputes. But they emerge quite naturally from an understanding of the characteristic pathologies of modern regulation, and they give a large degree of guidance.

In all of these cases, background norms are value-laden, and they may be controversial. But some of them can be shown to be ill-adapted to the modern regulatory state, and others can be justified as reasonable or even necessary responses to characteristic failings in the regulatory process and to contemporary views of the relationship between the citizen and the state. A clarification of the purposes and pathologies of regulatory legislation helps to provide a background against which interpretive debates can be understood.

All of these sources of interpretive norms provide criteria for evaluating various principles, and they help to resolve disagreements when there are fissures within the interpretive community. The existence of widely accepted or justified background norms and of criteria of this sort furnishes a decisive response to those who view legal (and other) texts as inevitably indeterminate. "Deconstruction" within the law—like its more carefully elaborated predecessor in philosophy and literary criticism[65]—is inadequate in large part because it neglects such norms and criteria, whether the deconstructive claims are intended as positive or normative. In law, and elsewhere, texts have relatively fixed meanings because of shared interpretive principles; and even where meaning is contested, standards are available by which to mediate among conflicting views.

The Postcanonical Legal Universe

What would regulatory law and statutory interpretation be like if all of these proposals were accepted? In one sense, the world would not be dramatically different from the one we inhabit. All of the principles suggested here have some foundations in contemporary law. Yet current law is far more chaotic and far less attuned to the nature and performance of modern government: some courts rely on altogether different interpretive norms, and no unitary set of norms emerges from the cases. A legal system that self-consciously adopted the principles described here would have a far greater degree of uniformity and coherence; and it would be especially responsive to constitutional norms and to the functions and failures of the regulatory state. Above all, it would rely on norms that are well-adapted to the aspirations that underlie the statutory regime and well-informed about its failings, and it would use the process of statutory construction as a partial corrective against some of the pervasive weaknesses of modern regulation. By contrast, some of modern law rests on principles that are incompatible with modern government, or that impair rather than improve its performance.

In all likelihood, a set of explicitly articulated interpretive norms would call forth administrative and legislative responses. In time, members of Congress and others involved in the lawmaking process would be aware of those norms. The enactment of legislation would be done in their shadow. One might expect some statutes to look quite different after these norms were adopted, since legislators and affected interests would be aware that courts would, in the face of statutory silence or ambiguity, press legislation in one direction rather than another. The ultimate consequence of judicial adoption of interpretive norms of this sort would be to shift the burden of legislative inertia—giving justice and rationality the benefit of the doubt—and at the same time to offer legislators and others a clear rather than murky background against which to do their work.

To a significant degree, the interpretive norms suggested here would convert hard cases into easy ones, providing principles with which to decide cases that might otherwise be in equipoise. But the norms would also make some easy cases into hard ones by shifting the legal backdrop and requiring clear legislative instructions before certain results could be reached. For this reason, a legal framework pervaded by explicit background norms of the sort outlined here would in a few settings create rather than diminish legal uncertainty. This is, however, a small price to pay for the increase in clarity in a variety of contexts, and, more fundamentally, an increase in rationality and in sensitivity to constitutional backdrop, statutory function, and regulatory failure. Most important, adoption of these principles would promote many of the goals of the original constitutional system, while at the same time remaining hospitable to the values reflected in the New Deal reformation and the rights revolution.

CHAPTER

6

Applications, the New Deal, and Statutory Construction

To give more specific content to the approach set out thus far, I will begin by discussing a set of disputed cases of statutory interpretation, explaining how reliance on background principles might aid in their resolution. After this, I shall deal in more general terms with the relation between the New Deal reformation and modern interpretive disputes. A number of such disputes call into question the appropriate baselines for statutory construction, especially when common law principles conflict with the values that underlie regulatory regimes.

A large task for the future is to develop interpretive principles that build on the logic of those regimes, rather than on the private law they are designed in large part to replace.[1] Moreover, the resolution of many questions of interpretation requires a judgment about the relation between the New Deal reformation and central aspects of the original constitutional structure. As we will see, the development of interpretive principles calls for an act of synthesis—in recognition that some aspects of the original structure, though thrown into doubt during the New Deal, retain considerable vitality. In particular cases, interpretation will require courts to fill gaps or resolve ambiguities with principles that are congenial to the assumptions underlying the modern regulatory state. In general, courts will be required to bring to bear, on statutory construction, judgments about the relation between the New Deal reformation and original understandings of federalism, private rights, legalism, and checks and balances.

Particulars

Occupational Safety and Health Act

In two remarkable cases the Supreme Court has been asked to decide on the meaning of OSHA in the context of toxic substance regulation. The pertinent language of the statute asks the Secretary to issue the standard that "most adequately assures, to the extent feasible . . . that no employee will suffer material impairment of health or functional capacity even if such employee has regular exposure to the hazard . . . for the period of his working life." The statute also contains a general definition of "occupational safety and health standard," which says that the term refers to measures that require "conditions . . . reasonably necessary or appropriate to provide safe or healthful employment and places of employment." [2]

In *Industrial Union Department, AFL-CIO v. American Petroleum Institute*,[3] the Court was confronted with an OSHA regulation of benzene. Its consequences were sharply contested, but there was reason to believe that the regulation would impose enormous costs for small or speculative gains. OSHA itself concluded that compliance would require capital investments of $266 million, first-year operating costs of $187 to $205 million, and recurring annual costs of $34 million. The consensus appeared to be that the state of scientific knowledge precluded a clear prediction of significant benefits. One study suggested that the regulation would save two lives every six years. The benefits, in the Court's view, "may be relatively small." [4]

A plurality of the Court concluded that the Secretary of Labor must establish a "significant risk" before regulating a toxic substance. The plurality relied for its conclusion on the definition of safety and health standards as those "reasonably necessary or appropriate to provide safe or healthful employment." In this view a standard was not "reasonably necessary or appropriate" if OSHA was unable to show that there was a significant risk.[5]

There was little direct basis for the plurality's conclusion in the text or history of the Act. Congress did not impose a requirement that OSHA show a "significant risk" in anything like explicit terms. The Court found that such a requirement was implicit in the definitional clause, but the clause need hardly be read in that way. It is more naturally treated, like most definitional clauses, as having no substantive content, or as having substantive content defined by other provisions of the Act. It is most unusual for the Court to read such a definitional clause as creating a limitation on administrative power. It is even more unusual for the Court to do so when the definition, so interpreted, flies in the face of the governing, and far more specific, substantive provision, which in this case says that toxic substance standards must ensure "to the extent feasible . . . that *no employee will suffer material impairment of health or functional capacity*." [6] The reference to "no employee" seems to suggest that the statute forbids OSHA from permitting risks from toxic substances even if only a few workers would face "material impairment of health." The function of the judicially created "significant risk" requirement, by contrast, is to forbid regulation unless many workers will be affected. Nothing in the legislative history, moreover, supports the Court's interpretation of the definitional clause; if anything, the historical record argues against that interpretation.

Unable to point to a solid textual basis for its "significant risk" requirement, the plurality invoked a clear statement principle:

> In the absence of a clear mandate in the Act, it is unreasonable to assume that Congress intended to give the Secretary the unprecedented power over American industry that would result from the Government's view . . . Expert testimony that a substance is probably a human carcinogen . . . would justify the conclusion that the substance poses some risk of serious harm no matter how minute the exposure and no matter how many experts testified that they regarded the risk as insignificant. That conclusion would in turn justify pervasive regulation limited only by the constraint of feasibility . . . The Government's theory would give OSHA power to impose enormous costs that might produce little, if any, discernible benefit.[7]

The plurality went on to suggest that the government's interpretation would give the Secretary of Labor "open-ended" policymaking authority that might amount to an unconstitutional delegation of legislative power. In his concurring opinion, Justice Powell, advocating an interpretation of the OSHA act that would call for cost-benefit balancing, suggested that "a standard-setting process that ignored economic considerations would result in a serious misallocation of resources and a lower effective level of safety than could be achieved under standards set with reference to the comparative benefits available at a lower cost."[8]

If the *Industrial Union* case were approached in formalist or textualist terms, the plurality's conclusion is exceptionally difficult to defend. The "significant risk" requirement cannot be found in the statute, at least not in any ordinary sense. It was a judicial creation. It would therefore be possible to caricature the result in the case as an impermissible judicial amendment of the statute. Moreover, a background principle in favor of interpreting words in accordance with their plain meaning would point toward acceptance of the government's position.

But the plurality's conclusion was nonetheless sound. Realistically speaking, the language of the statute cannot alone be made to resolve the problem. It is simply a myth to suggest that the Congress that enacted OSHA focused on the question of imposing enormous expenditures to redress minimal risks. Despite the broad language of the toxic substances provision, Congress never dealt with or focused on that problem. (We might recall here Wittgenstein's game of dice, discussed in Chapter 4.) In this light, the statutory language need not be read to require OSHA to regulate minor risks at the expense of billions of dollars.

In the context of *Industrial Union,* the plurality was therefore correct in seeing itself free to interpret the statute to contain an implicit "significant risk" requirement. The fundamental point here is that it would make little sense to interpret the statute so as to allow—indeed, require—OSHA to regulate to the point of "feasibility" merely because one or a few employees might suffer "material health impairment" as a result of a lifetime of exposure. Such an interpretation would make the Department of Labor reluctant to embark on a course of regulation at all. As we have seen, this interpretation would result in practice in less, not more, protection of workers.

In these circumstances, on what basis should the Court have resolved the case? The clear statement principle on which the plurality relied supplies the beginnings of an answer. We have seen that there is good reason for a background principle calling for de minimis exceptions to social and economic regulation; the *Industrial Union* case provided an excellent setting for the application of that principle. Moreover, the proportionality principle and the background rule counseling avoidance of irrationality argue in favor of the plurality's reading. A plausible argument can be made as well that draconian regulation of the workplace had become perverse in the light of changed circumstances of the 1980s, when the economic consequences of regulation appeared to be taking a major toll on the nation's economy. Finally, the beneficiaries of OSHA regulation were extremely well-organized and fully able to protect themselves in the implementation process. There was therefore a ready political corrective to the plurality's conclusion if it ran in the face of public consensus.

For all of these reasons, the plurality was correct to interpret the Act to require a showing of a significant risk as a predicate for regulation.[9] Its analysis of the problem tracked the approach suggested here with considerable precision.

In *American Textile Manufacturers Inst. v. Donovan*[10] the Supreme Court decided a question left open in *Industrial Petroleum:* did the OSHA statute require a cost-benefit analysis? In arguing that it did, the industry contended that the word "feasible" meant that the Secretary must not only show a significant risk, but also prove that the benefits of regulation justified the costs. "Feasibility," in industry's view, contemplated a balancing of costs and benefits. The government contended that once OSHA had shown a significant risk, it could regulate to the point where the survival of the regulated industry would be endangered by additional controls. For the government, the term "feasibility" connoted not cost-benefit balancing, but instead meant "possible."

In accepting the government's argument, the Court relied on the dictionary definition of "feasible," concluding that the term meant "capable of being done, executed, or effected," rather than justified by a balancing of costs and benefits.[11] This approach was not entirely unreasonable. The structure of the toxic substances provision—consider the "no employee shall suffer" language—is in considerable tension with the industry's construction. Moreover, Congress has sometimes used the term "feasible" as a self-conscious alternative to cost-benefit balancing, making it clear that the two terms do not have the same meaning. But the same principles that support the decision in *Industrial Petroleum* cast serious doubt on *American Textile Manufacturers.*

The first point is that notwithstanding the statute's language, it is probably unrealistic to believe that Congress actually focused on, and resolved, the question of whether the government's approach was to be favored over some kind of balancing of costs and benefits. That question never arose during the debates. In addition, there is real irrationality in a system in which the Secretary of Labor is required to find a significant risk but prohibited from undertaking a cost-benefit analysis. Whether a risk is significant depends in large part on the costs of eliminating it. A risk that is relatively small might call for regulation if the costs are also small; but even a large risk might best be left unregulated if the costs are enormous. A rational system of regulation takes account not of the magnitude of the risk alone, but of the risk in comparison to the costs.

These considerations would deserve little weight if the statute dictated a contrary result, but the word "feasible" was probably capacious enough to accommodate a kind of proportionality requirement. To be sure, the case was a difficult one. But by its reading of the statute, the Supreme Court has contributed to the irrationality of the OSHA—irrationality that has harmed workers, employers, consumers, and the public at large.

The Delaney Clause

I have referred on several occasions to the Delaney Clause, which prohibits the sale of food additives that "induce cancer when ingested by man or animal" or are found "after tests which are appropriate for the evaluation of the safety of food additives, to induce cancer in man and animal." As we have seen, the drafters of the Clause believed that only a few additives caused cancer but that they were extremely dangerous. By the 1980s, however, it was clear that many substances were carcinogenic, but many of them created exceptionally minor risks. These substances included natural dietary constituents posing dangers that surpass those of artificial chemicals.

These developments severely undermined the assumptions of the Congress that enacted the Delaney Clause, and indeed made it appear quite perverse in many of its applications—banning as it did substances that posed little or essentially no risk to health. One consequence is that some new products have been kept off the market because modern testing techniques can find carcinogenic contents, whereas more dangerous older products, tested by more primitive methods, remain available. On balance, health risks are thus increased. Another consequence is that manufacturers, having been forbidden to use food additives posing a de minimis risk of cancer, use instead additives that cause more serious risks of other diseases—thus creating what is quite possibly an increase in illnesses and deaths from food additives.

In response, the Food and Drug Administration—invoking background principles that reject obsolescence and favor de minimis exceptions—interpreted the Clause to permit exemptions of trivial risks. It said that it would approve food additives that posed a de minimis risk of cancer.

The United States Court of Appeals for the District of Columbia held that the FDA's position was unlawful.[12] In the court's view, the Delaney Clause was wholly unambiguous on the point. But this interpretation was far from inevitable. If the statute is read in its context, there is no such clarity. Congress simply did not focus on the question of de minimis risks. It is far from clear that the court's mechanical reading of the statute was sensible from the perspective of its original authors, whose assumptions did not hold in the 1980s. The background against which the Delaney Clause was written was so different from present circumstances that the statutory terms "induce cancer" should be treated as ambiguous. Whether a substance "induces" cancer within the meaning of the Clause might well be a function of the degree of risk that it posed. In these circumstances, interpretation of the Clause to permit de minimis exceptions seems consistent with permissible understandings of judicial interpretation, and quite sensible to boot. The court's decision to the contrary was misguided.

The Pennhurst Case

In *Pennhurst State School and Hospital v. Halderman,*[13] a group of mentally retarded people brought suit against a facility that was found to contain dangerous conditions. Many of the residents had been physically abused, brutally mistreated, or drugged, and the facility was utterly inadequate for the treatment of the retarded. As the basis of their legal claim, the plaintiffs invoked the "bill of rights" in the Developmental Disabilities Assistance and Bill of Rights Act.[14] The bill of rights contained a set of legislative findings, including the following:

1. Persons with developmental disabilities have a right to appropriate treatment, services, and habilitation for such disabilities.
2. The treatment, services, and habilitation for a person with developmental disabilities should be designed to maximize the developmental potentials of the person and should be provided in the setting that is least restrictive of the person's personal liberty.

3. The Federal Government and the States both have an obligation to assure that public funds are not provided to any institution . . . that does not provide treatment, services, and habilitation which is appropriate to the needs of such persons.[15]

The question in *Pennhurst* was whether the bill of rights created legally enforceable rights, or whether it set out a set of goals or aspirations that could not be vindicated in court. Whether the bill of rights was legally enforceable was uncertain in light of the text and history of the Act. The history provided the basis for a plausible argument that Congress intended to create legally cognizable rights.[16] Yet it was not unreasonable to suggest that the bill of rights should be taken as an essentially precatory statement of congressional aspirations—a statement that captured a goal, not an instrument that would permit the developmentally disabled to bring suit against a facility for the mentally retarded that failed to respect the bill of rights. Without a background interpretive principle, the case was probably impossible to decide.

In holding for the institution, the Supreme Court did not deny that the conventional sources of interpretation left the case in equipoise. Instead it invoked a background principle: "If Congress intends to impose a condition on the grant of federal moneys, it must do so unambiguously. By insisting that Congress speak with a clear voice, we enable the States to exercise their choice knowingly, cognizant of the consequences of their participation."[17] *Pennhurst* was thus decided as a result of an interpretive norm that was produced by the Court's understanding of the constitutional background. This norm could not be connected to the statute at issue in the case.

For reasons explored above, principles of federalism, at least in ordinary settings, require a clear statement from Congress for the imposition of significant duties on the states. If the bill of rights had been held legally enforceable, the states would have faced an enormous financial burden, one that they had not, in view of the ambiguity of the statute, necessarily agreed to incur. But two considerations suggest that *Pennhurst* was incorrectly decided.

First, the restraints of federalism have much less force when Congress is attempting to protect a traditionally disadvantaged group from state political processes. Here the ordinary presumption in favor of state autonomy is countered by the history and implementation of the fourteenth amendment—a self-conscious limitation on state power. Invocation of principles of state autonomy to justify a narrow reading of a statute enacted on behalf of a socially subordinated group is wrongheaded in light of constitutional structure and history.

To be sure, this conclusion depends on the controversial view that the developmentally disabled should for these purposes be treated the same as blacks, the group most obviously protected by the fourteenth amendment against state politics. And while a full-scale defense of that view is beyond the scope of the present discussion, it should not be difficult to support that position in light of the past and present treatment of the developmentally disabled—treatment that led to the very statute at issue in *Pennhurst*.

Second, an underenforced constitutional norm calls for aggressive construction of statutes involving the developmentally disabled. The Court has been extremely cautious in using the Constitution to protect the disabled, largely for institutional reasons. In holding that the equal protection clause does not entitle the mentally retarded to special protection, for example, the Court stressed that federal and state legislatures have in fact responded to the pervasive mistreatment of the retarded, and that courts should be reluctant to intrude in so dramatic a way into democratic processes.[18] In these circumstances, it remains possible to argue that the best substantive theory of the equal protection clause does accord special protection to the disabled, and that when other branches offer such protection, they are carrying out their constitutional responsibilities.

It follows that when Congress has taken steps to provide safeguards for that group, the Court should take into account the underenforced character of the equality norm and give statutes involving the disabled a hospitable rather than grudging interpretation. It is puzzling indeed that the *Pennhurst* Court invoked the constitutional principle of state autonomy in order to conclude that a statute appearing to protect the developmentally disabled provided no protection at all.

The Weber Case

In *Steelworkers v. Weber*,[19] the Court was asked to decide whether Title VII of the Civil Rights Act of 1964 made it unlawful for a private employer voluntarily to adopt a race-conscious affirmative action program. Among the disputed statutory provisions in the case, by far the most important made it an unlawful employment practice "for any employer . . . to discriminate against any individual because of his race." [20] Also relevant was a provision saying that "nothing contained in this title shall be interpreted to require any employer . . . to grant preferential treatment to any individual or to any group because of the race . . . of such individual or group." [21]

A divided Supreme Court held that despite the statute's explicit prohibition of discrimination because of race, a voluntary race-conscious program did not violate Title VII. The Court noted that the statutory disclaimer of a requirement of preferential treatment was far from a prohibition of such treatment. Indeed, the disclaimer would have been unnecessary if the basic antidiscrimination principle already prohibited preferential treatment. The statutory structure thus suggested that such treatment might be permissible.

More fundamentally, however, the Court said that the statutory prohibition of discrimination must be understood in terms of its underlying purposes and against its immediate background, which involved the imposition, by employers, of a variety of obstacles to the employment of blacks. The statute should be read in its context, not in the abstract. The Court concluded that the statutory goal of promoting black participation in the workplace was not violated by voluntary affirmative action, but would on the contrary be promoted by it. In the critical passage, the Court said that it "would be ironic indeed if a law triggered by a Nation's concern over centuries of racial injustice and intended to improve the lot of those who had 'been excluded from the American dream for so long,' constituted the first legislative prohibition of all voluntary, private, race-conscious efforts to abolish traditional patterns of racial segregation and hierarchy." [22]

In his concurring opinion, Justice Blackmun pointed to "considerations, practical and equitable, only partially perceived, if perceived at all," by the Congress that enacted the statute. [23] For Justice Blackmun, the particular problem was that an employer facing a potential suit for past discrimination against blacks might well choose a race-conscious program in order to avoid litigation. If those who have arguably violated the statute could not undertake voluntary remedies, the statute would require litigation in cases in which the courtroom can and should be avoided. Justice Blackmun emphasized that this problem could not have been anticipated by Congress. In the absence of a clear legislative resolution, he said, the problem argued in favor of allowing affirmative action.

In a vigorous dissenting opinion, Justice Rehnquist invoked the statutory history and above all its language to support a reading that would disallow all race-conscious measures. For Justice Rehnquist, the Court's approach was "Orwellian" because inconsistent with the "plain language" of the statute.[24] In his view, the text of the statute meant precisely what it said; and what it said was that employers could not discriminate on the basis of race.

At first glance, there is much to be said in favor of Justice Rehnquist's position. The civil rights act was enacted largely on the basis of a principle of color-blindness, and that principle was articulated over and over again during the debates.[25] The statutory prohibition of "discrimination against an individual because of his race" might well be taken as an unambiguous statement on the issue.

In fact, however, the issue in *Weber* could not realistically be resolved solely on the basis of the text and history of Title VII. In this respect, the case raised issues akin to those introduced by OSHA, the Delaney Clause, and Wittgenstein's game of dice. The statutory language was surely capacious enough to justify invalidation of affirmative action programs. But understood in its context, it need not have been read in that way. It was clear that Congress had not foreseen or focused on the possibility that employers would voluntarily engage in affirmative action in favor of blacks, whether to fend off litigation, to overcome societal discrimination, to improve the efficacy of the workplace, or for some other reason. In the racial setting, Congress understood the term "discrimination" in reference to race-conscious measures harming blacks. Indeed, the term drew its very meaning from that setting. Aside from a few comments in the debate, most of them ambiguous when taken in context, Congress did not specifically attend to the question whether its prohibition should be understood to include a general ban on racial differentiation. The statutory statement that affirmative action was not required hardly meant that affirmative action was proscribed.

Moreover, it is fully plausible to suggest that the notion of discrimination has the connotations it does precisely because of its association with the purposes and effects characteristic of measures subordinating disadvantaged groups.[26] It is by no means clear that a prohibition of discrimination should also be read to bar measures favoring such groups. Measures advantaging members of minority groups quite arguably have purposes and effects exactly opposite to those of measures that discriminate against blacks. On this view, the purposes animating Title VII—properly characterized—are not compromised by such measures and if anything argue in favor of their validation. It is no answer to say that an argument of this sort invokes a controversial view about public policy; the notion that the language and history dispose of the case is simply a myth. There is revision in precisely the same sense either way. The statute must be interpreted; the idea that it should be "followed" produces indeterminacy.

To say this is not to supply a full argument in favor of the *Weber* result. It would be at least plausible to argue that Title VII should be taken to incorporate a general prohibition on racial differentiation. To be persuasive, however, that argument would have to appeal to considerations other than those unambiguously embodied in the text and history of the statute: indeed, it would have to be that such a reading of Title VII would lead to the most sensible system of antidiscrimination law. Resorting to ideas of this sort is inescapable in *Weber*.

The best criticism of *Weber* would suggest that extratextual considerations argue against the Court's decision; the defense would suggest that such considerations argue in its favor. The ideal of color-blindness has considerable appeal, but as Justice Blackmun emphasized, circumstances had changed significantly since the original enactment of Title VII, adding to the ambiguity of the text on the question, read in its context. Moreover, there is a sharp distinction, in principle, between the purposes and effects of measures discriminating against blacks and the purposes and effects of remedial programs.

Indeed, the attack on affirmative action depends on premises reminiscent of those that led to the New Deal attack on market ordering. For the critics of affirmative action, it is not neutral to understand antidiscrimination statutes as permitting distinctions between discrimination against blacks and discrimination against whites. Such an understanding makes the outcome depend on "whose ox is gored." This view, like the attack on New Deal regulation, treats the status quo as the baseline from which to measure neutrality or inaction. In the case of affirmative action, government intervention to redress only one form of discrimination is impermissibly partisan. But if the current distribution of benefits and burdens as between blacks and whites is thought not to represent the state of nature but to be a product of unjust past and present social choices, the argument for affirmative action—like the argument for redistributive regulation in general—becomes far more powerful. No requirement of "neutrality" would be seen as mandating measures that are (or seem) indifferent to race. There is no antecedent entitlement to distributions based on market ordering pursuant to the status quo.

In fact, the very term "affirmative action"—ironically, embraced by defenders of the practice—is based on pre-New Deal assumptions. The term suggests that indifference to race (understood here as "inaction") is natural; that discriminatory effects deriving from colorblind rules are simply "there"; and that an effort to counter those effects should be labeled "affirmative." The terms "affirmative" and "action" both rest on status quo baselines that could easily, in the post-New Deal, post-Title VII world, be objects of attack. And as we have seen, statutes enacted to protect traditionally disadvantaged groups suffer from a range of obstacles to effective implementation. Considerations of this sort are not realistically avoidable in *Weber*. In these circumstances it would have been wrong indeed for the Court to interpret an ambiguous statute, not embodying an explicit legislative judgment on the point, as prohibiting affirmative action undertaken voluntarily by a private employer. *Weber* was correctly decided.

The Wards Cove Case

Related issues were raised in *Wards Cove Packing Co. v. Atonio*,[27] which involved the standards governing cases brought under Title VII. In its earlier decision in *Griggs v. Duke Power Co.*[28] the Court had held that once a plaintiff showed that an employment practice had a discriminatory effect on members of racial minority groups, the burden shifted to the defendant to demonstrate that the practice was justified by "business necessity." In *Wards Cove*, the Court altered this test in two ways. First, it held that the defendant's burden is producing evidence, not persuading the factfinder; the plaintiff must carry the burden of persuasion. Second, and more fundamentally, the Court said that the defendant need not show that a "challenged practice [is] 'essential' or 'indispensable' to the employer's business." The question is instead "whether a challenged practice serves, in a significant way, the legitimate employment goals of the employer." This determination of whether the practice "was based on a legitimate neutral consideration" makes disparate impact cases quite similar to disparate treatment cases. The question is whether the practice operates as a pretext or proxy for intentional discrimination. *Wards Cove* makes it extremely difficult to make such a showing.

The dispute between the *Wards Cove* majority on the one hand and the *Griggs* Court on the other cannot be resolved by reference to the text and history of the statute. The basic problems here are to decide what constitutes "discrimination," and how to ensure that it does not occur. The textual proscription of "discrimination" does not tell us whether discriminatory effects are in themselves impermissible; whether such effects might shift some or all of the relevant burdens to the defendant, not because they are objectionable in themselves, but in order to flush out discriminatory purpose; or whether such effects are only mildly probative of discriminatory purpose. To be sure, the legislative history reveals that the legislators were thinking largely of obvious cases of racial preference. But it does not say whether the statutory proscription does not also apply when the defendant adopts practices, not justified by business necessity, that " 'freeze' the status quo of prior discriminatory practices," or when the practice has a disproportionate effect on blacks that the employer would not be willing to tolerate if the burdened group consisted of whites.[29] In short, the history leaves a gap on the application of the statute to these cases.

The *Wards Cove* case therefore raises questions about implementing devices and gaps, questions that the text and history of the statute inform but do not answer. For this reason, the decision must be regarded as a form of federal common law, akin to the implementation of the Sherman Act and section 1983. Here the case can be resolved only by asking the value-laden question about what sorts of devices best implement the nondiscrimination guarantee, or put it in its best light.[30] That question is certainly not a simple one; the *Wards Cove* Court offered no reasons in support of its conclusions.

Probably the best argument against the Court's approach would begin by noting that discriminatory purpose is exceptionally difficult to show even when it exists. Discrimination exists, moreover, when an employer has not been neutral in the sense that it has adopted a practice having a discriminatory effect on blacks that it would have rejected if the burden had fallen on whites. While the *Griggs* approach might invalidate some practices that should, given perfect implementing devices, be upheld, *Wards Cove* will validate many practices that should, given such devices, be struck down. Various systemic barriers hinder the implementation of antidiscrimination statutes, and overenforcement of such statutes is highly unlikely. In the circumstances, *Griggs* was a better method of implementing the statutory proscription.

The New Deal and Statutory Construction

Many disputes about statutory construction amount to a confrontation between regulatory regimes and the pre-New Deal premises they appear to repudiate. These disputes characteristically take the form of a disagreement about the appropriate background principle in cases of statutory silence. Though seemingly narrow, such disagreements in fact reflect broad questions about the New Deal reformation and the consequences of government regulation for constitutional democracy. Some courts, for example, invoke common law baselines as a source of interpretation, whereas others reject those baselines as anachronistic. Such disputes should, I suggest, be resolved through an act of synthesis—treating modern regulation with hospitality, but at the same time attempting to promote aspects of the original constitutional system that have the strongest claim to contemporary support.

In an illustrative case, a state enacts a law providing for workers' compensation; in the aftermath of enactment an employer attempts to discharge employees who file workers' compensation claims.[31] Suppose that state law generally permits employers to fire employees "at will"—for whatever reasons they choose. Should the creation of the workers' compensation statute be understood to prevent the employer from discharging an employee for filing a claim?

On one view, the answer is negative.[32] The statute was written against the backdrop of at-will employment, and unless it expressly entitles employees not to be discharged for filing workers' compensation claims, they do not yet have that entitlement. This view leans heavily on the common law background, which is said to be controlling unless and until specifically displaced. The common law, that is, serves to fill statutory gaps. It provides the rule against which statutory silence must be read.

We may doubt, however, if an interpretive strategy of this sort is consistent with the values that underlie social and economic legislation. Workers' compensation is of course designed to permit employees to recover in the event of an injury. If employers could discharge employees who filed such claims, the workers' compensation program, most plausibly characterized, would be substantially undermined. The deterrent effect of even a few discharges would probably be enormous. For this reason it is extremely doubtful that the common law rule should serve as the gap-filler. A preferable approach would be for courts to explore whether that rule is consistent with the logic of the workers' compensation program. Because discharge would interfere significantly with the program, the proper conclusion is that employers cannot discharge employees for filing claims.

To say this is not to neglect the existence of legislative compromise, to deny that the legislature has the power to preserve the at-will rule in this context, or to say that the enactment of a workers' compensation scheme necessarily or by definition eliminates an employer's power of discharge. An advocate of the "deals" approach might suggest, for example, that the failure of the relevant groups to obtain a legal prohibition on discharge for filing a claim indicates that the deal did not include a right against such discharge. In this view, the legislature sought to protect the right to file workers' compensation claims, but only to a certain extent.

One could not argue, then, that purely as a logical matter, a workers' compensation statute resolves the ambiguity. But the "deals" approach depends on the view that legislative silence on freedom to discharge should be understood as a resolution of the question, when it might merely mean inadvertence, failure to focus on the issue, or a delegation to the courts. The "deals" approach also depends on reflexive incorporation of common law principles as the baseline against which to read statutory silence, when the relevant baseline is the question to be decided. Some value judgment, informing legislative silence, must be made either way. The better presumption is that the creation of a workers' compensation program implicitly carries with it a right to file claims without fear of dismissal by the employer.

Problems of this general sort arise quite frequently. Consider, for example, whether an employee discharged in violation of the National Labor Relations Act (NLRA) must "mitigate damages" by seeking alternative work.[33] The issue is of enormous importance to labor law. If employees must seek alternative work, their legally recoverable damages will generally be quite low, and the deterrent value of the various provisions of the NLRA will be greatly reduced. Employers will be able to engage in unfair labor practices at relatively low cost. Courts have nonetheless held that the common law principle in favor of mitigation of damages provides the appropriate background rule. This holding quite plausibly weakens the statutory regime.

A similar issue arose in *Independent Federation of Flight Attendants v. Zipes*.[34] The Court was asked to decide whether a successful plaintiff in a civil rights case could obtain attorney's fees against an intervening party in a case in which the intervener had litigated the case after the defendant had agreed to settle. The relevant provision says that a "court, in its discretion, may allow the prevailing party, other than the United States, a reasonable attorney's fee as part of the costs." The Court concluded that interveners could not be liable to a prevailing plaintiff. According to the Court, the fee-award provision is subject to "the competing equities that Congress normally takes into account," and those equities called for a rule that would permit an intervener—who after all was not a wrongdoer—to participate free from liability for fees.

The dissenting opinion argued that in light of the general purpose of the fee-shifting statute—to encourage civil rights plaintiffs to bring suit by allowing them to recover fees—interveners should be liable. The dissenters stressed that the contrary rule would require victorious plaintiffs to pay the sometimes large costs of litigating against interveners, an outcome that would undermine effective enforcement of the law. The Court responded that "the essential difference" between the two sides had to do with whether Title VII should be interpreted as reconciling "competing rights" in the traditional way, or rather as placing civil rights plaintiffs at the highest point of a hierarchy.

On this score, the statutory language and history offered no direct answers. Here was a problem to which Congress simply did not speak. The case therefore turned on the selection of background rules, or on federal common law. The Court's resolution depended on its assumption that the fee-shifting provisions of Title VII should be interpreted against the backdrop of open-ended balancing that preceded the statute's enactment. This decision—highly reminiscent of the use of common law baselines to decide the reach of public law— was probably mistaken in light of the adverse effects of the traditional approach on civil rights enforcement. In view of the pervasive difficulties in encouraging victims of discrimination to bring suits, and Congress' sensitivity to precisely those difficulties, *Zipes* was wrongly decided. The enactment of Title VII in general and of its fee-shifting provision in particular should have been taken as a repudiation of the more open-ended balancing that preceded it.

My basic conclusion is that in the filling in of statutory silences, it is necessary to ask to what extent the regulatory regime is in tension with the principles that underlie the preexisting network of law, most prominently the common law. To say this is not to say that common law rules are never helpful. Sometimes they complement regulatory systems quite well, and in any case they provide a readily available and often carefully elaborated body of law with which to fill the interstices of social and economic regulation. But it is necessary to look quite carefully at the relationship between the regulatory regime and the common law rule at issue. Frequently the regime is built on premises that call for an alternative baseline. Decisions of this sort cannot be made deductively or by reference to any precise metric; they call for a form of practical reason. But that fact should be no embarrassment to the enterprise.

New Deal and Common Law Baselines in Regulatory Law

In a number of important areas statutory interpretation involves the relationship between social and economic regulation and the common law principles that it displaced. In such cases it is necessary to synthesize principles of the New Deal reformation with the preexisting legal framework. An exploration of these issues calls for an assessment of such major problems as the value of administrative autonomy, the current role of federalism, and the relationship between social and economic regulation and older ideas about legal controls.

"Standing"

"Standing" has to do with what sorts of persons, invoking what sorts of injuries, may have access to federal court. Under current law, for example, it is clear that an industry affected by government regulation has standing to challenge the regulation on legal grounds. Indeed, a denial of standing to regulated industries might well violate the due process clause. It is equally clear that a taxpayer in Oregon is without standing to challenge the government's failure to eliminate workplace risks in Iowa. But in numerous areas questions of standing are sharply disputed, and their resolution calls for an interpretation of regulatory statutes involving both substance and procedure. Many of the central questions here have to do with whether and when regulatory benefi-

ciaries—victims of pollution, discrimination, and other harms—
should be able to invoke the courts on terms equal to those of regulated entities.

The Rise of the Private Law Model. For most of the nation's history, there was no separate body of standing doctrine. Whether a person could invoke the judiciary turned on whether the relevant law
created a "legal right" on his behalf. If government had conferred a
legal right on X, then X would be entitled to seek legal relief. On this
view, those having either common law interests or rights protected by
statute could invoke the federal courts.

In the early period of administrative law, courts used common law
principles to define the judicial role in public law cases.[35] If administrators intruded on interests protected by common law, judicial review was available to test whether the legislature had authorized
what would otherwise be a common law wrong. But if no common
law right was at stake, judicial review was unavailable. A traditional
liberty or property right was thus a prerequisite for legal intervention.

It is not surprising that this framework operated at the same time
as—indeed was a part of—the set of ideas associated with the *Lochner* era, discussed in Chapter 1. When the Supreme Court invalidated
social and economic regulation growing out of the progressive and
New Deal periods, it invoked common law categories to test the validity of public law. As we have seen, governmental departures from
the common law status quo—for example, a minimum wage or maximum hour law—seemed to be impermissible partisanship: a "taking" from A for B. Common law baselines played an important role
not only in *Lochner*-era decisions interpreting the due process clause,
but also in cases resolving the question of who was entitled to invoke
judicial protection.

In the context of standing, this view had two principal implications. First, regulated entities—industries and others who were the
object of regulation—had access to court to challenge agency action.
It was they whose common law rights, mostly in the form of private
property, were endangered by modern regulation. Second, the interests of beneficiaries of regulatory programs were not legally cognizable; they were treated as privileges or legal gratuities. They could
be protected through the political process, but not through the courts.

This basic model was accepted by the critics of the New Deal reformation, who sought to invoke private law as a limitation on public
law, as well as by its advocates, who voiced the prevailing belief that

traditional conceptions of the rule of law were incompatible with administrative regulation. Believers in judicial control of the sort reflected in *Lochner,* hostile as they were to administrative regulation, saw no need for judicial intervention to safeguard the interest in regulatory protection. And in light of the contemporary history, those favoring regulation were highly suspicious of legal controls and the courts—a suspicion that formed an important part of New Deal constitutionalism. In particular, Justices Brandeis and Frankfurter were instrumental in developing limitations on the power to invoke the judiciary to control administration, and they embraced restrictions on standing.[36] The resulting framework amounted to a private law model of standing, requiring a common law interest for the invocation of the judiciary. The private law model, traced by many current observers to the founding generation, was in fact a creation of the New Deal period.

A Public Law of Standing. Inroads on the private law model took place before the enactment of the Administrative Procedure Act (APA) in 1946; the model was largely abandoned in the 1960s and 1970s. The APA—the basic framework governing judicial review of administrative action—granted standing to anyone "suffering legal wrong" or "adversely affected or aggrieved . . . within the meaning of a . . . statute." [37] The term "legal wrong" referred to harm to common law interests and also to interests protected by statute. If Congress had required an agency to protect an interest, those suffering injury to that interest would have standing to sue.[38] At the same time, the "adversely affected or aggrieved" phrase recognized that Congress sometimes allowed people to act as private "attorneys general" even if their interests were not legally relevant under the governing statute—as, for example, in the case of a disappointed applicant for a radio license bringing suit to protect the interests of listeners. The APA provided a system that went well beyond the private law model, enabling those without common law interests to invoke the courts.

In the 1960s courts interpreted the APA to permit beneficiaries of regulation to vindicate claims of administrative illegality. Thus, for example, viewers of television, victims of housing discrimination, and users of wilderness parks were able to bring suit to challenge inadequate regulation, because their interests were statutorily protected.[39] According to the emerging view, a belief in the rule of law and in judicial controls was entirely compatible with a system of administrative regulation. Legal limits on regulatory agencies seemed well adapted to or even necessary for the successful implementation of statutory programs. In their rejection of the use of common law baselines in the law of standing, judges were conforming to the beliefs that gave rise to regulation in the first place. But the new synthesis was a firm repudiation of the New Deal belief in an inevitable disjunction between the realm of law and the realm of administrative government. The beneficiaries of regulation, no less than members of regulated industries, were entitled to invoke the courts.

This shift reflected three more particular ideas. First, statutes could be defeated not only by overzealous implementation, but also by unlawful failure to regulate and by administrative hostility to statutory programs. Agency inaction, or inadequate implementation, posed a major threat to the goals of regulatory statutes, an idea that drew on some of the empirical work discussed in Chapter 3. If congressional ends could be undermined by agency inaction, it seemed natural to conclude that courts ought to be available to counteract this form of illegality as well.

The second idea came from widespread evidence of the influence of regulated industries over regulatory programs. In the face of such evidence, it was most peculiar that regulated industries, and not regulatory beneficiaries, should have access to courts. As we have seen, political remedies are no more obviously available to regulatory beneficiaries than to regulated entities; indeed, beneficiaries face particularly severe obstacles to political organization. In these circumstances, a body of standing doctrine that restricted the judiciary to regulated industries seemed thoroughly perverse.

The final idea was that from the standpoint of the legal system, the interests of regulatory beneficiaries were of no less importance than those of regulated entities. This conclusion was a natural—indeed inevitable—outgrowth of the New Deal, which, as we have seen, arose from a belief that the common law catalogue of interests was inadequate. People needing recourse to prevent (for example) pollution or discrimination, no less than those invoking traditional property rights, were entitled to judicial protection. As a result the legal system dramatically altered standing principles, so that they no longer owed their shape to common law categories or distinguished between the rights of regulated entities and regulatory beneficiaries.

Indeed—and this is the central point—that very distinction depended on a conceptual foundation that had become anachronistic precisely because it was dependent on common law baselines.

Whether someone is the object of regulation or its beneficiary cannot be decided without an independent theory outlining what government ordinarily or properly does. Regulated entities are themselves the beneficiaries of legal limits on administrative power—and the common law—insofar as these sources of law protect them from public or private incursions into their legally created spheres. The beneficiaries are the objects of regulation insofar as the law authorizes such intrusions and restricts private conduct. It is not surprising that in the wake of the New Deal attack on the common law, it became impossible to sustain the assumptions underlying the distinction between beneficiaries and regulated entities. Eventually the Supreme Court concluded that for a plaintiff to have standing, it was necessary only to show an "injury in fact" that was "arguably within the zone of interests protected or regulated" by the statute—an expansive test that obliterated the distinction between regulatory beneficiaries and objects.[40]

The Return of Private Law. In the 1980s the Supreme Court reinvigorated private law principles in order to limit the ability of regulatory beneficiaries to bring suit. Ironically, the "injury in fact" requirement was the source of the limitation.

In the more recent cases the Court has said that in order to satisfy that requirement, the plaintiff must show (1) that a judicial ruling in his favor is likely to redress his injury, and (2) that the injury was caused by the unlawful acts of which he complains. These causation requirements are unobjectionable in the abstract, but they have turned out to raise hard questions about what sorts of injuries are legally cognizable and what kind of connection must be made out between the relevant injury and the acts of the governmental defendant. In some cases, courts have said that the APA and governing substantive statutes require a plaintiff to show an injury of the sort recognized in the common law and a tight causal connection between that injury and the alleged illegality. Sometimes the Court has said that these requirements are rooted in the Constitution as well. In these respects, the causation requirements have reintroduced private law principles of standing, forbidding regulatory beneficiaries from bringing suit.

Conspicuous examples are cases in which plaintiffs seek to redress what we might describe as regulatory harms: injuries in the form of increased risks. Consider these examples: poor people, denied medical services, object to the failure of the Internal Revenue Service (IRS) to provide adequate incentives to hospitals to offer services to the poor; parents of black children in districts undergoing desegregation challenge tax exemptions to segregated schools; prospective purchasers of fuel-efficient automobiles attack an EPA policy that might reduce the number and increase the price of such automobiles.[41] In all of these cases, the question is whether the plaintiffs have met the requirement of showing an "injury in fact" as a result of governmental conduct. In the first two cases, a badly divided Supreme Court denied standing. In the third, the United States Court of Appeals for the District of Columbia Circuit was evenly divided on the issue and therefore unable to resolve it.

The argument for denial of standing in these cases was that the injury should be characterized in highly particularized, common law-like terms and once it was so characterized, it would not be redressed by a decision favorable to the plaintiff. Thus, for example, parents of black children attending public schools undergoing desegregation could not show that the denial of tax exemptions to private schools would affect them in particular; prospective purchasers of fuel-efficient cars could not point to a particular automobile that would be unavailable as a result of the government's decision. The argument in favor of standing was that the injury was in the form of a decreased opportunity or an increased risk, and that the relevant statutes should be interpreted to allow plaintiffs to seek judicial protection against that injury.

The question of statutory construction depends, in short, on whether common law conceptions of injury should play a continuing role in public law regimes. In such regimes, however, the legal harms are quite generally probabilistic or systemic. The purpose of the regulatory program is to reduce risks of precisely that sort. Because nineteenth-century conceptions of injury are inconsistent with the principles that underlie modern regulation, they should not be used to resolve issues of standing in contemporary administrative law. A system in which regulatory harms were not judicially cognizable would allow regulated industries, and not regulatory beneficiaries, to have access to court—thus imposing a perverse set of ex ante incentives on administrators by inclining them against regulatory implementation. Such a tilt would defeat congressional purposes.

Finally, a refusal to treat regulatory harms as legally cognizable would disregard the collective action problems that characteristically give rise to statutory protection and also impair implementation.[42] It follows that common law principles do not provide the appropriate baseline for deciding questions of standing. Where there is ambiguity in the statute, probabilistic or regulatory harms should be sufficient to invoke judicial protection.

The Constitutional Backdrop. Conclusions of this sort are sometimes challenged on the ground that the constitutional framework allows for legal protection of traditional property and liberty interests, but not of the new interests safeguarded by regulatory statutes.[43] The Constitution restricts federal courts to "cases or controversies"; and it delegates to the President, and no one else, the power to "take Care that the laws be faithfully executed." On one view, courts may not be invoked to protect the broad public interests of those who seek more environmental protection or regulation of broadcasting. Those public interests should be vindicated through politics, not through the judiciary. On this view, which may well underlie the Court's recent decisions, the private law model has constitutional status.

For several reasons, this view is unsound. First, it depends on an inaccurate understanding of the original constitutional regime, which did not require litigants to show a private law interest. If the law created a right to bring suit, actions brought by people without traditional private rights, including taxpayers, were fully permissible. Indeed, the old prerogative writ of mandamus allowed for suits against government officials to compel them to do their jobs.[44] No separate body of statutory doctrine and no private law model even existed before the twentieth century. It is sometimes said that the Constitution was designed to protect only negative rights—rights against the government—but as we saw in Chapter 1, protection by the government was a prominent theme of the founding period. Legal protection against depredations by private parties, not merely against governmental action, has a long pedigree. The private law model thus finds no solid roots in the original document.

Second, it is most doubtful that courts should interpret the Constitution to forbid Congress from granting standing to beneficiaries even if the Constitution's framers actually believed that traditional liberty and property interests would provide the exclusive basis for invocation of courts. The private law model is not in the text of the Constitution. As we saw in Chapters 4 and 5, translation of any unenacted belief in the primacy of private law ideas into a dramatically different period—with a vastly expanded federal bureaucracy protecting novel interests through unforeseen and indeed unforeseeable methods—is enormously difficult. Those interests may be the functional equivalents of the original ones under current conditions. It is quite plausible to think that the Constitution, here as elsewhere, is best taken to set out a general principle capable of change over time. Even if the historical record supported the private law model, it would not at all follow that fidelity to the document requires current courts to invalidate legislative grants of standing to beneficiaries of regulation.

Advocates of the private law model sometimes introduce functional rather than historical arguments in support of their view. They argue, for example, that democratic principles suggest that courts should protect traditional or individual rights, but not public or collective rights. There is considerable ambiguity in this view. It is not clear whether standing is to be denied whenever many people are affected, or instead, whenever an interest in regulatory protection—an interest not protected by common law—is at stake. If numbers are the crucial concern, this view would foreclose standing not only for regulatory beneficiaries but often for regulated entities as well. The industries challenging (for example) a carcinogen regulation are usually numerous. The view that they should be denied standing because of their numbers is hard to sustain; indeed, in that view standing ought to be denied even when traditional property interests are at stake. Yet no one seems to argue for that result.

Numbers, then, cannot be decisive. Hence the nature of the injury, which involves a failure to afford regulatory protection, becomes the critical issue. And for reasons given above, the distinction between regulatory interests and traditional private rights cannot be sustained. The interests of beneficiaries are no more general or societal, and no less individual, than those of regulated entities.

It is especially odd to invoke considerations of democracy in support of the private law model when that model has been expressly repudiated by the democratic branches of government, and when Congress seeks to allow for judicial relief to ensure bureaucratic compliance with legislative directives. Nor does the constitutional authority of the President support the private law model. The constitutional provision calling on the President to "take Care that the Laws Be faithfully executed" is a duty, not a license. It would be most peculiar for courts to subvert legislative goals by invoking pre-New Deal conceptions of private right in order to prevent Congress from enabling the legal system to vindicate the interests that regulatory regimes have been created to protect.

Reviewability

Courts are frequently confronted with a question closely related to that of standing: whether administrative decisions are subject to judicial review. The question is not who may seek review, but what sorts of decisions are cognizable in court. We have seen that the basic presumption is in favor of review—an idea that draws on constitutional concerns and fears about agency failure. Judicial interpretation of regulatory statutes is done in the shadow of ideas of this sort.

Judicial Controls and Bureaucracy. The precise strength of the presumption in favor of review is in some question. In the New Deal period, courts hospitable toward regulation saw in principles of administrative accountability and expertise a good reason to find that Congress had "implicitly" precluded review. In the labor area, for example, judicial concerns about the adverse effects of legal intervention led courts to construe statutes so as to bar judicial review.[45] In the 1960s and 1970s, by contrast, agency expertise was frequently thought to be susceptible to regulated interests, and agencies no longer appeared accountable. The presumption of review became much stronger as courts saw legal control as a necessary check on agency failure.

More recently, courts have been willing to find implicit preclusion of review when judicial intervention would plausibly disrupt the statutory framework. Contemporary judges enthusiastic about implicit preclusion of review recall the New Deal's hospitality toward autonomous administration; those who find the presumption of review to be nearly irrebuttable repeat the attack on administration made by the antagonists of New Deal reforms. Ironically, however, the political constellation has been entirely reversed, as the presumption of review has recently been criticized most sharply by conservative judges unfavorably disposed toward administrative regulation. Statutory construction on the question of reviewability thus raises large issues about the relationship between legal controls and social and economic regulation.

Experience over the last half-century suggests that as a general rule, the contemporary judicial enthusiasm for administrative autonomy is as myopic as that of the progressives in the 1930s. There is no inconsistency between adherence to law and administrative regulation, so long as judges are well-informed about the nature, performance, and malfunctions of regulatory programs. Legal controls can be harmful if courts call for what is characteristically a requirement of a system of compensatory justice, a clear relationship between regulation and injury. In the context of regulatory programs, the evidence often does not allow for such a demonstration.[46] And an unduly aggressive judicial posture may increase delays and paperwork in a way that threatens implementation.

But so long as courts take these considerations into account, judicial review ought to be the general rule, operating as an important ex ante deterrent and occasional ex post corrective. Statutory requirements will sometimes call for or proscribe agency action. If they do so, courts should be available, at least in the absence of a clear congressional statement to the contrary.

Coercion and Private Rights Revisited. The law of reviewability distinguishes between defendants seeking to fend off governmental intervention and plaintiffs seeking to obtain review of inadequate regulatory protection. In the second context, the presumption of review is far more controversial. Indeed, the Supreme Court has held, in *Heckler v. Chaney,* that there is a presumption against judicial review of agency inaction.[47] In so holding, the Court said that agency inaction is not "coercive" and is therefore not reviewable unless Congress has said so.

Although the reach of the decision is uncertain, its implications are potentially enormous. A rule that would immunize the regulatory agencies against legal challenge for inaction in such areas as environmental law, discrimination, securities, and communications would remove an important incentive for executive compliance with law, and at the same time skew administrative incentives against implementation. Here a clear commonality unites the debates over standing and those involving reviewability.

The Supreme Court's reasoning in *Heckler v. Chaney* depends on pre-New Deal ideas finding coercion only in cases of government infringement of common law rights; the common law is the baseline against which to measure whether coercion has occurred. But the enactment of the very statute at issue repudiates that understanding and calls for a different interpretive principle. As we have seen, the New Deal reformation and the existence of social and economic regulation are often attributable to a belief that the market creates a kind of coercion from which government must protect its citizens, and a corresponding belief that governmental inaction is hardly neutral, but a conscious social choice. Ideas of this sort make it quite troublesome to use common law principles of coercion as the basis for creating a presumption against review of agency inaction.

To be sure, there are plausible reasons to treat agency inaction in a different way from agency action, most notably the fact that administrators cannot redress all violations and must allocate resources among numerous potential objects of regulation. If the agency has acted responsibly, there is no basis for saying that it has acted unlawfully. But this does not support a general conclusion that administrative inaction is unreviewable. For reasons explored in Chapter 2, the distinction between agency action and inaction is especially problematic in cases involving traditionally disadvantaged groups, public aspirations, and collective action problems. In such cases judicial review is an important safeguard against inadequate implementation. It might be for this reason that the distinction has often yielded in such cases.[48] A sharp distinction between agency action and agency inaction is thus not useful for purposes of reviewability. And even if such a distinction were plausible under some statutory regimes, it is quite implausible when statutory beneficiaries are especially at risk. The distinction is a holdover from anachronistic conceptions of the relations between citizens and the state.

In Chapter 4, we noted more generally that some observers argue for a background rule in favor of private ordering and that many participants in the legal culture rely on such a rule without seeming to be aware of it. But in view of the multiple statutory intrusions into the sphere of private autonomy—indeed of the New Deal attack on the idea of a prepolitical private sphere—a general background rule in favor of laissez-faire is no longer defensible. In the abstract, it is not possible to claim that common law principles are the appropriate background against which to read statutory silence.

Injunctions versus Other Relief

In several recent cases courts have been asked to decide whether environmental statutes require district judges to issue injunctions against unlawful polluting behavior, or whether instead they permit courts to retain their traditional discretion to "balance the equities" before issuing such injunctions. Under the latter approach, monetary penalties will be the sanction for pollution. In the relevant cases, the Supreme Court has adopted a strong clear statement principle against compulsory injunctions. This approach expresses the common law preference for damages relief and for balancing the equities, even though the contexts involve congressional rejection of common law principles.

In *Weinberger v. Romero-Barcelo*,[49] the Navy had violated the Federal Water Pollution Control Act by discharging pollutants into the sea without a permit. Balancing the costs and benefits of the polluting activity, the district court refused to enjoin the activity. The court of appeals reversed; because the statute required a permit before discharge, the traditional balancing process was no longer appropriate. The Supreme Court held that old principles of equitable balancing, with the criteria of "irreparable injury" and a balance in favor of the complainants, would apply "unless a statute in so many words, or by a necessary and inescapable inference, restricts the court's jurisdiction in equity." Therefore no injunction was forthcoming.

Likewise, in *Amoco Production Co. v. Village of Gambell*,[50] the Supreme Court concluded that an injunction would not be issued against polluting activity associated with oil and gas leases in Alaska—notwithstanding the fact that the Secretary of the Interior had failed to comply with federal law protecting areas in Alaska. The Court said that an injunction would not be forthcoming to prevent admitted illegality unless the equitable balancing so indicated.

Both *Weinberger* and *Amoco* turned on the importation of common law principles into the public law of environmental remedies. But in view of the relevant federal statutes, it is far from clear that those principles provide the appropriate background rule. In environmental cases it may have been better to issue an injunction to prevent unlawful polluting behavior unless Congress had indicated otherwise. Indeed, some courts have so held.[51]

The strongest argument against this approach would invoke the proportionality norm for the conclusion that when Congress has not spoken, courts ought not to impose large costs for small benefits. In the environmental arena, however, there is a severe collective action problem, and environmental harms that are trivial in the individual case might be collectively disastrous. In these circumstances courts should probably issue injunctions unless the polluter can make a persuasive argument that the costs are grossly disproportionate to the benefits.

Implied Causes of Action

In common law the violation of a statutory standard amounts to negligence per se: the violation would be found negligent regardless of the existing common law standard. For much of this century, federal courts used precisely this idea to conclude that if an agency failed to enforce a statutory mandate, a private litigant could bypass the agency and bring suit directly against a private defendant who was acting in violation of federal law.[52] This was the ordinary outcome if Congress had been silent on a private right of action. Where there is a right, the courts said, there is a remedy. For example, a victim of pollution could initiate an action directly against a polluter; a victim of securities fraud could bring suit against a company alleged to have violated the securities acts. This conclusion directly transferred common law conceptions of entitlement to public law regimes. In this setting, in contrast to the matter of standing, a private law model of public law operated to help regulatory beneficiaries.

In many cases, however, the judicial implication of a private action could cause serious problems for social and economic regulation. It is possible, for example, that Congress failed to create such rights because it wanted to control the aggregate level of enforcement through the appropriations process. If so, a private right of action could increase enforcement beyond that intended by Congress, producing overdeterrence. Suppose, for example, that Congress intended the securities laws to be enforced only to a limited degree; the creation of an implied cause of action would therefore bypass legislative limitations on enforcement levels. The regulatory program could reflect a complex system of compromises among enactment, sanction, and enforcement levels, and those compromises might be disrupted by creating a private remedy.

This conclusion is probably artificial in most contexts. Especially in the face of an ambiguous background rule, legislative silence on the question of implied causes of action might signify inattention, inadvertence, or a delegation to the courts rather than a careful calibration of optimal enforcement levels. Even so, judicial creation of private remedies might be highly undesirable for other reasons. Private remedies, in bypassing the agency, will frequently prevent centralized and coordinated enforcement, force unspecialized judges to decide complex technical questions de novo, and overcome the various democratic controls that are placed on administrative enforcement.

Imagine, for example, the multiple problems that would arise if private litigants were permitted to bring suit against "unfair and deceptive" advertising in the event that the Federal Trade Commission refused to act. Courts would be required to define in the first instance the statutory terms "unfair" and "deceptive." The process of regulatory implementation would be removed from the agency. Administrative expertise and accountability, so important in giving content to open-ended statutory terms, would be unavailable. All of the factors that gave rise to the agency would be undermined by independent judicial decisions. A general rule in favor of implied causes of action would therefore be inconsistent with the assumptions that typically underlie administrative regulation.

These considerations make it tempting to support an across-the-board rule against implied causes of action, foreclosing them unless Congress said specifically that it wanted private suits.[53] Such a rule would have the virtue of simple administration; it would put Congress on notice about the relevant background rule; and it would respond to the multiple dangers of private suits in disrupting a regulatory system. Notwithstanding substantial arguments in its favor, however, such a rule would not clearly be sound in light of the absence of legislative authorization and the likelihood that implied causes of action would provide a complement or corrective to the regulatory regime. For some programs private rights are a valuable supplement, sought by agencies themselves; in other cases they correct for administrative inaction, torpor, or inadequate resources. It is not valid to say that courts have no authority to create such rights, since a judicial role here is time-honored, and legislative silence is not plausibly taken as an implicit decision not to allow such rights.

No approach is perfect; every possibility has serious drawbacks. An alternative to a bright-line rule against implied rights would call on courts, in the event of legislative silence, to examine particular statutes to see if private suits would comport with the administrative framework.[54] The principal disadvantage is that this would require courts to undertake complex, value-laden inquiries of principle and policy into the regulatory scheme. Even a rule forbidding implied causes of action must, however, depend on some such inquiries, though conducted in a general way rather than case-by-case; and in time, particularized rules would emerge from case-by-case inquiries themselves.

For example, a vague or ambiguous statutory standard makes an extremely weak case for an implied cause of action, since judicial construction might well deviate from administrative interpretation, creating two competing enforcement schemes. That is one reason why civil rights statutes, containing relatively clear proscriptions, quite generally are held to create private actions, while ordinary economic regulation, with vague standards, is not.[55] In cases in which inadequate implementation is peculiarly likely, the argument for an implied cause of action is also strengthened. In this way, an understanding of collective action problems and other situation-specific obstacles to enforcement might prove helpful to courts deciding on implied causes of action.

Deference to Agency Interpretations of Law

In Chapter 4 I explored the view, expressed in the *Chevron* case, that courts should defer to agency interpretations of law. In this view, with its clear roots in the New Deal period, administrative expertise and accountability are reasons to accept agency interpretations so long as they are plausible.

But the *Chevron* position is far too crude. It treats ambiguities as equivalent to delegations of lawmaking power; the two are very different. When Congress has provided no such delegation, legal questions are for the courts. Even more fundamentally, the *Chevron* rule is inconsistent with the constitutional background. A cardinal principle of American constitutionalism is that those who are limited by law should not be empowered to decide on the meaning of the limitation: foxes should not guard henhouses. The *Chevron* rule disregards this principle by permitting agencies to interpret laws that limit and control their authority. The need for an independent judicial arbiter is especially urgent here in light of the awkward constitutional position of the administrative agency.

These considerations might be accommodated through an approach that would call for courts to defer to agency interpretation when there has been a legislative delegation of law-interpreting power, or, in the absence of clear legislative guidance, by inferring such a delegation in cases involving mixed questions of law and fact, rather than pure questions of law. For mixed questions, involving the application of law to fact, the agency's factfinding and policymaking competence is highly relevant. For purely legal questions, it is much less so. Such a rule would respect underlying constitutional principles while at the same time allowing agencies to deploy their specialized knowledge when it bears on the problem at hand.

Preemption

Courts are often asked whether state law regulating, for example, pollution or nuclear power can continue to operate in the face of federal law governing the same subject matter. The legacy of the New Deal is evident in a number of cases, particularly in the 1960s, which aggressively construe federal statutes so as to preempt state law.[56] On this view, federal law should be taken to "occupy the field," whether or not Congress has said so expressly. State law is presumed to have been displaced.

In this approach the courts placed a premium on the need for uniform federal regulation and saw state law as an unnecessary obstacle to federal goals. But as a general rule the approach was badly misguided, for reasons that cannot be fully elaborated in this space; a brief statement will suffice.[57] By any standard, the New Deal actors were far too cavalier in their treatment of federalism. For them, the presidency, or perhaps the executive branch, had a democratic pedigree far superior to that of the states. Both theory and practice reveal, however, that national institutions in general, and federal regulators in the executive branch in particular, are at best imperfect means for enabling the citizenry to achieve self-determination. The New Dealers' faith that autonomous administration would serve democratic goals was unjustified. The modern administrative agency has attenuated the links between citizens and governmental processes. In retrospect, the original framework of dual sovereignty was far superior to the New Deal system.

Moreover, uniform federal controls have often proved inefficient, clumsy, and rigid. As we have seen, regulatory uniformity has been a significant cause of regulatory failure. The presidency itself, though visible, is hardly a forum for republican self-government. In the interest of efficiency, democracy, and systemic rationality, states and localities should ordinarily be permitted to tailor regulatory programs to local needs and desires.

For these reasons, the New Deal reformation and the rights revolution ought not be taken as across-the-board repudiations of the system of dual sovereignty that was built into the original constitutional regime. This judgment bears most fundamentally on the question of regulatory reform, but it also suggests that state law should not be held preempted in the absence of a clear statement from Congress.

The weight and applicability of this principle will turn on the nature of the regulatory scheme. When a national moral commitment is involved, the case for uniformity is much stronger. As we saw in Chapter 5, a statute protecting disadvantaged groups calls for a different understanding of federalism than does a statute embodying ordinary social and economic regulation. A constitutional commitment trumps the otherwise controlling structural considerations supporting state autonomy. The case for state autonomy is also weakened when there are interstate spillovers or competition among the states for revenue-producing business and industry; such competition, often an important safeguard against tyranny, may also drive regulation below the optimal point. But outside of these settings, state autonomy should be the guiding principle. It follows that a general presumption against preemption of state law is appropriate in most contexts.

Functions, Failures, and the New Deal Reformation

Many disputes over the meaning of statutes are disagreements about the extent to which the legal background has been altered by the New Deal reformation. Pre-New Deal understandings are frequently invoked to define the reach of regulatory statutes and the class of people entitled to invoke their protections. In general, interpretive strategies of this sort are improper, since they rest on premises inconsistent with the values of the regulatory state.

An understanding of the relationship between the constitutional system and modern regulation and a review of statutory functions and failures should prove helpful to the resolution of these questions. Principles governing such issues as standing, reviewability, preemption, and implied causes of action can be informed by an appreciation of constitutional commitments, the purposes and failures of regulatory intervention, and the possibility of respecting those commitments and correcting those failures through statutory construction. In this way, the process of interpretation might help to synthesize the New Deal reformation and the rights revolution with those aspects of the original constitutional structure that have the strongest claim to continuing support.

Conclusion

The Constitution of the Regulatory State— and Its Reform

The national regulatory state, which originated in the New Deal and culminated in the rights revolution of the 1960s and 1970s, has renovated the American constitutional structure. With the rejection of common law baselines for distinguishing between neutrality and partisanship, or inaction and action, a social order based on the common law no longer seemed a natural or spontaneous arrangement, but a sometimes inefficient and unjust series of collective choices. The ultimate consequence of this shift of perception has been a transformation of the original constitutional commitments to checks and balances, federalism, and individual rights.

The transformation notably included the rise of a massive bureaucratic apparatus and a dramatically strengthened presidency. Both of these significantly altered the original system of tripartite government: governmental powers of legislation, execution, and adjudication were frequently concentrated into single institutions; powers originally thought to be within the domain of the states came to be exercised by the national government; and individual rights included not simply traditional liberty and property, but also nondiscrimination, clean air and water, a "social safety net," and freedom from unreasonable risks in the workplace, consumer products, and elsewhere.

Despite these developments, the problem of regulatory legislation has not yet been incorporated into the culture of modern political science and public law. For too long regulatory statutes have been approached as an undifferentiated mass, or as a crazy-quilt of unprincipled, ad hoc repudiations of the foundational principles of private property and freedom of contract. This view, pervasive even today, has roots in the early period of legal hostility to regulation, when statutes were treated as disruptive elements in the carefully elaborated system of the common law. After more than a half-century of experience, however, it is possible to fit social and economic regulation into a framework that takes account of the characteristic functions of law in contemporary liberal democracies.

Understood in terms of these functions, the modern regulatory system is superior not only to more highly collectivist alternatives but also to its common law predecessor. The numerous attacks on the regulatory state have been far too crude, whether they purport to be based on principle or on the facts. To be sure, the basic principles of welfare and autonomy argue powerfully in favor of respect for voluntary interactions and arrangements. But a system based exclusively on private ordering and private markets is undesirable in light of the multiple breakdown of markets, the existence of public aspirations, the injustice of current distribution of wealth, and the inevitable role of law, even in a system of private ordering, in allocating entitlements and wealth and in shaping the content of preferences themselves. In many settings, regulation that apparently overrides private choice is actually a means of facilitating private choice in light of collective action and coordination problems. Regulation may also vindicate democratic aspirations and altruistic goals, or counter preferences that have adjusted to the lack of information and opportunities, to existing consumption patterns, or to unjust background conditions. In all of these contexts, considerations of autonomy and welfare argue in favor of regulatory controls.

If modern regulation is approached in these terms, it emerges not as a crazy-quilt but as a series of patterns with integrity and coherence of their own. We have seen that social and economic regulation has been designed to promote economic efficiency, to redistribute resources in a public-spirited fashion, to reduce or eliminate social subordination, to reflect collective aspirations, to protect future generations from irreversible losses, and to alter preferences that are produced by various motivational or cognitive defects. Ideas of this sort account for regulation in such diverse areas as the environment, broadcasting, endangered species, occupational safety and health, consumer products, and discrimination. Nothing is to be gained by treating regulatory regimes as undergirded by a single rationale or as mere interest-group transfers. Approaches that begin from laissez-faire premises and rely exclusively on neoclassical economics are bound to misinterpret the modern regulatory state, relying as they do on criteria that cannot capture the diverse legitimate reasons for regulatory controls.

In principle, then, the modern fabric of regulatory programs has much to be said in its favor; this is so even though considerations of welfare and autonomy point toward fewer controls in some areas and greater controls in others. Moreover, some regulatory regimes have been highly successful in practice, producing important social gains unobtainable through exclusive or near-exclusive reliance on markets. The claim that regulation has generally been perverse is indefensible in view of its salutary effects in many areas, including the environment, automobile safety, and racial discrimination.

Many such programs, however, have performed poorly, and the failings of statutory regimes fall into distinctive patterns. Many of these are traceable to the awkwardness of treating collective goods as individual rights; others are a product of regulatory strategies that are self-defeating, in the sense that they aggravate the very problems they are supposed to solve. Some of the failings of regulation occur in the drafting process, as statutes reflect a misdiagnosis of the problem, are insensitive to the inevitability of tradeoffs, have unanticipated side effects, operate perversely because the marketplace can counteract regulatory controls, suffer as a result of interest-group power, treat programs involving risk reduction as vindicating individual "rights," or are insufficiently coordinated. Other regulatory failures are a product of inadequate implementation, as statutes are either under- or overenforced, redistribute resources in a perverse way, reduce economic productivity, and produce undemocratic processes and outcomes. Some statutes, moreover, become obsolete over time. Most of these forms of regulatory failure reflect institutional defects of the sort that the original constitutional regime was intended to counter.

One of the major tasks of modern public law is to develop structures to decrease the likelihood of regulatory failure and to introduce original constitutional safeguards into a dramatically changed system of government. For the most part, remedies must come from nonjudicial institutions. Structural reform should be high on the agenda here. Its overriding purpose should be to incorporate the constitutional goals of promoting deliberation and coordination in government and protecting against factionalism and self-interested representation. Substantive reforms, sometimes including a return to market ordering and always based on an understanding of how markets affect regulatory controls, are also an important strategy.

An understanding of the constitutional backdrop and of regulatory functions and failures has a series of concrete implications for both structural and substantive change. I have argued in favor of (1) flexible incentive systems, disclosure strategies, and performance standards rather than rigid command-and-control regulation, technological requirements, and design standards; (2) a constant focus on the practical advantages and disadvantages of various regulatory strategies, including possible adverse side effects; (3) a general rejection of conceptions of regulation as founded in individual rights in favor of a conception based on the management and reduction of social risks; (4) presidential coordination of the regulatory process, including both executive and independent agencies; (5) the creation of an office within the White House or Congress to coordinate long-range planning of regulatory agencies, to encourage research, and to operate as a brake on undesirable initiatives and as a spur to necessary controls; (6) a revival of checks and balances, in the form of greater legislative specification of regulatory ends and tradeoffs; and (7) increased reliance on federalism and decentralization, in the place of the inefficient and often unjust uniformity that has become characteristic of federal regulation.

The goal of these strategies is to bring some of the understandings of the original constitutional system to bear on current problems of institutional design. A regime built on this foundation would reflect enthusiasm about the use of national governmental power to promote economic productivity and to help the disadvantaged. In this respect, it would wholeheartedly embrace important elements of the New Deal reformation and the rights revolution. At the same time, it would be sensitive, as those developments were not, to the multiple dangers posed by modern bureaucratic government and to the risks of failure that are built into current regulatory strategies. The ultimate task of reconstruction carries with it all the possibilities and risks faced by reformers at critical points in American history, and all of the tools are available with which to bring about significant improvements.

Interpreting the Regulatory State

In this process of reconstruction the courts might prove helpful as well. We have seen that the traditional understandings of statutory construction are inadequate: textualism, structural approaches, purposive interpretation, use of congressional intent, and legal process approaches depend on fictions, leave enormous interpretive gaps, or both. Efforts to approach statutes as "deals" and attempts to justify a general background rule in favor of either "private ordering"[1] or deference to agency interpretations cannot be defended. Such approaches produce indeterminacy, lead to an inferior system of law, or depend on values that are inconsistent with the congressional decision to create the regulatory regime in the first instance.

Because language alone is without meaning, and because obvious gaps or ambiguities exist in hard cases, interpretive norms of various sorts are inevitable. Interpretation cannot go forward without background principles that orient reader to text, fill gaps in the face of legislative silence, or provide the backdrop against which to read linguistic commands. Some principles aid courts in discerning the meaning of particular statutes and help to implement Congress' actual or probable interpretive instructions; others are rooted in constitutional concerns; others are based on assessments of institutional performance; others depend on selection of baselines against which to read statutory silence; and still others attempt to respond to characteristic failings of regulatory legislation. Because of all these functions, "canons" of statutory construction, far from being obsolete, must occupy a prominent place in the theory and practice of statutory interpretation.

The eventual task is to develop a set of background understandings—sensitive to the constitutional structure, institutional design, the New Deal and the rights revolution, and the diverse functions and failings of governmental actors and statutory regimes—with which to approach social and economic regulation in a system that has largely abandoned common law categories. It is possible to generate a series of interpretive principles, all with support in current law, that can help accomplish some of the goals of deliberative government and a liberal republic in the period after the New Deal and the rights revolution. In this way, statutory construction can serve as an ally of more ambitious strategies aiming to promote some of the original constitutional goals in a novel legal environment. It is far too much to expect statutory construction to respond to all the failings of the modern regulatory state. But it is not too much to expect that the process of interpretation can make the situation better.

The discussion of background norms of statutory construction has broad implications. It bears, for example, on questions of interpretation in general; such norms provide a clue to the derivation of meaning of legal and other texts. The process of ascertaining meaning is inevitably a function of the principles with which interpreters approach legal enactments. No text can have meaning apart from the precepts held by those who must construe it, and those precepts cannot be found in any code. Disagreements over background norms play a role in common law and constitutional adjudication as well as in statutory construction, and inform debates over literary, historical, and philosophical texts. In all of these areas, the dispute frequently hinges on competing conceptions of the appropriate background principles with which to approach the text. But this perception provides no support for the claim that texts are indeterminate, or have the meaning they do merely because of arbitrary whim or intractable convention. On the contrary, it is possible to mediate among competing norms by reference to their consequences for the efficient, just, and democratic operation of the regulatory state.

The interpretive principles suggested here are directed to the President, regulatory agencies, Congress, and ordinary citizens, as well as to the courts. In particular, the President and regulatory agencies are entrusted with administering regulatory statutes in the first instance, and here interpretive norms are indispensable. Even more fundamentally, they provide a basis for understanding and evaluating the principles that underlie the fabric of the modern regulatory state. Indeed, the background ideas about interpretation help define our understandings not only of the New Deal reformation and the rights revolution, but of American constitutionalism and democracy as a whole.

In dealing with these issues it is especially important to avoid three common errors. The first is to treat interpretive principles as the illegitimate intrusion of discretionary policy judgments into ordinary, norm-free interpretation; as we have seen, there is no such thing. The second is to assume that the existence of competing, and value-laden, principles is reason enough to give up on the enterprise of statutory construction altogether, and in hard cases to resort to a supposedly "plain language" or to treat interpretation as inevitably indeterminate. Even in hard cases, it is possible to mediate among competing principles and to assess them in terms of their sensitivity to constitutional structure, to institutional arrangements, and to regulatory function and failure.

The third and final error is to use traditional norms of private law—carried over from anachronistic conceptions of the relationship between the citizen and the state—to resolve disputes about the meaning of modern enactments. The task for those charged with developing principles for the regulatory state is to promote, simultaneously, the diverse but ultimately compatible purposes of constitutional government and regulatory legislation.

Appendix A: Interpretive Principles

I. A Typology of Existing and Defunct Principles

A. *Principles designed to reveal statutory meaning in particular cases*

    1. plain meaning (questionable)
    2. words understood in context of statutory structure
    3. specific provision overcomes general provision
    4. expressio unius (questionable)
    5. statutes construed in context of and harmoniously with other statutes
    6. ejusdem generis

B. *Principles designed to reflect the actual or probable interpretive instructions of Congress*

    1. 1 U.S.C. 1–6
    2. appropriations statutes narrowly construed
    3. statutes construed so as to avoid constitutional invalidity
    4. judicial review of administrative decisions presumed available
    5. statutes interpreted so as to take account of changed circumstances

C. Principles designed to promote institutional goals or to improve lawmaking

1. plain meaning (questionable)
2. appropriations statutes narrowly construed
3. narrow construction of exemptions from taxation or antitrust
4. deference to agency interpretations of law, or to agency decisions where discretion has been conferred
5. statutes construed so as to limit administrative discretion and force decision by Congress or President
6. judicial review of agency decisions presumed available
7. congressional refusal to disrupt longstanding judicial or administrative interpretations of statutes will be taken as acquiescence

D. Principles designed to promote substantive goals

1. federal statutes not lightly taken to preempt state law (questionable when discrimination is at stake)
2. presumption against implied repeals
3. statutes construed so as to harmonize with one another
4. statutes in derogation of common law narrowly construed (obsolete)
5. statutes abrogating sovereign immunity narrowly construed (obsolete)
6. statutes construed in favor of Indian tribes
7. statutes construed not to create implied causes of action (questionable)
8. judicial review of agency inaction presumed unavailable (questionable)
9. rule of lenity in criminal cases
10. laws presumed to apply only within the United States
11. standing presumed unavailable for "regulatory harms" (questionable)
12. remedial statutes should be broadly construed (indefensible except as a corrective to 4 above)
13. presumption against implied rights of action
14. presumption against retroactivity
15. presumption against interference with traditional powers of President and of federal courts

II. Proposed Principles for the Regulatory State

A. Constitutional principles

    1. in favor of federalism
    2. political deliberation; the constitutional antipathy to naked interest-group transfers
    3. avoiding constitutional invalidity and constitutional doubts
    4. political accountability; the nondelegation principle
    5. disadvantaged groups
    6. hearing rights
    7. property and contract rights
    8. welfare rights
    9. rule of law

B. Institutional concerns

    1. appropriations statutes narrowly construed
    2. presumption in favor of judicial review
    3. implied exemptions from taxation disfavored
    4. presumption against implied repeals
    5. question of administrative discretion
    6. cautious approach to legislative history

C. Counteracting statutory failure

    1. *Generic principles:*
    a. in favor of political accountability
    b. against subversion of statute through collective action problems
    c. in favor of coordination and consistency
    d. against obsolescence
    e. narrow construction of procedural qualifications of substantive rights
    f. understand systemic effects of regulatory controls
    g. against irrationality and injustice
    2. *For market-failure statutes and statutes responding to short-term public outcry*
    a. proportionality (to counteract overzealous implementation)
    b. de minimis exceptions (same)

3. *For statutes protecting traditionally disadvantaged groups and noncommodity values:* broad construction (to counteract likely implementation failure)

4. *Narrow construction of statutes embodying interest-group transfers* (to counteract "deals")

III. Priority and Harmonization

A. *Political accountability and political deliberation as meta-principles*

B. *Principles with constitutional foundations (e.g., protect disadvantaged groups, prevent interest-group deals, ensure against procedural unfairness)*

C. *Nonconstitutional principles (with proportionality, systemic effects, and de minimis exceptions at the top)*

Appendix B: Selected Regulations in Terms of Cost Per Life Saved

Agency	Regulation	Net cost per death prevented
FDA	DES ban in cattlefeed	$132 million
OSHA	coke oven emissions	$63 million
EPA	uranium mill tailings	$55 million
OSHA	vinyl chloride	$40 million
OSHA	acrylonitrile	$39 million
EPA	arsenic/copper smelter	$28 million
OSHA	coke oven	$6 to 50 million
EPA	radionuclides/uranium mines	$7 million
OSHA	arsenic	$4.8 to 38 million
OSHA	ethylene oxide	$1.1 to 9 million
EPA	mobile source regulation of 1970 Clean Air Act	$2.7 million
OSHA	hazard communication	$2 million
NHTSA	side doors	$1.4 million
FAA	floor emergency lighting	$735,000
FAA	seat cushion flammability	$630,000
OSHA	servicing wheel rims	$525,000
OSHA	asbestos	$400,000
EPA	trihalomethanes	$315,000
OSHA	underground construction	$315,000
NHTSA	fuel system integrity	$300,000

OSHA	servicing wheel rims	$260,000
FAA	cabin fire protection	$210,000
HHS	sacharine ban	$136,000
NHTSA	steering column protection	$105,000
CPSC	unvented space heaters	$105,000
OSHA	oil and gas well service	$105,000
CPSC	mandatory smoke detectors	$0 to $85,000
EPA	stationary source regulations of 1970 Clean Air Act	$70,000
CPSC	regulation of space heaters	$70,000
NHTSA	55 mph speed limit	$59,000
NHTSA	compulsory seatbelt usage law (not adopted)	$0
NHTSA	roadside hazard removal	$0
CPSC	clothing flammability	$0

The costs are in 1985 dollars. Some of the calculations are of course controversial and depend on uncertain assumptions. When a range is given, it reflects disagreements among different sources or scientific uncertainty about the number of lives saved. When the net cost is $0, it is because the gains in terms of health and related savings exceed the costs. The figures for OSHA are limited to cancers prevented. The sources are John Graham and James Vaupel, "The Value of a Life: What Difference Does It Make?" 1 *Risk Analysis* 89 (1981); John Mendeloff, *The Dilemma of Toxic Substance Regulation* 24–25 (1988); Executive Office of the President, Office of Management and Budget, *Regulatory Program of the U.S. Government* xxi (April 1, 1986–March 1, 1987); Ivy Border and John Morrall, "The Economic Basis for OSHA's and EPA's Generic Carcinogen Regulations," in *What Role for Government?* 242, Richard Zeckhauser and Derek Leebaert, eds. (1983); John Morrall, "A Review of the Record," 10 *Regulation* 25 (November/December 1986).

It is possible that some of these seemingly irrational regulations reflect different, and quite rational, societal assessments of the underlying activity. For example, it would be plausible to say that motorcycle riders ought not to be required to wear helmets even if the costs per life saved were low, because riders engage in that activity freely and with good information about the relevant risks, or because riding without a helmet is part and parcel of the pleasure of riding and therefore something that government ought not to discourage without special justification. Whatever one thinks of any particular example, it is important to understand that it is entirely rational to decide on the appropriate amount of regulation not simply by looking at the cost per life saved, but by looking more fully and contextually at the particular setting of the regulated activity and at social judgments about the benefits and the nature of the relevant risks. Such considerations would probably justify significant disparities in expenditures per life saved. It would, however, be exceptionally difficult to justify the status quo, described above, in these terms.

Appendix C. The Growth of Administrative Government

This appendix contains some data on the rise of administrative regulation from the nation's beginning through the decade of the 1970s; it is designed to supplement Chapter 1. The principal source of both the raw data and the charts is the Directory of Federal Regulatory Agencies (2d edition 1980), compiled by Ronald J. Penoyer for the Center for the Study of American Business, Washington University, St. Louis, Missouri.

Only six major regulatory agencies existed in the federal government before 1900, prominently including the Interstate Commerce Commission (1887) and the Comptroller of the Currency (1863), and excluding the Cabinet-level departments. In the decade between 1900 and 1910, only one regulatory agency, the Antitrust Division in the Department of Justice, was established. The period from 1910 to 1920 saw five more agencies, notably the Federal Trade Commission (1914) and the Federal Power Commission (1920); the decade between 1920 and 1930 saw only two. During the decade of the New Deal, Congress created no fewer than ten new agencies (not including a range of additional entities not qualifying as directly regulatory entities but performing spending, taxing, insurance, and similar functions).

From 1940 to 1960, Congress created only four agencies, three of them between 1950 and 1960. The 1960s saw seven agencies, including the Equal Employment Opportunity Commission (1964), the National Transportation Safety Board (1966), and the Council on Environmental Quality (1969). No fewer than twenty-one agencies were

:reated in the 1970s, by far the most explosive period of regulatory growth in the nation's history. (See Chapter 1, Tables 1 through 4, for some details.)

In the period 1970–1980 the most dramatic changes occurred in the area of social regulation (defined to include consumer safety and health, job safety and working conditions, and environment and energy) rather than economic regulation (defined to include finance and banking, industry-specific regulation, and general business controls). In actual dollars, for example, expenditures on social regulation increased from $539 million in 1970 to $1.5 billion in 1979, an increase of 760%; for economic regulation, the corresponding change was from $327 million in 1970 to $885 million, a total increase of 171%. In terms of staffing, social regulation saw an increase of 555%, from 9,707 employees in 1970 to 63,574 in 1979; economic regulation saw an increase of only 33%, ranging from 17,954 (at that point substantially higher than the corresponding level for social regulation) in 1970 to 23,960 in 1979 (at that point substantially lower than the corresponding figure).

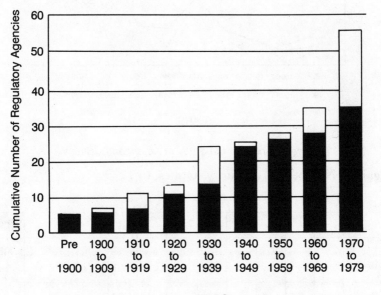

Source: Center for the Study of American Business

Figure 1. Number of regulatory agencies, to 1979

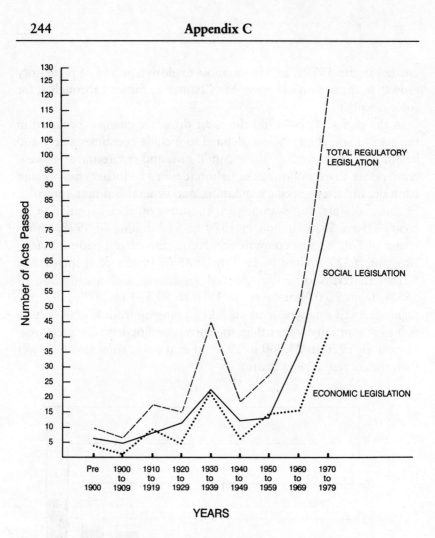

Source: Center for the Study of American Business

Figure 2. Number of regulatory statutes, to 1979

	1970	1971	1972	1973	1974	1975	1976	1977	1978	1979	1980	% Change 1970-79
Expenditures in 1970 dollars (millions of dollars)	$866	$1,163	$1,834	$1,976	$2,231	$2,348	$2,456	$2,627	$2,963	$3,054	$3,062	+374%
Total full-time staff positions	77,661	29,105	54,353	66,960	70,697	84,006	77,319	74,006	86,185	87,534	89,950	+216%

Figure 3. Expenditures and staffing in regulatory agencies, 1970–1980

Notes

Introduction

1. See *Johnson v. Southern Pacific Co.*, 117 F. 462, 466 (8th Cir. 1902); *Shaw v. Railroad Co.*, 101 U.S. 557, 565 (1880); *United States v. Elgin, J. & E. Ry.*, 298 U.S. 492 (1936); *FTC v. Gratz*, 253 U.S. 421, 427–428 (1920); *FTC v. Eastman Kodak Co.*, 274 U.S. 619, 623–625 (1927); *FTC v. American Tobacco Co.*, 264 U.S. 298, 305–306 (1924); the labor cases discussed in Felix Frankfurter and Nathan Greene, *The Labor Injunction* 168–182 (1930). See the critical remarks in Roscoe Pound, "Common Law and Legislation," 21 *Harv. L. Rev.* 383, 384, 387–388, 400–403 (1908); Roscoe Pound, "Courts and Legislation," 7 *Am. Polit. Sci. Rev.* 361, 374–375 (1913). See generally Jefferson B. Fordham and J. Russell Leach, "Interpretation of Statutes in Derogation of the Common Law," 3 *Vand. L. Rev.* 438 (1950), and cases cited therein.

2. See Frank H. Easterbrook, "Statutes' Domains," 50 *U. Chi. L. Rev.* 533, 549–550 (1983); Jeremy A. Rabkin, *Judicial Compulsions: How Public Law Distorts Public Policy* (1989). See also Antonin Scalia, "Vermont Yankee: The APA, the D.C. Circuit, and the Supreme Court," 1978 *Supreme Court Review* 345, 389, where the defense of an aggressive judicial role is said to be weakest in a case involving regulatory beneficiaries.

3. See, e.g., *Wards Cove Packing Co. v. Atonio*, 109 S.Ct. 2115 (1989); *Pennhurst State School and Hospital v. Halderman*, 451 U.S. 1 (1981); *Grove City College v. Bell*, 465 U.S. 555 (1984); *Amoco Production Co. v. Village of Gambell*, 480 U.S. 531 (1987).

4. See Frank H. Easterbrook, "Foreword: The Court and the Economic System," 98 *Harv. L. Rev.* 4, 15 (1984); Richard Posner, *The Federal Courts: Crisis and Reform* 285–290 (1985).

5. See, e.g., Charles Plott, "Axiomatic Social Choice Theory: An Overview and Interpretation," in *Rational Man and Irrational Society?* Brian Barry and Russell Hardin, eds. (1982); Kenneth J. Arrow, *Social Choice and Individual*

Values (1952); James M. Buchanan and Gordon Tullock, *The Calculus of Consent* (1972). The celebrated treatment in Henry M. Hart and Albert M. Sacks, *The Legal Process* (1958), runs into severe difficulties because of its failure to appreciate the complications raised by work of this sort. My ultimate goal, however, is to revive important elements of the approach in Hart and Sacks, rather than to celebrate its demise or to emphasize its occasional naivete about politics and interpretation.

6. This view is currently enjoying a renaissance in the courts. See Chapter 4.

7. See Roberto Unger, *Knowledge and Politics* 88–100 (1975); see also Duncan Kennedy, "Freedom and Constraint in Adjudication: A Critical Phenomenology," 36 *J. Legal Educ.* 518 (1985).

8. See Stanley Fish, *Doing What Comes Naturally* (1989).

9. See Karl N. Llewellyn, "Remarks on the Theory of Appellate Decision and the Rules or Canons About How Statutes Are to Be Construed," 3 *Vand. L. Rev.* 395 (1950); Ronald Dworkin, *Law's Empire* (1986).

1. Why Regulation?

1. In recent writings, liberalism and republicanism have been said to conflict; see e.g. Joyce Appleby, *Capitalism and a New Social Order* (1984); but the conflict between liberalism and republicanism is a false one in the American constitutional tradition. The perception of a conflict disserves both traditions—converting liberalism into a commitment to politics as civil war, to possessive individualism, or to the sacred character of existing property rights; and converting republicanism into a nightmarish, totalist vision that rejects rights altogether. On the alliance between American liberalism and American republicanism, see Cass R. Sunstein, "Beyond the Republican Revival," 97 *Yale L. J.* 1539 (1988).

2. See Joseph M. Bessette,"Deliberative Democracy: The Majority Principle," in *How Democratic Is the Constitution?* Robert A. Goldwin and William A. Schambra, eds. (1983). The role of republican thought in the constitutional design is disputed. For other views, see, e.g., Robert Dahl, *A Preface to Democratic Theory* (1956); Bruce A. Ackerman, "The Storrs Lectures: Discovering the Constitution," 93 *Yale L. J.* 1013 (1984); Martin Diamond, "Ethics and Politics: The American Way," in *The Moral Foundations of the American Republic* 75, Robert H. Horwitz, ed. (2nd ed. 1979); J. G. A. Pocock, *The Machiavellian Moment* (1975); Joyce Appleby, "Republicanism in Old and New Contexts," 43 *Wm. & Mary Q.* 20 (1986); James Kloppenberg, "The Virtues of Liberalism: Christianity, Republicanism, and Ethics in Early American Political Discourse," 74 *J. Am. Hist.* 9 (1987); John P. Diggins, *The Lost Soul of American Politics: Virtue, Self-Interest, and the Foundations of Liberalism* (1986).

3. See generally Bruce Ackerman, *Discovering the Constitution* (forthcoming).

4. See generally Frank P. Bourgin, *The Great Challenge: The Myth of Laissez-Faire in the Early Republic* (1989).

5. See *The Federalist* No. 10.

6. Ibid. See also James Madison, "Property and Suffrage: Second Thoughts on the Constitutional Convention," in *The Mind of the Founder: Sources of the Political Thought of James Madison* 501, Marvin Meyers, ed. (rev. ed. 1981).

7. See *The Federalist* No. 51, the classic locus of this argument.

8. Consider in this connection Madison's view that "in our Governments the real power lies in a majority of the Community, and the invasion of private rights is chiefly to be apprehended, not from acts of Government contrary to the sense of its constituents, but from acts in which the Government is the mere instrument of the major number of its constituents." Madison to Jefferson, Oct. 17, 1788, in 11 James Madison, *Papers of James Madison* 298, Robert A. Rutland and Charles Hobson, eds. (1977).

9. See ibid. and note 7.

10. Ideas of these sorts were exploited by the New Deal reformers. Seeing government in the conventional protection of life, liberty, and property, they argued that government was already implicated in the distribution of wealth and entitlements, that governmental protection was a constitutional guarantee, and that there was nothing illegitimate about a governmental role in protecting economic security. See below; see also Stephen Holmes, "Liberal Guilt: Some Theoretical Origins of the Welfare State," in *Responsibility, Rights, and Welfare,* J. Donald Moon, ed. (1988).

The framers also placed a high premium on political equality, and Madison and Jefferson both expressed a desire for the government to eliminate wide disparities in wealth. Thus Madison listed among the means of combating the "evil of parties": "1. By establishing a political equality among all. 2. By withholding *unnecessary* opportunities from a few, to increase the inequality of property, by an immoderate, and especially an unmerited, accumulation of riches. 3. By the silent operation of laws, which, without violating the rights of property, reduce extreme wealth towards a state of mediocrity, and raise extreme indigence toward a state of comfort." 14 *Papers of James Madison* 197, Robert A. Rutland, ed. (1983; emphasis in original).

Thus Jefferson wrote: "I am conscious that an equal division of property is impracticable. But the consequences of this enormous inequality producing so much misery to the bulk of mankind, legislators cannot invent too many devices for subdividing property, only taking care to let their subdivisions go hand in hand with the natural affections of the human mind . . . Another means of silently lessening the inequality of property is to exempt all from taxation below a certain point, and to tax the higher portions of property in geometrical progression as they rise. Whenever there is in any country, uncultivated lands and unemployed poor, it is clear that the laws of property have been so far extended as to violate natural right. The earth is given as a common stock for man to labor and live on." 8 *Papers of Thomas Jefferson* 682, Julian P. Boyd, ed. (1953).

11. See William E. Nelson, "The Impact of the Antislavery Movement upon Styles of Judicial Reasoning in Nineteenth-Century America," 87 *Harv. L. Rev.* 513 (1974). On statelessness and the early period, see Stephen Skowronek,

Building a New American State: The Expansion of National Administrative Ca-pacities, 1877–1920 (1982). On the traditional role of the national government, see Theodore Lowi, *The Personal President* (1985).

12. See Lowi, *The Personal President;* on the pre-New Deal developments, see Skowronek, *Building a New American State.*

13. See *Lochner v. New York,* 198 U.S. 45 (1905); Sunstein, "Lochner's Legacy," 87 *Colum. L. Rev.* 783 (1987).

14. *Lochner v. New York,* 198 U.S. 45 (1905); *Adkins v. Children's Hospital,* 261 U.S. 525 (1923).

15. Franklin D. Roosevelt, "Message to Congress, June 8, 1934," (H.R. Doc. 397, 73d Cong; 2d Sess.), reprinted in *Statutory History of the United States: Income Security* 61, Robert B. Stevens, ed. (1970).

16. Franklin D. Roosevelt, "Speech Accepting the Nomination for the Presidency" (July 2, 1932), in 1 *The Public Papers and Addresses of Franklin D. Roosevelt* 657 (1938).

17. This was a prominent theme in the legal realist movement. See Robert L. Hale, "Coercion and Distribution in a Supposedly Non-Coercive State," 38 *Pol. Sci. Q.* 470 (1923).

18. See *West Coast Hotel v. Parrish,* 300 U.S. 379 (1937); *Miller v. Schoene,* 276 U.S. 272, 279 (1928); *Erie R.R. Co. v. Tompkins,* 304 U.S. 64 (1938); *Shelley v. Kraemer,* 334 U.S. 1 (1948).

19. See *West Coast Hotel v. Parrish,* 300 U.S. 379, 399 (1937).

20. Franklin D. Roosevelt, "Message to the Congress on the State of the Union" (Jan. 11, 1944), in 13 *The Public Papers and Addresses of Franklin D. Roosevelt* 41 (1969).

Consider also Pound, "Common Law and Legislation," at 404 (referring to judges as influenced by "the prejudices which the individualism of common law institutional writers, the dogmas learned in a college course in economics, and habitual association with the business and professional class, must inevitably produce").

21. See James M. Landis, *The Administrative Process* (1938); Pound, "Common Law and Legislation," at 403: "The political occasions for judicial interference with legislation have come to an end. In the sixteenth and seventeenth centuries the judiciary stood between the public and the crown. It protected the individual from the state when he required that protection. Today, when it assumes to stand between the legislature and the public and thus again to protect the individual from the state, it really stands between the public and what the public needs and desires, and protects individuals who need no protection against society which does need it. Hence the side of the courts is no longer the popular side."

22. Roscoe Pound, "Spurious Interpretation," 7 *Colum. L. Rev.* 379, 384 (1907).

23. See, e.g., *Home Building & Loan Assn. v. Blaisdell,* 290 U.S. 398 (1934); *Wickard v. Filburn,* 317 U.S. 111 (1942); *NLRB v. Jones & Laughlin Steel Corp.,* 301 U.S. 1 (1937); *United States v. Carolene Products Co.,* 304 U.S. 144 (1938).

24. See David Vogel, "The 'New' Social Regulation in Historical and Com-

parative Perspective," in *Regulation in Perspective* 155, Thomas K. McCraw, ed. (1981).

25. "Annual Message to the Congress on the State of the Union" (January 22, 1970), reprinted in *Public Papers of the President: Richard M. Nixon* 8, 13 (1970). The need for an active federal role in protecting the environment is among the most striking themes of the Nixon presidency; it recurs throughout his statements between 1969 and 1972. See also President Nixon's subsequent suggestion that "clean air and clean water, the wise use of our land, the protection of wildlife and natural beauty, parks for all to enjoy" are "part of the birthright of every American. To guarantee that birthright, we must act, and act decisively. It is literally now or never." Richard M. Nixon, "Statement on Transmitting a Special Message to Congress Outlining the 1972 Environmental Program" (Feb. 8, 1972), in *Public Papers of the President: Richard M. Nixon* (1972).

26. See, e.g., *Motor Vehicle Mfrs. Ass'n v. State Farm Mutual Ins. Co.,* 463 U.S. 29 (1983); *Natural Resources Defense Council, Inc. v. Train,* 510 F.2d 692 (D.C. Cir. 1975); *Adams v. Richardson,* 480 F.2d 1159 (D.C. Cir. 1973); *National Congress of Hispanic Am. Citizens v. Marshall,* 626 F.2d 882 (D.C. Cir. 1979).

27. Executive Order 12,291, 3 C.F.R. 127 (1981); Executive Order 12,298, 3 C.F.R. 323 (1985).

28. See, most notably, *Chevron USA, Inc. v. Natural Resources Defense Council, Inc.,* 467 U.S. 837 (1984); *Heckler v. Chaney,* 470 U.S. 821 (1985).

29. John Rawls, *A Theory of Justice* (1971). See also Brian N. Barry, *Theories of Justice* (1989); Jürgen Habermas, *The Philosophical Discourse of Modernity* (1987); Bruce A. Ackerman, *Social Justice in the Liberal State* (1987).

30. See Rawls at 134–135, n. 10: "What is lacking is a suitable definition of a status quo that is acceptable from a moral point of view. We cannot take various contingencies as known and individual preferences as given and expect to elucidate the concept of justice (or fairness) by theories of bargaining. The conception of the original position is designed to meet the problem of the appropriate status quo."

31. I do not discuss here an evaluation of government action from another starting-point, such as an ethic of care, see Carol Gilligan, *In a Different Voice* (1982); a belief in virtue, see Alasdair C. MacIntyre, *After Virtue* (1984); or a form of Aristotelian practical reason, see Martha Nussbaum, *The Fragility of Goodness* (1986). It would not be surprising, however, if people using such different starting points reached conclusions broadly in accord with those suggested here.

32. See John Stuart Mill, *Utilitarianism* (1863); John Dewey, *The Quest for Certainty* 259, 265, 272–273 (1929) (claiming that there is a need for critical reflection on the "conditions under which objects are enjoyed" and on the "consequences of esteeming and liking them," and arguing that *"judgments about values are judgments about that which should regulate the formation of our desires, affections and enjoyments"*; emphasis in original); see also Robin L. West, "Liberalism Rediscovered: A Pragmatic Definition of the Liberal Vision," 46 *U. Pitt. L. Rev.* 673 (1985). Thus understood, this form of utilitarianism merges

into certain forms of Aristotelian thought; the two are concerned with "welfare" in analogous senses. See Martha Nussbaum, "Perceptive Equilibrium: Literary Theory and Ethical Theory," 8 *Logos* 55 (1987).

33. See H. Geoffrey Brennan and James M. Buchanan, *The Reason of Rules* 136–137 (1985); and James M. Buchanan, *Liberty, Market, and State* 179–180 (1986). Some of Buchanan's work is ambiguous on this point, suggesting that unanimous consent must be obtained only at some ideal early stage, for the basic ground-rules (or Constitution) after which private action will occur. At this point his approach takes on Rawlsian dimensions, attempting to provide a just status quo from which market ordering might take place. See, e.g., "Rules for A Fair Game: Contractarian Notes on Distributive Justice," in *Liberty, Market, and State* at 123. If taken more seriously, and used more pervasively, this aspect of Buchanan's work would lead him in quite different directions.

34. See James M. Buchanan, *Freedom in Constitutional Contract* 83 (1977).

35. See Russell Hardin, *Morality Within the Limits of Reason* (1988).

36. See the Introduction above.

37. The qualification is necessary because some cognitive or motivational distortion may justify disruption of voluntary transactions even when both parties think that they will be made better off. See Chapter 2.

38. The effects of endowments on both wealth and preferences suggest that the influential Coase theorem, see Ronald Coase, "The Problem of Social Cost," 3 *J. L. & Econ.* 1 (1960), will in some cases be erroneous. The opposite phenomenon may also occur; the "grass is greener" mechanism may make people value something precisely because it has not been allocated to them.

39. See Jon Elster, *Sour Grapes: Studies in the Subversion of Rationality* (1983). See also Martha Nussbaum, "Shame, Separateness, and Political Unity: Aristotle's Criticism of Plato," in *Essays on Aristotle's Ethics* 395, A. Rorty, ed. (1988).

40. On deliberation, cognition, and democracy, see S. L. Hurley, *Natural Reasons: Personality and Polity* 314–360 (1989). On first- and second-order preferences, see Amartya K. Sen, "Rational Fools: A Critique of the Behavioral Foundations of Economic Theory," 6 *Phil. & Pub. Aff.* 317 (1977); Thomas Schelling, "Enforcing Rules on Oneself," 1 *J. L. Econ. & Org.* 357 (1985); Harry Frankfurt, "Freedom of the Will and the Concept of a Preference," 68 *J. Phil.* 5 (1971).

Collective judgments may likewise be myopic, overriding individual choices that are considered. The framers' emphasis on political deliberation was in large part a product of fear of public passions emphasizing the short term at the expense of the long term. In a case of this sort, of course, the argument for protection of the collective decision is much weaker.

41. See the description in Chapter 2.

42. See the highly illuminating treatment in Edna Ullmann-Margalit, *The Emergence of Norms* (1977), which, however, is marred by the claim that one could give a causal explanation of norms by reference to the social functions they serve; for a valuable catalogue and discussion of social norms that is critical of functionalist reasoning, see Jon Elster, *The Cement of Society* (1989).

43. See Robin L. West, "Liberalism Rediscovered," 46 *U. Pitt. L. Rev.* 673 (1985).

2. The Functions of Regulatory Statutes

1. See Gary S. Becker, "Public Policies, Pressure Groups, and Dead Weight Costs," 28 *J. Pub. Econ.* 329 (1985); and Gary S. Becker, "A Theory of Competition Among Pressure Groups for Political Influence," 98 *Q. J. Econ.* 371 (1983). On the extent to which statutes are public-regarding, compare Arthur Maass, *Congress and the Common Good* (1983), Steven Kelman, *Making Public Policy* (1987), and Martha Derthick and Paul J. Quirk, *The Politics of Deregulation* (1985), with Sam Peltzman, "Toward a More General Theory of Regulation," 19 *J. L. & Econ.* 211 (1976) and George J. Stigler, "The Theory of Economic Regulation," 2 *Bell J. Econ. & Mgmt. Sci.* 3 (1971).

2. The problem with such arguments is that the notion of rent-seeking, if used normatively, is hopelessly unattractive in this context. See below.

3. See Stephen Breyer, *Regulation and Its Reform* (1981), for more detailed discussion.

4. See Russell Hardin, *Collective Action* (1982), for a general discussion; see also David P. Gauthier, *Morals by Agreement* (1986).

5. On the controversial character of the description of pollutees as victims, see the discussion of Coase, immediately below.

6. For lucid treatments, see Jon Elster, *The Cement of Society* (1989); *Rational Choice,* Jon Elster, ed. (1986); Edna Ullmann-Margalit, *The Emergence of Social Norms* (1977).

7. See the discussion of hockey helmets in Thomas C. Schelling, *Micromotives and Macrobehavior* 213–214, 223–224 (1978).

8. See the discussion in Ullmann-Margalit, *The Emergence of Social Norms.*

9. Thomas Nagel, "Moral Conflict and Political Legitimacy," 16 *Phil. & Pub. Affairs* 215, 224 (1987); see also Hardin, "Political Obligation," in *The Good Polity: Normative Analysis of the State* 103, 106–107, Alan Hamlin and Philip Pettit, eds. (1989).

10. See Peter Asch, *Consumer Safety Regulation* (1988), on which I draw here.

11. See George A. Akerlof, "The Market for 'Lemons': Quality Uncertainty and the Market Mechanism," 84 *Q. J. Econ.* 488 (1970).

12. See Daniel Kahneman, Paul Slovic, and Amos Tversky, eds., *Judgment Under Uncertainty* (1982).

13. See Amos Tversky and Daniel Kahneman, "Judgment Under Uncertainty: Heuristics and Biases," 185 *Science* 1124 (1974); see generally *Judgment and Decision Making: An Interdisciplinary Reader,* Hal R. Arkes and Kenneth R. Hammond, eds. (1986).

14. See Elliot Aronson, *The Social Animal* (5th ed. 1988).

15. This lesson emerges from Ronald H. Coase, "The Problem of Social Cost," 3 *J. L. and Econ.* 1 (1960).

16. See the discussion in Russell Hardin, *Morality within the Limits of Reason* 92–93 (1988); see also John Stuart Mill, *Principles of Political Economy* 958, J. M. Robson, ed. (1965).

17. See Finis Welch, *Minimum Wages: Issues and Evidence* (1978).

18. See Steven Shavell, "A Note on Efficiency vs. Distributional Equity in Le-

gal Rulemaking: Should Distributional Equity Matter Given Optimal Income Taxation?" 71 *Am. Econ. Rev.* 414 (1981).

19. Cf. Bernard Manin, "On Legitimacy and Political Deliberation," 15 *Pol. Theory* 338 (1987); Jon Elster, *Sour Grapes* (1983).

20. See Howard Margolis, *Selfishness, Altruism, and Rationality* (1982).

21. See Richard B. Stewart, "Regulation in a Liberal State: The Role of Non-Commodity Values," 92 *Yale L. J.* 1537 (1983).

22. See Robert M. Entman, *Democracy Without Citizens* (1989).

23. Consider in this regard John Rawls, *A Theory of Justice* 102 (1971): "[We] may reject the contention that the ordering of institutions is always defective because the distribution of natural talents and the contingencies of social circumstances are unjust, and this injustice must inevitably carry over to human arrangements. Occasionally this reflection is offered as an excuse for ignoring injustice, as if the refusal to acquiesce in injustice is on a par with being unable to accept death. The natural distribution is neither just nor unjust; nor is it unjust that persons are born into society at some particular position. These are simply natural facts. What is just and unjust is the way that institutions deal with these facts. Aristocratic and caste societies are unjust because they make these contingencies the ascriptive basis for belonging to more or less enclosed and privileged social classes. The basic structure of these societies incorporates the arbitrariness found in nature. But there is no necessity for men to resign themselves to these contingencies. The social system is not an unchangeable order beyond human control but a pattern of human action."

24. See Gary Becker, *The Economics of Discrimination* (2d ed. 1971); Finis Welch, "Labor-Market Discrimination: An Interpretation of Income Differences in the Rural South," 75 *J. Pol. Econ.* 584 (1967). Both of these approaches see discrimination as persisting, in spite of economic incentives, because of employers' taste for discrimination. See also Jennifer Roback, "Southern Labor Law in the Jim Crow Era: Exploitative or Competitive?" in *Labor Law and the Employment Market: Foundations and Applications* 217, Richard A. Epstein and Jeffrey Paul, eds. (1985).

25. See "The Economics of Caste and of the Rat Race and Other Woeful Tales," in George A. Akerlof, *An Economic Theorist's Book of Tales* 23 (1984). This may account for the striking findings in James J. Heckman and Brook Paynor, "The Impact of Federal Antidiscrimination Policy on the Economic Status of Blacks: A Study of South Carolina," 79 *Am. Econ. Rev.* 138 (1989) (showing no change in black employment in southern textile industries until Title VII). For discussion of the relationship between markets and discrimination, see also Kenneth Arrow, "The Theory of Discrimination," in *Discrimination in Labor Markets* 3–33, Orley Ashenfelter and Albert Rees, eds. (1973); Kenneth Arrow, "Models of Job Discrimination," in *Racial Discrimination in Economic Life,* A. H. Pascal, ed. (1972); Shelly Lundberg and Richard Startz, "Private Discrimination and Social Intervention in Competitive Labor Markets," 73 *Am. Econ. Rev.* 340 (1983); George Akerlof, "Discriminatory, Status-Based Wages among Tradition-Oriented, Stochastically Trading Coconut Producers," 93 *J. Polit. Econ.* 265 (1985); John J. Donohue, "Prohibiting Sex Discrimination in the Workplace: An Economic Perspective," 56 *U. Chi. L. Rev.* 1337 (1989); Paul

Milgrom and Sharon Oster, "Job Discrimination, Market Forces, and the Invisibility Hypothesis," 102 *Q. J. Econ.* 453 (1987).

26. See David A. Strauss, "The Myth of Colorblindness," 1986 *Supreme Court Review* 99.

27. See below.

28. See below. For some vivid examples, see Leon Litwack, *Been in the Storm So Long* (1977), which discusses the complex adaptive mechanisms of slaveowners and slaves to emancipation; see also Jane J. Mansbridge, *Why We Lost the ERA* 107 (1986).

29. See Catharine A. MacKinnon, *Toward a Feminist Theory of the State* (1989).

30. See Menahem Yaari, "Endogenous Changes in Tastes: A Philosophical Discussion," in *Decision Theory and Social Ethics* 59, Hans W. Gottinger and Werner Leinfellner, eds. (1978).

31. T. C. Schelling, "Egonomics, or the Art of Self-Management," 68 *Am. Econ. Rev.* 290 (Papers and Proceedings) (1978); Jon Elster, "Weakness of Will and the Free-Rider Problem," 1 *Econ. & Phil.* 231 (1985).

32. See Elster, "Weakness of Will and the Free-Rider Problem."

33. See George A. Akerlof and William T. Dickens, "The Economic Consequences of Cognitive Dissonance," 72 *Am. Econ. Rev.* 307 (1982); Aronson, *The Social Animal* 162–164; see also Chapter 1, note 39. But see W. Kip Viscusi, *Risk by Choice* (1983).

Note in this regard that in the aftermath of the Three Mile Island nuclear power plant accident in 1979, those who lived nearest the plant most believed the assurances of the Nuclear Regulatory Commission—a phenomenon consistent with cognitive dissonance theory, but hard to explain on other grounds. See Aronson, *The Social Animal* 176–178. On cognitive dissonance, see Leon Festinger, *A Theory of Cognitive Dissonance* (1957); on its implications for political theory, with particular reference to utilitarianism, see generally Jon Elster, *Sour Grapes* (1983).

34. "One of the most striking findings that has been carefully documented recently is the extent to which people will alter their self-esteem in order to believe they deserve their fate, even when, by any objective assessment, that fate has been inflicted on them by external forces beyond their control. Other investigators have documented the way people afflicted with an 'objectively' terrible fate . . . typically remove the experience of injustice associated with their fate by discovering fully compensating rewards, usually spiritual in nature, associated with the injury." Melvin J. Lerner, "The Justice Motive in Human Relations," in *The Justice Motive in Social Behavior* 11, 21, Melvin J. Lerner and Sally C. Lerner, eds. (1981). See also the discussion of the complex reactions of newly freed slaves in Litwack, *Been in the Storm So Long*.

See Elaine McCrate, "Gender Difference: The Role of Endogenous Preferences and Collective Action," 78 *Am. Econ. Rev.* 235 (Papers and Proceedings) (1988); see generally *The Justice Motive in Social Behavior*, Lerner and Lerner, eds. (exploring implications for belief formation of a general belief in the justice of the world); Adrian Furnham and Barrie Gunter, "Just World Beliefs and Attitudes Towards the Poor," 23 *British J. Soc. Psych.* 265 (1984) (exploring negative attitudes toward the poor among people who believe that the world is just).

35. See Melvin J. Lerner, *The Belief in a Just World: A Fundamental Delusion* (1980); Melvin J. Lerner and James R. Meindl, "Justice and Altruism," in *Altruism and Helping Behavior* 213, J. Philippe Rushton and Richard M. Sorrentino, eds. (1981).

36. See S. Rubin and A. Pepau, "Belief in a Just World and Reaction to Another's Lot: A Study of Participants in the National Draft Lottery," 29 *J. of Soc. Issues* 73 (1973); see also the discussion in Jon Elster, *Solomonic Judgments* 53–60 (1989). On reactions by victims generally, see Lerner, *The Belief in a Just World*.

37. See Ronnie Janoff-Bulman, Christine Timko, and Linda L. Carli, "Cognitive Biases in Blaming the Victim," 21 *J. Exper. Soc. Psych.* 161 (1985).

38. See Jonathan L. Freedman, "Long-Term Behavioral Effects of Cognitive Dissonance," 1 *J. Exper. Soc. Psych.* 145 (1965); Keith E. Davis and Edward E. Jones, "Changes in Interpersonal Perception as a Means of Reducing Cognitive Dissonance," 61 *Abnormal and Soc. Psych.* 402 (1960); Aronson, *The Social Animal* 156–162. Aronson discusses rumors that spread after the slaying of students at Kent State University by members of the Ohio National Guard, to the effect that their bodies were crawling with lice and that they were so ridden with syphilis that they would have died within several weeks in any case. A local high school teacher said that "anyone who appears on the streets of a city like Kent with long hair, dirty clothes or barefooted deserves to be shot" (p. 157). Aronson deals with the implications of this phenomenon for the question of racism, pp. 161–162. See also Litwack, *Been in the Storm So Long*.

39. See Paul Gewirtz, "Choice in the Transition," 86 *Colum. L. Rev.* 728 (1986).

40. See generally E. J. Mishan, "The Economics of Disamenity," 14 *Nat. Resources J.* 55 (1974); cf. Derek Parfit, *Reasons and Persons* (1984). On the issues discussed in this section, see generally Peter Wenz, *Environmental Justice* (1988); Holmes Rolston, *Environmental Ethics: Duties to and Values in the Natural World* (1988); Tom Regan, *The Case for Animal Rights* (1983); Peter Singer, *Animal Liberation* (1975), Ernest Partridge, ed., *Responsibilities to Future Generations* (1981); Bryan Norton, *Why Preserve Natural Variety?* (1988).

41. See Geoffrey P. Miller, "Interstate Banking in the Court," 1985 *Supreme Court Review* 179 (identifying interest-group forces behind prohibition of interstate banking); Jonathan R. Macey, "Special Interest Group Legislation and the Judicial Function: The Dilemma of Glass-Steagall," 33 *Emory L. J.* 1 (1983).

42. See Keith Schneider, "Cost of Farm Law Might Be Double Original Estimate," *New York Times*, July 22, 1986, p. 1 (fiscal year 1986 cost of new farm legislation to reach $35 billion). See also Reuben A. Kessel, "Economic Effects of Federal Regulation of Milk Markets," 10 *J. L. & Econ.* 51 (1967); Richard A. Ippolito and Robert T. Masson, "The Social Cost of Government Regulation of Milk," 21 *J. L. & Econ.* 33 (1978); see also Geoffrey P. Miller, "The True Story of Carolene Products," 1987 *Supreme Court Review* 397.

43. See generally *Chicago Studies in Political Economy*, George J. Stigler, ed. (1988); Richard A. Epstein, *Takings* (1985).

44. See John Stuart Mill, *Considerations on Representative Government* (1867).

45. Cf. Dworkin, *Law's Empire* (discussing interpretive character of law).

3. How Regulation Fails

1. See, e.g., Office of Management and Budget, *Regulatory Program of the U.S. Government* (1986); *Chicago Studies in Political Economy,* George J. Stigler, ed. (1988).

2. See the analysis in Sam Peltzman, "The Effects of Automobile Safety Regulation," 83 *J. Polit. Econ.* 677 (1975). The magnitude of this effect has, however, been shown to be much less great than Peltzman suggested. Thus the benefits of seatbelt requirements are far greater than the costs. See Robert W. Crandall, *Controlling Industrial Pollution: The Economics and Politics of Clean Air* (1983); *Auto Safety Regulation,* Henry G. Manne and Roger LeRoy Miller, eds. (1976).

3. See Center for Policy Alternatives at M.I.T., *Benefits of Environmental, Health, and Safety Regulation,* prepared for the Committee on Governmental Affairs, United States Senate (1980).

For other discussion of the social benefits from social and economic regulation, see, e.g., Aaron Wildavsky, *Searching for Safety* (1988); John M. Mendeloff, *The Dilemma of Toxic Substance Regulation* 22 (1988) (suggesting that asbestos regulation saves 396 lives per year from cancer and that coke oven emissions regulation saves between 8 and 36 lives per year); Crandall, *Controlling Industrial Pollution;* John D. Graham and James W. Vaupel, "The Value of a Life: What Difference Does It Make?" 1 *Risk Analysis* 89 (1981) (outlining lives saved at relatively low expense as a result of CPSC mandatory smoke detectors, EPA regulation of stationary source pollution); Robert Crandall et al., *Regulating the Automobile* (1986) (suggesting significant safety benefits as a result of automobile safety regulation); Center for Policy Alternatives at M.I.T., *Benefits of Regulation* (describing reduced injuries by 28% to belted drivers and 11% to unbelted drivers as a result of 55 mph speed limit; injury reductions of 44% and mortality reductions of 33% as a result of crib safety standard). Robert Crandall, "Learning the Lessons," 11 *The Wilson Quarterly* 69–80 (1987).

4. See Thomas Crocker et al., *Methods Development for Assessing Air Pollution Control Benefits,* vol. 1: *Experiments in the Economics of Air Pollution Epidemiology* 71 (1979).

5. See Council of Environmental Quality, *Environmental Quality: The 17th Annual Report* C-72—C-79 (1988).

6. See The Conservation Foundation, *State of the Environment: A View Toward the Nineties* (1987); Council on Environmental Quality, *Environmental Quality: The 18th and 19th Annual Report* (1989).

7. See Barry Commoner, "Failure of the Environmental Effect," 6 *Env. L. Rep.* 10195 (1988); Council on Environmental Quality, *The 17th Annual Report* C-104—C-112.

8. For the details, see The Conservation Foundation, *State of the Environment.*

9. See Crandall, *Regulating the Automobile* 155 (1986); Joan Claybrook and David Bollier, "The Hidden Benefits of Regulation: Disclosing the Auto Safety Payoff," 3 *Yale J. Reg.* 87 (1985).

10. Crandall, *Regulating the Automobile* 78.

11. Center for Policy Alternatives at M.I.T., *Benefits of Regulation* 39.

12. Ibid. For questions about these results, and on the poor general record of the CPSC, see W. Kip Viscusi, *Regulating Consumer Product Safety* (1984).

13. See John Mendeloff, *The Dilemma of Toxic Substance Regulation* 22 (1988).

14. See John Mendeloff, *Regulating Safety* (1979). But see W. Kip Viscusi, *Risk by Choice* (1983).

15. See *The Question of Discrimination,* Steven Shulman and William Darity, eds. (1989), especially the essays by John Bound and Richard Freeman, James Heckman, and Finis Welch; Charles Brown, "Black-White Earnings Ratios Since the Civil Rights Act of 1964: The Importance of Labor Market Dropouts," 99 *Q. J. Econ.* 31 (1984); James J. Heckman and Brook S. Paynor, "Determining the Impact of Federal Antidiscrimination Policy on the Economic Status of Blacks: A Study of South Carolina," 79 *Am. Econ. Rev.* 138 (1989); National Research Council, *A Common Destiny: Blacks and American Society* 315–319 (1989); and Jonathan Leonard, *The Effectiveness of Equal Employment Law, Report to the Subcommittee on Employment Opportunity,* U.S. Congress (1989). But see James Smith and Finis Welch, *Closing the Gap* (1986).

16. See Richard B. Freeman, "The Changing Labor Market for Black Americans," *Brookings Papers on Economic Activity* (1973); Stanley H. Masters, *Black-White Income Differentials* (1975); Daniel Vronman, "Changes in Black Workers' Relative Earnings: Evidence for the 1960s," in *Patterns of Racial Discrimination,* chap. 11, George M. Von Furstenberg, ed. (1974).

17. Orley Ashenfelter and James Heckman, "Measuring the Effect of an Antidiscrimination Program," in *Evaluating the Labor Market Effects of Social Programs,* Orley Ashenfelter and James Blum, ed. (1976).

18. See Stephen Burman, "The Economics of Discrimination: The Effects of Public Policy," Ph.D. Thesis, University of Chicago, 1973; James J. Heckman and Kenneth I. Wolpin, "Does the Contract Compliance Program Work? An Analysis of Chicago Data," 29 *Indust. & Labor Relations Rev.* 544 (1976).

19. See Richard B. Freeman, "Black Economic Progress After 1964: Who Has Gained and Why?" in *Studies in Labor Markets,* Sherwin Rosen, ed. (1981); see also sources in note 15.

20. Ibid. 282.

21. See Heckman and Paynor, "Impact of Federal Antidiscrimination Policy," 143.

22. See National Research Council, *A Common Destiny: Blacks and American Society* 316–317 and citations therein.

23. On sex discrimination, see Morley Gunderson, "Male-Female Wage Differentials and Policy Responses," 27 *J. Econ. Lit.* 46 (1989); James J. Koch and John F. Chizmar, Jr., "Sex Discrimination and Affirmative Action in Faculty Salaries," 14 *Econ. Inquiry* 16 (1976); Andrea H. Beller, "Occupational Segregation by Sex: Determinants and Changes," 17 *J. Human Res.* 371, 388–390 (1982);

Jonathan S. Leonard, "The Impact of Affirmative Action on Employment," 2 *J. Labor Econ.* 439 (1984).

24. See Graham and Vaupel, "Value of a Life: What Difference Does It Make?"

25. See the discussion in Thomas H. Tietenberg, *Emissions Trading: An Exercise in Reforming Pollution Policy* (1985); Bruce A. Ackerman and Richard B. Stewart, "Reforming Environmental Law," 37 *Stan. L. Rev.* 1333, 1337–1339 (1985).

26. For this statement and in the following paragraph I draw on Crandall, *Regulating the Automobile* 43, 113–15, 139.

27. See Martha Derthick and Paul J. Quirk, *The Politics of Deregulation* (1985); Stephen Breyer, *Regulation and Its Reform* (1981).

28. See the discussion in Viscusi, *Regulating Consumer Product Safety;* Congressional Quarterly, Inc., *Consumer Protection: Gains and Setbacks* (1978).

29. See generally Henry G. Grabowski and John M. Vernon, *The Regulation of Pharmaceuticals* (1983).

30. See Mendeloff, *Toxic Substance Regulation* 22.

31. See Viscusi, *Risk by Choice.*

32. See ibid. 73–104.

33. See, e.g., John Mendeloff, "Regulatory Reform and OSHA Policy," 5 *J. Policy Analysis & Management* 440 (1986); Crandall, *Controlling Industrial Pollution;* Viscusi, *Risk by Choice;* Crandall, *Regulating the Automobile; Chicago Studies in Political Economy.*

34. See Bruce A. Ackerman and William T. Hassler, *Clean Coal/Dirty Air* (1981); see also Peter Pashigian, "Environmental Regulation: Whose Self-Interests Are Being Served," in *Chicago Studies in Political Economy.*

35. See Crandall, *Controlling Industrial Pollution* 110–130.

36. See Crandall, *Regulating the Automobile.*

37. I draw here on the discussion in Bruce A. Ackerman and Richard B. Stewart, "Reforming Environmental Law: The Democratic Case for Market Incentives," 13 *Colum. J. Env. L.* 171 (1988).

38. See Richard Liroff, *Reforming Air Pollution Regulation* (1986); Thomas Tietenberg, *Emissions Trading* (1985).

39. See note 38.

40. See Stephen Breyer, *Regulation and Its Reform* (1980).

41. See Mendeloff, *Toxic Substance Regulation.*

42. Edward D. Berkowitz, *Disabled Policy: America's Programs for the Handicapped* 1 (1987). See also Robert A. Katzmann, *Institutional Disability* (1986).

43. See generally Peter Huber, "Electricity and the Environment: In Search of Regulatory Authority," 100 *Harv. L. Rev.* 1002 (1987).

44. See John D. Graham, Laura C. Green, and Marc J. Roberts, *In Search of Safety: Chemicals and Cancer Risk* (1988); Robert E. Litan and William D. Nordhaus, *Reforming Federal Regulation* (1983); Office of Technology Assessment Task Force, *Identifying and Regulating Carcinogens* 199 (1988). See also Executive Office of the President, Office of Management and Budget, *Regulatory Program of the U.S. Government* xxi (April 1, 1986–March 31, 1987).

45. See Graham and Vaupel, "The Value of a Life" (listing expenditures per life saved among thirty-seven agencies).

46. See Ernest Gellhorn, "Regulatory Reform and the Federal Trade Commission's Antitrust Jurisdiction," 49 *Tenn. L. Rev.* 471 (1982).

47. See Donald C. Langevoort, "Study in Statutory Obsolescence and the Judicial Process," 85 *Mich. L. Rev.* 56 (1987).

48. Cf. David Strauss, "Discriminatory Intent and the Taming of Brown," *U. Chi. L. Rev.* 935 (1989); Charles R. Lawrence II, "The Id, the Ego, and Equal Protection: Reckoning with Unconscious Racism," 39 *Stan. L. Rev.* 632 (1987).

49. 42 U.S.C. § 7423(c).

50. See Jerry L. Mashaw and David Harfst, *The Struggle for Auto Safety* (1990).

51. See Mendeloff, *Toxic Substance Regulation*.

52. See Ernest Gellhorn, "Regulatory Reform and the Federal Trade Commission's Antitrust Jurisdiction," 49 *Tenn. L. Rev.* 471 (1982).

53. See ibid.; American Bar Association, *Report of the ABA Commission to Study the Federal Trade Commission* (1969); Roger L. Faith, Donald R. Leavens, and Robert D. Tollison, "Antitrust Pork Barrel," in *Public Choice and Regulation: A View from Inside the Federal Trade Commission* 15, Robert J. Mackay, James C. Miller, and Bruce Yandle, eds. (1987).

54. See Ackerman and Hassler, *Clean Coal/Dirty Air*.

55. Kay Lehman Schlozman and John T. Tierney, *Organized Interests and American Democracy* (1986); James Q. Wilson, "The Politics of Regulation," in *The Politics of Regulation*, James Q. Wilson, ed. (1980); Richard B. Stewart, "The Reformation of American Administrative Law," 88 *Harv. L. Rev.* 1667 (1975).

56. See William A. Niskanen, *Bureaucracy and Representative Government* (1971).

57. See David P. McCaffrey, *OSHA and the Politics of Health Regulation,* 16–19, 77–80 (1982).

58. Mendeloff, *Toxic Substance Regulation* 74–102 (1988); Susan Rose-Ackerman, "Progressive Law and Economics," 98 *Yale L. J.* 341 (1988).

59. See Kristin Bumiller, *The Civil Rights Society* (1988); Drew Days, "Turning Back the Clock: The Reagan Administration and Civil Rights," 19 *Harv. C.R.-C.L. L. Rev.* 309 (1984); Comment, "The Rise and Fall of the United States Commission on Civil Rights," 22 *Harv. C.R.-C.L. L. Rev.* 449 (1987); see also below.

60. See below.

61. See Mashaw and Harfst, *The Struggle for Auto Safety*.

62. See generally Erwin G. Krasnow, Lawrence D. Longley, and Herbert A. Terry, *The Politics of Broadcast Regulation* 35–48, 53–61 (1982).

63. See Michael Pertchuck, *Revolt against Regulation* (1982).

64. See, e.g., Grabowski and Vernon, *The Regulation of Pharmaceuticals;* Peter Huber, "The Old-New Division in Risk Regulation," 64 *Virginia Law Review* 613 (1984); Sam Peltzman, "An Evaluation of Consumer Protection Legislation: The 1962 Drug Amendments," in *Chicago Studies in Political Economy.*

65. See Crandall, *Controlling Industrial Pollution;* Peter Pashigian, "Environmental Regulation: Whose Self-Interests Are Being Served," 23 *Economic Inquiry* 551 (1985).

66. See Crandall, *Regulating the Automobile.*

67. Some carcinogen regulations are key examples here.

68. See generally Derthick and Quirk, *The Politics of Deregulation.*

69. The classic statement is James M. Landis, *The Administrative Process* (1938).

70. See Stewart, "The Reformation of American Administrative Law."

71. See James D. Freedman, *Crisis and Legitimacy* (1978); Gerald E. Frug, "The Ideology of Bureaucracy in American Law," 97 *Harv. L. Rev.* 1277 (1984).

72. Wilson, "The Politics of Regulation."

73. See David Wood, "The Equal Opportunity Commission (1972–1987): Bureaucratic Responsiveness to Changing Political Conditions" (unpublished paper delivered at 1988 meeting of the American Political Science Association) 7.

74. See Bumiller, *The Civil Rights Society.*

75. See Edward A. Tomlinson, "Report on the Experience of Various Agencies with Statutory Time Limits Applicable to Licensing or Clearance Functions and to Rulemaking," in Administrative Conference of the United States, *Recommendations and Reports* 119, 122–123 (1978).

76. See L. A. Scott Powe, *American Broadcasting and the First Amendment* (1987).

77. For more general discussion, see Cass R. Sunstein, "Paradoxes of the Regulatory State," 56 *U. Chi. L. Rev.* (forthcoming 1990).

78. Compare the discussion of how the "best interests of the child" standard in family law turns out to be self-defeating, because the determination is itself harmful to the child, in Jon Elster, *Solomonic Judgments* (1989).

79. See Walter Gellhorn, *Ombudsmen and Others: Citizens' Protectors in Nine Countries* (1966).

80. See Chapter 1.

81. See Paul Weiler, *The Law at Work* (forthcoming 1990); Daniel Spulber, *Regulation and Markets* 392–399 (1989); Viscusi, *Risk by Choice.*

4. Courts, Interpretation, and Norms

1. See *Hirschey v. Federal Energy Regulatory Comm'n,* 777 F.2d 1, 7–8 (D.C. Cir. 1986) (Scalia, J., concurring); Address by Judge Antonin Scalia, "Speech on Use of Legislative History" (1985); compare Daniel A. Farber and Philip P. Frickey, "Legislative Intent and Public Choice," 74 *Va. L. Rev.* 423 (1988).

2. In this sense, the debate over formalism in statutory construction replicates a similar debate in constitutional law. See, e.g., Paul Brest, "The Misconceived Quest for the Original Understanding," 60 *B.U.L. Rev.* 204 (1980).

3. 1 *Holmes-Laski Letters* 249, Mark DeWolfe Howe, ed. (1953).

4. See, e.g., *McLaughlin v. Richland Shoe Co.,* 108 S. Ct. 1677 (1988); *Goodyear Atomic Corp. v. Miller,* 108 S. Ct. 1704 (1988).

5. Its inadequacy has been pointed out in many places. For philosophical treatments, see Ludwig Wittgenstein, *Philosophical Investigations,* G. E. M. Anscombe, trans. (1972); Hans-Georg Gadamer, *Truth and Method* (trans. 2d ed. 1975). For legal discussion, see, e.g., John H. Wigmore, 9 *Evidence* 2470, at 227 (3d ed. 1940); Frank E. Horack, Jr., "The Disintegration of Statutory Construc-

tion," 24 *Ind. L. J.* 335, 338 (1949); Jerome Frank, "Words and Music: Some Remarks on Statutory Interpretation," 47 *Colum. L. Rev.* 1259, 1263 (1947); Henry M. Hart, Jr., and Albert M. Sacks, *The Legal Process* (1958); Stanley Fish, "Don't Know Much About the Middle Ages: Posner on Law and Literature," 97 *Yale L. J.* 777, 778–780 (1988).

Consider Learned Hand's view: "Words are not pebbles in alien juxtaposition; they have only a communal existence; and not only does the meaning of each interpenetrate the other, but all in their aggregate take their purport from the setting in which they are used." *NLRB v. Federbush Co.,* 121 F.2d 954, 957 (2d Cir. 1941).

There is a difference, at least in principle, between the sorts of understandings that make ordinary words intelligible and the sorts of interpretive principles that give meaning to statutory gaps, as, for example, in the norms in favor of state autonomy or judicial review. Participation in the set of practices that make ordinary words intelligible is probably best conceived not as interpretation at all. See Wittgenstein, *Philosophical Investigations* section 201 (discussing ways "of grasping a rule which is *not* an *interpretation,* but which is exhibited in what we call 'obeying the rule' and 'going against it' in actual cases") (emphasis in original). This point holds even though one's participation in those practices is conditional on a wide range of background understandings that are not "part" of those ordinary words.

The distinction is important because it is sufficient, for purposes of background understandings of this sort, that there be a social consensus on their behalf; communication is possible only because of that consensus. But with respect to interpretive principles that are part of interpretation—for example, the idea that silence on preemption means that state law continues to exist—a consensus may be inadequate if the arguments on behalf of that consensus are not good ones. In these cases, interpretive principles are at least in theory subject to evaluation and to replacement by alternatives. A pervasive problem with conventionalist approaches to legal interpretation is that they treat all principles as if they fell within the category of norms that make communication possible.

6. U.S. Const. art II, §1, cl. 5.

7. See *Weinberger v. Romero-Barcelo,* 456 U.S. 305 (1982); *Amoco Production Co. v. Village of Gambell,* 107 S. Ct. 1396 (1987).

8. See *Cannon v. University of Chicago,* 441 U.S. 677, 730–731 (1979) (Powell, J., dissenting); *Thompson v. Thompson,* 108 S. Ct. 513, 520–523 (1988) (Scalia, J., concurring).

9. See, e.g., *Industrial Union Dep't, AFL-CIO v. American Petroleum Inst.,* 448 U.S. 607 (1980) (meaning of "feasible"); *Steelworkers v. Weber,* 443 U.S. 193 (1979) (discrimination).

10. See, e.g., *National Society of Professional Engineers v. United States,* 435 U.S. 679, 688 (1978).

11. See ibid.; *Business Elecs. Corp. v. Sharp Elecs. Corp.,* 108 S.Ct. 1515, 1519–24 (1988); *Broadcast Music, Inc. v. CBS,* 441 U.S. 1, 19–22 (1979); *Continental TV, Inc. v. GTE Sylvania, Inc.,* 433 U.S. 36, 51–59 (1977).

12. 42 U.S.C. §1983.

13. See, e.g., *Wood v. Strickland,* 420 U.S. 308, 316–318 (1975); *City of Newport v. Fact Concerts, Inc.,* 453 U.S. 247, 258 (1981).

14. See Larry Kramer and Alan O. Sykes, "Municipal Liability Under §1983: A Legal and Economic Analysis," 1987 *Supreme Court Review* 249, 261–266; Jack Beerman, "A Critical Approach to Section 1983," 42 *Stan. L. Rev.* 51 (1989).

15. 78 Stat. 241, 253–266 (1964) (codified as amended at 42 U.S.C. §§2000e to 2000e-17 (1982)).

16. The example is drawn from H. L. A. Hart, *The Concept of Law* 121–132 (1961).

17. *United States v. Wells Fargo Bank,* 485 U.S. 351 (1988). For judicial rejections of literalism, see *Public Citizen v. U.S. Dept. of Justice,* 109 S.Ct. 2558, 2573–74 (1989); *United States v. American Trucking Assns.,* 310 U.S. 534, 543 (1940); *Armstrong Co. v. Nu-Enamel Corp.,* 305 U.S. 315, 333 (1933); *Sorrells v. United States,* 287 U.S. 435, 446–448 (1932); *United States v. Ryan,* 284 U.S. 167, 175 (1931); *Perry v. Strawbridge,* 209 Mo. 621, 108 S.W. 641 (1908). See also note 19 below.

Consider the following view: "Frequently words . . . broad enough to include an act . . . [are used in a statute], and yet a consideration . . . of the absurd results which follow . . . makes it unreasonable to believe that the legislator intended to include the particular act." *Church of the Holy Trinity v. United States,* 143 U.S. 457, 459 (1892).

18. *Mackey v. Lanier Collections Agency & Serv.,* 108 S. Ct. 2182 (1988).

19. See *California Fed. Sav. & Loan Ass'n v. Guerra,* 479 U.S. 272 (1987); *O'Connor v. United States,* 479 U.S. 27 (1986); *Offshore Logistics, Inc. v. Tallentire,* 477 U.S. 207, 220–221 (1986); *Church of the Holy Trinity v. United States,* 143 U.S. 457, 459 (1892); *Steelworkers v. Weber,* 443 U.S. 193, 201 (1979); *Kelly v. Robinson,* 479 U.S. 36, 43–44 (1986); *Perry v. Strawbridge,* 209 Mo. 621, 108 S.W. 641 (murderer may not inherit as a result of death caused by his crime, notwithstanding clear statutory language). See also *Arizona v. California,* 373 U.S. 546 (1963) (interpreting statute against meaning of plain text because text was clearly an error). *United States v. Locke,* 471 U.S. 84, was wrongly decided for this reason. See also the discussion of "plain verbal errors" in Ernst Freund, "Interpretation of Statutes," 65 *U. Pa. L. Rev.* 207, 219–220 (1917).

20. Wittgenstein, *Philosophical Investigations* 33.

21. 69 F.2d 809 (2d Cir. 1934), aff'd, 293 U.S. 465 (1935).

22. See, e.g., *Helvering v. Gregory,* 69 F.2d 809 (2d Cir. 1934), aff'd, 293 U.S. 465 (1935); *Commissioner v. Court Holding Co.,* 324 U.S. 331 (1945); *Goldstein v. Commissioner,* 364 F.2d 734 (2d Cir. 1966), cert. denied, 385 U. S. 1005 (1967). Outside of the area of taxation, there are many examples as well. See, e.g., *Stoner v. Hudgins,* 568 S.W.2d 898 (Tex. Civ. App. 1978). See generally Joseph Isenbergh, "Musings on Form and Substance in Taxation" (book review), 49 *U. Chi. L. Rev.* 859 (1982). The decision in *Johnson v. Southern Pacific Co.,* 117 F. 462 (8th Cir. 1902), rev'd, 196 U. S. 1 (1904) is persuasively criticized in Hart, Jr., and Sacks, *The Legal Process* 1173–1174 on this ground.

23. *Olmstead v. United States,* 277 U.S. 438, 469 (1928) (Holmes, J., dissenting).

24. See the discussion of *Bob Jones University v. United States* in Chapter 6.

25. For a powerful demonstration in the context of environmental law, see R.

Shep Melnick, *Regulation and the Courts: The Case of the Clean Air Act* (1983), which shows the constant resort to statutory text in cases in which text is at best indeterminate, and in which judges are acting according to policy considerations—perhaps laudable and legitimate, but unarticulated and uninformed.

26. See, e.g., *Community for Creative Non-Violence v. Reid,* 109 S. Ct. 2166 (1989).

27. Lon L. Fuller, "Positivism and Fidelity to Law: A Reply to Professor Hart," 71 *Harv. L. Rev.* 630 (1958); Hart, Jr., and Sacks, *The Legal Process.*

28. See *United States v. Turkette,* 452 U.S. 576, 588–593 (1981).

29. See, e.g., *United States v. Elgin, J. & E. Ry.,* 298 U.S. 492 (1936).

30. See Antonin Scalia, "Vermont Yankee: The APA, the D.C. Circuit, and the Supreme Court," 1978 *Supreme Court Review* 345, 381–382, arguing in favor of such "bending."

31. See the discussion in Donald C. Langevoort, "Statutory Obsolescence and the Judicial Process: The Revisionist Role of the Courts in Federal Banking Regulation," 85 *Mich. L. Rev.* 672, 687–719 (1987).

32. See Richard A. Posner, *The Federal Courts: Crisis and Reform* 289 (1985).

33. *Missouri v. Holland,* 252 U.S. 416, 433 (1920).

34. 461 U.S. 574 (1983).

35. This point is insufficiently emphasized in Guido Calabresi, *A Common Law for the Age of Statutes* (1982), which treats the problem of obsolescence as one of "overruling" statutes, when the issue is frequently the consequence of changed circumstances for interpretation.

36. On how to handle the problem of changed circumstances, see Chapter 5.

37. See, e.g., *Train v. Colorado Pub. Interest Research Group, Inc.,* 426 U.S. 1 (1976); *Thompson v. Thompson,* 108 S. Ct. 513 (1988).

38. See, e.g., *Green v. Boch Laundry Mach. Co.,* 109 S.Ct. 1981, 1994 (1989) (Scalia, J., concurring in the judgment); *United States v. Stuart,* 109 S.Ct. 1183, 1193–1197 (1989) (Scalia, J., concurring in part); *United States v. Taylor,* 108 S.Ct. 2413, 2423–2424 (1988) (Scalia, J., concurring in part). See also the critical discussion in Max Radin, "Statutory Interpretation," 43 *Harv. L. Rev.* 863, 866 (1930).

39. As a self-conscious example, consider these words: "Mr. Speaker, having received unanimous consent to extend my remarks in the *Record,* I would like to indicate that I am not really speaking these words . . . As a matter of fact, I am back in my office typing this out on my own hot little typewriter . . . Such is the pretense of the House that it would have been easy to just quietly include these remarks in the RECORD, issue a brave press release, and convince thousands of cheering constituents that I was in there fighting every step of the way, influencing the course of history in the heat of debate." 117 Cong. Rec. 36506 (1971) (statement of Rep. Heckler).

40. Pub. L. No. 414, §212(a)(4), 66 Stat. 163, 182 (1952), 8 U.S.C. §1182(a)(4) (1964), amended by Pub. L. No. 89-236, §15(b), 74 Stat. 911, 919 (1965), to read "psychopathic personality, or sexual deviation, or a mental defect," 8 U.S.C. §1182(a)(4) (1982 & Supp. V 1987).

41. See Alexander Aleinikoff, "Updating Statutory Interpretation," 87 *Mich. L. Rev.* 20 (1988).

42. "We do not inquire what the legislature meant; we ask only what the statute means." Oliver Wendell Holmes, "The Theory of Legal Interpretation," 12 *Harv. L. Rev.* 417, 419 (1899); see also Frank H. Easterbrook, "The Role of Original Intent in Statutory Construction," 11 *Harv. J. L. & Pub. Policy* 59 (1988). As noted, however, a reference to history can help in clearing up ambiguities, correcting unintended absurdities, and avoiding irrationality. For examples, see *Green v. Boch Laundry Mach. Co.,* 109 S.Ct. 1981 (1989); *Public Citizen v. U.S. Dept. of Justice,* 109 S.Ct. 2558 (1989).

43. See Hart, Jr., and Sacks, *The Legal Process* 1415.

44. Karl N. Llewellyn, "Remarks on the Theory of Appellate Decision and the Rules or Canons about How Statutes Are to Be Construed," 3 *Vand. L. Rev.* 395, 399 (1950) (emphasis in original).

45. Ernst Freund, "Interpretation of Statutes," 65 *U. Pa. L. Rev.* 207, 231 (1917). Freund continued: "That object is far more important than a painstaking fidelity to the supposed legislative intent. This intent is in reality often a fiction, and the legislature is fully aware that any but the most explicit language is subject to the judicial power of interpretation. That power might, therefore, as well be frankly and vigorously used as a legitimate instrument of legal development and of balancing legislative inadvertence by judicial deliberation."

46. Max Radin, "Statutory Interpretation," 43 *Harv. L. Rev.* 863, 884 (1930).

47. See Daniel Bell, *The End of Ideology* (1960); see the discussion in Richard A. Posner, "The Decline of Law as an Autonomous Discipline: 1962–1987," 100 *Harv. L. Rev.* 761 (1987).

48. See Ronald Dworkin, *Law's Empire* 313–354 (1986).

49. Posner, *The Federal Courts* 287 (1985).

50. See ibid. 289.

51. To make this observation is not to deny that there are many democratic defects in Congress, some of which are discussed in Chapter 3. Both disparities in political influence and the difficulties, described by Arrow, in aggregating private desires into a social welfare function make it necessary to be cautious in identifying even democratic outcomes with the public will.

52. In civil law systems, this point is a conventional one. Courts are far more willing explicitly to interpret statutes so as to create systemic rationality. See Konrad Zweigert and Hans-Jürgen Puttfarken, "Statutory Interpretation—Civilian Style," 44 *Tul. L. Rev.* 704, 707–08 (1970); William N. Eskridge, Jr., "Public Values in Statutory Interpretation," 137 *V. Pa. L. Rev.* 1007, 1011–1012 (1989).

53. See *The Federalist* No. 78, at 528, J. Cooke, ed. (1961): "But it is not with a view to infractions of the Constitution only that the independence of judges may be an essential safeguard against the effects of occasional ill humours in the society. These sometimes extend no farther than to the injury of the private rights of particular classes of citizens, by unjust and partial laws. Here also the firmness of the judicial magistracy is of vast importance in mitigating the severity and confining the operation of such laws. It not only serves to moderate the immediate mischiefs of those which may have been passed, but it operates as a check upon the legislative body in passing them; who, perceiving that obstacles to the

success of an iniquitous intention are to be expected from the scruples of the courts, are in a manner compelled by the very motives of the injustice they mediate, to qualify their attempts." See also Richard A. Posner, discussing civilizing effect of interpretation in *Foundations of Jurisprudence* (forthcoming); Dworkin, *Law's Empire* 313–354.

54. Consider, for example, the fact that canons of construction have played a central role in statutory interpretation throughout the history of Anglo-American law. See also 1 William Blackstone, *Commentaries on the Laws of England* 87–92 (1765) (discussing statutory interpretation in a nonformal way, with principles of construction); Eskridge, Jr., "Public Values," 1007, 1010–11 and sources cited in note 8.

55. The seminal work here is Kenneth J. Arrow, *Social Choice and Individual Values* (1951). For a more recent collection, see *Rational Man and Irrational Society?* Brian Barry and Russell Hardin, eds. (1982).

56. See James M. Buchanan and Gordon Tullock, *The Calculus of Consent* (1962); Jonathan R. Macey, "Competing Economic Views of the Constitution," 56 *Geo. Wash. L. Rev.* 50 (1987).

57. See the discussion in Frank H. Easterbrook, "Foreword: The Court and the Economic System," 98 *Harv. L. Rev.* 4, 42–51 (1984).

58. See William M. Landes and Richard A. Posner, "The Independent Judiciary in an Interest-Group Perspective," 18 *J. L. & Econ.* 875, 877–879 (1975).

59. See, e.g., Martha Derthick and Paul J. Quirk, *The Politics of Deregulation* (1985); Joseph P. Kalt and Mark A. Zupan, "Capture and Ideology in the Economic Theory of Politics," 74 *Am. Econ. Rev.* 279 (1984); Daniel A. Farber and Philip P. Frickey, "The Jurisprudence of Public Choice," 65 *Tex. L. Rev.* 873 (1987).

60. On Madisonian republicanism, see Cass R. Sunstein, "Interest Groups in American Public Law," 38 *Stan. L. Rev.* 29, 38–48 (1985); on the norm against naked interest-group transfers, see Cass R. Sunstein, "Naked Preferences and the Constitution," 84 *Colum. L. Rev.* 1689 (1984) and Cass R. Sunstein, "Political Self-Interest in Constitutional Law," in *Beyond Self-Interest*, Jane Mansbridge, ed. (1990).

61. See the Introduction above.

62. *Chevron USA, Inc. v. Natural Resources Defense Council, Inc.*, 467 U.S. 837, 842 (1984); but see *INS v. Cardoza-Fonseca*, 480 U.S. 421, 446–448 (1987).

63. See Peter L. Strauss, "One Hundred Fifty Cases Per Year," 87 *Colum. L. Rev.* 1093, 1117–1129 (1987); Colin S. Diver, "Statutory Interpretation in the Administrative State," 133 *U. Pa. L. Rev.* 549 (1985); Antonin Scalia, "Judicial Deference to Agency Interpretations of Law," 1989 *Duke L. J.* 511.

64. See Henry P. Monaghan, "Marbury and the Administrative State," 83 *Colum. L. Rev.* 1 (1983).

65. See *The Federalist* No. 78.

66. See Chapter 6 for an effort to sort out the appropriate place of agency interpretations in regulatory law.

67. Jerome Frank, *Law and the Modern Mind* 190–192 (1930); Roberto Unger, *Knowledge and Politics* 94–110 (1975).

68. *Shaw v. Railroad Co.*, 101 U.S. 557, 565 (1879); but see *Isbrandtsen Co. v. Johnson*, 343 U.S. 779, 783 (1952).

69. 198 U.S. 45 (1905).

70. See Robert L. Hale, "Coercion and Distribution in a Supposedly Noncoercive State," 38 *Pol. Sci. Q.* 470 (1923); Morris R. Cohen, "Property and Sovereignty," 13 *Cornell L. Q.* 8 (1927).

71. See Llewellyn, "Remarks on the Theory of Appellate Decision and the Rules or Canons," 395, 401–406.

72. See Richard A. Posner, "Statutory Interpretation—In the Classroom and in the Courtroom," 50 *U. Chi. L. Rev.* 800, 805–817 (1983).

The dispute over canons of construction is not confined to the law. See the critical comments in E. D. Hirsch, *Validity in Interpretation* 198–207 (1967), especially the suggestion, with respect to literary canons of construction, that the "rules do not always contradict one another, but they do proliferate in the most diverse directions . . . Since all practical interpretive canons are merely preliminary probability judgments, two consequences follow with regard to their intelligent application. First, the canon is more reliable the narrower its intended range of application . . . Second, since any interpretive canon can be overturned by subsuming the text under a still narrower class in which the canon fails to hold or holds by such a small majority that it becomes doubtful, it follows that interpretive canons are often relatively useless baggage. When they are general, they cannot compel decision, and even when they are narrowly practical, they can be overturned"; pp. 199, 203.

The discussion in this chapter suggests that these conclusions are misconceived. Interpretive canons are an unavoidable part of the process of drawing meaning from text. Both general and narrow principles have critical consequences for statutory interpretation, as we will see in more detail below.

73. There are notable exceptions, including Hart, Jr., and Sacks, *The Legal Process* 1220–40; William Eskridge, Jr., "Public Values in Statutory Interpretation," 137 *U. Pa. L. Rev.* 1007 (1989); Jonathan R. Macey, "Promoting Public-Regarding Legislation Through Statutory Construction," 86 *Colum. L. Rev.* 223 (1986); Posner, "Statutory Interpretation," 805–817 (defending several canons while objecting to them as a general rule). An especially useful treatment can be found in William N. Eskridge, Jr., and Philip P. Frickey, *Cases and Materials on Legislation: Statutes and the Creation of Public Policy* 639–695 (1987).

Consider also the suggestion of Felix Frankfurter, in "Some Reflections on the Reading of Statutes," 47 *Colum. L. Rev.* 527, 544 (1947): "Canons give an air of abstract intellectual compulsion to what is in fact a delicate judgment, concluding a complicated process of balancing subtle and elusive elements . . . So far as valid, they are what Mr. Justice Holmes called them, axioms of experience . . . Insofar as canons of construction are generalizations of experience, they all have worth."

74. Llewellyn, "Remarks on the Theory of Appellate Decision and the Rules or Canons," 397, 399. See also Radin, "Statutory Interpretation," 863, 884, advising judges to ask: "Will the inclusion of this particular determinate in the statutory determinable lead to a desirable result? What is desirable will be what

is just, what is proper, what satisfies the social emotions of the judge, what fits into the ideal scheme of society which he entertains."

75. See generally Charles J. Goetz and Robert E. Scott, "The Limits of Expanded Choice: An Analysis of the Interactions Between Express and Implied Contract Terms," 73 *Calif. L. Rev.* 261 (1985).

76. See ibid. There is not universal agreement on this point. Sometimes implied terms might serve redistributive functions; sometimes they might be designed to shape and transform preferences; sometimes they might be paternalistic; sometimes it is impossible to decide on the legal rule by "mimicking the market" because the market will itself be a function of the legal rule and is not exogenous to it. See Chapter 1; Duncan Kennedy, "Distributive and Paternalist Motives in Contract and Tort Law, with Special Reference to Compulsory Terms and Unequal Bargaining Power," 41 *Md. L. Rev.* 563 (1982).

77. See *O'Connor v. United States*, 479 U.S. 27, 31–32 (1986).

78. See *Louisiana Pub. Serv. Comm'n v. FCC*, 476 U.S. 355, 370 (1986); *Washington Market Co. v. Hoffman*, 101 U.S. 112, 116 (1879).

79. See, e.g., *Jett v. Dallas School Dist.*, 109 S.Ct. 2702, 2722 (1989); *Northern Border Pipeline Co. v. Jackson County*, 512 F. Supp. 1261, 1264 (D. Minn. 1981).

80. See *Block v. Community Nutrition Services, Inc.*, 467 U.S. 340, 347, 349 (1984); *Steelworkers v. Weber*, 443 U.S. 193, 205–206 (1979); *National R.R. Passenger Corp. v. National Ass'n of R.R. Passengers*, 414 U.S. 453, 458 (1974).

81. 443 U.S. 193 (1979).

82. See, e.g., *TVA v. Hill*, 437 U.S. 153 (1978).

83. 1 U.S.C. §§1–6 (1982).

84. See, e.g., *United States v. Will*, 449 U.S. 200, 221–222 (1980); *TVA v. Hill*, 437 U.S. 153, 189–190 (1978).

85. See House Rule XXI (2) ("Nor shall any provision in any [appropriation] bill or amendment thereto changing existing law be in order"); Standing Rules of the Senate, Rule 16.4. See also Neal E. Devins, "Regulation of Government Agencies Through Limitations Riders," 1987 *Duke L. J.* 456, 458 n. 12 (supporting this point).

86. See, e.g., *Communications Workers of America v. Beck*, 108 S. Ct. 2641, 2657 (1988); *Commodity Futures Trading Comm'n v. Schor*, 478 U.S. 833, 841 (1986); *NLRB v. Catholic Bishop of Chicago*, 440 U.S. 490, 500 (1979); *American Airways Charters, Inc. v. Regan*, 746 F.2d 865, 873–874 (D.C. Cir. 1984).

87. See *Bowen v. Michigan Academy of Family Physicians*, 476 U.S. 667, 670 (1986); *Lindahl v. OPM*, 470 U.S. 768, 778 (1985); *Dunlop v. Bachowski*, 421 U.S. 560, 567 (1975); *Abbott Laboratories v. Gardner*, 387 U.S. 136, 139–141 (1967).

88. *Haig v. Agee*, 453 U.S. 280, 301 & n. 50 (1982); *Zemel v. Rusk*, 381 U.S. 1, 1213 (1965); *Dames v. Moore v. Regan*, 453 U.S. 654 (1981).

89. See, e.g., *Chevron USA, Inc. v. National Resources Defense Council*, 467 U.S. 837 (1984).

90. See above; Stephen Breyer, "Judicial Review of Questions of Law and Policy," 38 *Admin. L. Rev.* 363 (1986).

91. See Henry P. Monaghan, "Foreword: Constitutional Common Law," 89 *Harv. L. Rev.* 1 (1975).

92. See Lawrence Gene Sager, "Fair Measure: The Legal Status of Under-enforced Constitutional Norms," 91 *Harv. L. Rev.* 1212 (1978).

93. See, e.g., *Transamerica Mortgage Advisors, Inc. v. Lewis,* 444 U.S. 11 (1979); *Touche Ross & Co. v. Redington,* 442 U.S. 560 (1979); *Pennhurst State School & Hosp. v. Halderman,* 451 U.S. 1 (1981); Frank H. Easterbrook, "Statutes' Domains," 50 *U. Chi. L. Rev.* 533 (1983).

94. See, e.g., *California v. Cabazon Band of Mission Indians,* 480 U.S. 202, 216 (1987); *Three Affiliated Tribes v. Wold Engineering,* 467 U.S. 138, 149 (1984); *Montana v. Blackfeet Tribe,* 471 U.S. 759, 766 (1985).

95. See, e.g., *United States v. Wells Fargo Bank,* 108 S. Ct. 1179, 1182 (1988) (no implied exemptions from taxation); *Foley Bros., Inc. v. Filardo,* 336 U.S. 281, 285 (1949) (laws apply only within territory of United States); *Bowen v. Georgetown Univ. Hosp.,* 109 S. Ct. 468, 471 (1989) (presumption against retroactivity).

5. Interpretive Principles

1. Consider the shifting reaction to implied causes of action: compare *J. I Case Co. v. Borak,* 377 U.S. 426 (1964) (willingly creating such actions) with *Touche Ross & Co. v. Redington,* 442 U.S. 560 (1979) (suggesting that such actions will not be recognized without affirmative evidence of a congressional intent to do so). Consider also the changing attitudes toward preemption, set out in "Note, The Preemption Doctrine: Shifting Perspectives on Federalism and the Burger Court," 75 *Colum. L. Rev.* 623 (1975). The general shift in this period is remarked in "Note, Intent, Clear Statements, and the Common Law: Statutory Interpretation in the Supreme Court," 95 *Harv. L. Rev.* 892 (1982). The most prominent illustration is a shifting attitude toward civil rights law, involving the movement from broad to narrow construction. See below.

2. 476 U.S. 974 (1986).

3. See Cass R. Sunstein, "Interest Groups in American Public Law," 38 *Stan. L. Rev.* 29, 59–64 (1985).

4. See, e.g., *NLRB v. Catholic Bishop of Chicago,* 440 U.S. 490 (1979).

5. See Richard A. Posner, *The Federal Courts: Crisis and Reform* 285 (1985).

6. *Panama Refining Co. v. Ryan,* 293 U.S. 388, 421 (1935); *Schechter Poultry Corp. v. United States,* 295 U.S. 495, 529–530 (1935).

7. 357 U.S. 116 (1958).

8. 426 U.S. 88 (1976).

9. See *New York City Transit Auth. v. Beazer,* 440 U.S. 568, 597–611 (1979) (White, J., dissenting); *Regents of University of California v. Bakke,* 438 U.S. 265 (1978) (Powell, J.).

10. See *Myers v. United States,* 272 U.S. 52 (1926); *Sierra Club v. Costle,* 657 F.2d 298 (D.C. Cir. 1981).

11. See the classic discussion of how the rule of law fails in Lon L. Fuller, *The Morality of Law* (1965).

12. *Independent Fed'n of Flight Attendants v. Zipes,* 109 S.Ct. 2732, 2736 (1989) (emphasis in original).

13. See *Washington v. Davis,* 426 U.S. 229, 238–241 (1976); *Personnel Adm'r of Mass. v. Feeney,* 442 U.S. 256, 279 (1979).

14. The best demonstration of this point in the elaborate literature is David A. Strauss, "Discriminatory Intent and the Taming of Brown," 56 *U. Chi. L. Rev.* 935 (1989).

15. See *City of Cleburne v. Cleburne Living Center, Inc.*, 473 U.S. 432, 441–443 (1985); *Bowers v. Hardwick*, 478 U.S. 186, 194–195 (1986). See Cass R. Sunstein, "Sexual Orientation and the Constitution: A Note on the Relationship between Due Process and Equal Protection," 55 *U. Chi. L. Rev.* 1161 (1988).

16. See, e.g., *Home Bldg. & Loan Ass'n v. Blaisdell*, 290 U.S. 398 (1934); *Energy Reserves Group, Inc. v. Kansas Power & Light Co.*, 459 U.S. 400 (1983); *Penn Cent. Transp. Co. v. New York City*, 438 U.S. 104 (1978); *Hawaii Hous. Auth. v. Midkiff*, 407 U.S. 229 (1984).

17. For an emphatic negative answer, see Richard A. Epstein, *Takings: Private Property and the Power of Eminent Domain* (1985).

18. See, e.g., *Goldberg v. Kelly*, 397 U.S. 254 (1970); Richard H. Fallon, "Of Legislative Courts, Administrative Agencies, and Article III," 101 *Harv. L. Rev.* 915, 963–967 (1988); Henry M. Hart, Jr., "The Power of Congress to Limit the Jurisdiction of Federal Courts: An Exercise in Dialectic," 66 *Harv. L. Rev.* 1362 (1953).

19. See, e.g., *Johnson v. Robison*, 415 U.S. 361, 366–374 (1974); *Webster v. Doe*, 108 S.Ct. 2047, 2053–2054 (1988).

20. The most prominent efforts here are Frank I. Michelman, "Foreword: On Protecting the Poor Through the Fourteenth Amendment," 83 *Harv. L. Rev.* 7 (1969); Frank I. Michelman, "Welfare Rights in a Constitutional Democracy," 1979 *Wash. U.L.Q.* 659.

21. See, e.g., *Baltimore Gas & Elec. Co. v. Natural Resources Defense Council*, 462 U.S. 87 (1983).

22. *Hahn v. Gottlieb*, 430 F.2d 1243 (1st Cir. 1970); *Heckler v. Chaney*, 470 U.S. 821 (1985).

23. 458 F.2d 827 (D.C. Cir. 1972).

24. See *Chevron USA, Inc. v. National Resources Defense Council* 467 U.S. 837, 865–866 (1984).

25. See, e.g., cases cited in note 60 below; *Scenic Hudson Preservation Conference v. Federal Power Comm'n*, 354 F.2d 608 (2d Cir. 1965), cert. denied, 384 U.S. 941 (1966); *Citizens to Preserve Overton Park v. Volpe*, 401 U.S. 402 (1971); R. Shep Melnick, *Regulation and the Courts: The Case of the Clean Air Act* (1983), for a detailed catalogue.

26. See Cass R. Sunstein, "Deregulation and the Hard-Look Doctrine," 1983 *Supreme Court Review* 177. See also William N. Eskridge, Jr., "Politics Without Romance: Implications of Public Choice Theory for Statutory Interpretation," 74 *Va. L. Rev.* 275, 330–334 (1988).

27. See, e.g., *Industrial Union Dept, AFL-CIO v. American Petroleum Inst.*, 448 U.S. 607 (1980).

28. See *Flint Ridge Co. v. Scenic Rivers Assn of Okla.*, 426 U.S. 776 (1976); *Estate of Sanford v. Commissioner*, 308 U.S. 39 (1939); *Jones v. Illinois Dept of Rehabilitation Servs.*, 504 F. Supp. 1244 (N.D. Ill 1981), aff'd, 689 F.2d 724 (7th Cir. 1982); *Preston State Bank v. Ainsworth*, 552 F. Supp. 578 (N.D. Tex. 1982); *Daigneault v. Public Fin. Corp.*, 562 F. Supp. 194 (D. R.I. 1983).

29. *Bob Jones Univ. v. United States,* 461 U.S. 574 (1983).

30. See, e.g., *Industrial Union Dept, AFL-CIO v. American Petroleum Inst.,* 448 U.S. 607 (1980); *National Resources Defense Council v. EPA,* 824 F.2d 1146 (D.C. Cir. 1986).

31. See Eskridge, "Politics Without Romance"; T. Alexander Aleinikoff, "Updating Statutory Interpretation," 87 *Mich. L. Rev.* 20 (1988); William N. Eskridge, Jr., "Interpreting Legislative Inaction," 87 *Mich. L. Rev.* 67 (1988).

32. See Ronald Dworkin, *Law's Empire* (1986); Mark V. Tushnet, "Following the Rules Laid Down: A Critique of Interpretivism and Neutral Principles," 96 *Harv. L. Rev.* 781 (1983); William N. Eskridge, Jr., "Dynamic Statutory Interpretation," 135 *U. Pa. L. Rev.* 1479 (1987).

33. 392 U.S. 309 (1968).

34. See Chapter 4, note 11.

35. See Robert Bork, *The Antitrust Paradox* (1978); Richard A. Posner, *Economic Analysis of Law* (3d ed. 1986).

36. See, e.g., *Scenic Hudson Preservation Conference v. Federal Power Comm'n* 354 F.2d 608 (2d Cir. 1965), cert. denied, 384 U.S. 941 (1966).

37. See Ellen Ash Peters, "Common Law Judging in a Statutory World: An Address," 43 *U. Pitt. L. Rev.* 995, 1010 (1982).

38. See Donald C. Langevoort, "Statutory Obsolescence and the Judicial Process: The Revisionist Role of the Courts in Federal Banking Regulation," 85 *Mich. L. Rev.* 672 (1987).

39. See Guido Calabresi, *A Common Law for the Age of Statutes* (1982).

40. See generally Louis L. Jaffe, *Judicial Control of Administrative Action* (1965). There is a serious inconsistency between the Court's hostility to case-by-case implication of private rights of action and its occasional enthusiasm for case-by-case findings of preclusion of judicial review and preclusion of *Bivens* and 1983 actions. The inconsistency is probably best explained on the basis of a distinction between the rights of defendants and the rights of plaintiffs. See generally Daniel J. Meltzer, "Deterring Constitutional Violations by Law Enforcement Officials: Plaintiffs and Defendants as Private Attorneys General," 88 *Colum. L. Rev.* 247 (1988).

41. 344 F. Supp. 253 (D.C.C. 1972).

42. See the discussion in R. Shep Melnick, *Regulation and the Courts* (1983), cited in Chapter 4.

43. See *O'Connor v. United States,* 479 U.S. 27, 30–31 (1986); *Busic v. United States* 446 U.S. 398, 407 (1980); *Brock v. Pierce County,* 476 U.S. 253, 258–262.

44. 417 U.S. 156 (1974).

45. See citations in Chapter 4 (discussing textualism); and consider here the quotation from Wittgenstein, *Philosophical Investigations,* above.

46. See, e.g., *Industrial Union Dep't, AFL-CIO v. American Petroleum Inst.,* 448 U.S. 607 (1980); *National Resources Defense Council v. Thomas,* 805 F.2d 710 (D.C. Cir. 1986).

47. 29 U.S.C. §655(b)(5) (1982).

48. See *American Textile Mfrs. Inst. v. Donovan,* 452 U.S. 490 (1981).

49. See Chapter 3.

50. 805 F.2d 410 (D.C. Cir. 1986).

51. See *Bowen v. Yuckert,* 107 S.Ct. 2287 (1987) (severity regulation); *Weinberger v. Romero-Barcelo,* 456 U.S. 305 (1982); *Coalition on Sensible Transp. v. Dole,* 826 F.2d 60 (D.C. Cir. 1987); *Sierra Club v. United States Dept of Transp.,* 753 F.2d 120 (D.C. Cir. 1985); *Alabama Power Co. v. Costle,* 636 F.2d 323 (D.C. Cir. 1979). See generally Jeryl Mumpower, "An Analysis of the De Minimis Strategy for Risk Management," 6 *Risk Analysis* 437 (1986); Joseph Fiksel, "Toward a De Minimis Policy in Risk Regulation," 5 *Risk Analysis* 257 (1985).

52. See, e.g., *Cannon v. University of Chicago,* 441 U.S. 677 (1979); *Allen v. State Bd. of Elections,* 393 U.S. 544 (1969).

53. See the discussion in Robert Katzmann, *Institutional Disability* 152–187 (1986); see also *School Bd. of Nassau County v. Arline,* 480 U.S. 273 (1987).

54. See, e.g., *Griggs v. Duke Power Co.,* 401 U.S. 424 (1971); *Steelworkers v. Weber,* 443 U.S. 193 (1979).

55. On deregulation, see *Office of Communication of United Church of Christ v. FCC,* 779 F.2d 702 (D.C. Cir. 1985); *Office of Communication of United Church of Christ v. FCC,* 707 F.2d 1413 (D.C. Cir. 1983). On the public interest standard generally, see *Central Fl. Enter. v. FCC,* 598 F.2d 37 (D.C. Cir. 1978), cert. dismissed, 441 U.S. 957 (1979); *Citizens Communication Center v. FCC,* 447 F.2d 1201 (D.C. Cir. 1971); *Pasadena Broadcasting Co. v. FCC,* 555 F.2d 1046 (D.C. Cir. 1977); *Friends of the Earth v. FCC,* 449 F.2d 1164 (D.C. Cir. 1971); *Citizens Comm. to Save WEFM v. FCC,* 506 F.2d 246 (D.C. Cir. 1974); *Home Box Office, Inc. v. FCC,* 567 F.2d 9 (D.C. Cir. 1977); *California Coastal Comm'n v. Granite Rock Co.,* 480 U.S. 572 (1987); see also *United States v. Dion,* 476 U.S. 734 (1986).

See generally Richard B. Stewart, "Regulation in the Liberal State," 92 *Yale L. J.* 1537 (1983). But see the (questionable) decision in *Telecommunications Research and Action Center v. FCC,* 801 F.2d 501 (D.C. Cir. 1986), concluding that the fairness doctrine had not been codified.

56. See, e.g., *California Coastal Comm. v. Granite Rock Co.,* 480 U.S. 572 (1987); *Scenic Hudson Preservation Conference v. Federal Power Comm'n,* 354 F.2d 608 (2d Cir. 1965); *Citizens to Preserve Overton Park v. Volpe,* 401 U.S. 402 (1971); *Seacoast Anti-Pollution League v. Costle,* 572 F.2d 872 (1st Cir. 1982); *Sierra Club v. Ruckelshaus,* 344 F. Supp. 253 (D.D.C. 1972); *National Resources Defense Council v. EPA,* 489 F.2d 390 (5th Cir. 1974); *National Resources Defense Council v. Train,* 545 F.2d 320 (2d Cir. 1976); *Lead Indus. Ass'n v. EPA,* 647 F.2d 1130 (D.C. Cir. 1980); *Environmental Defense Fund v. Ruckelshaus,* 439 F.2d 584 (D.C. Cir. 1971).

The extraordinary role of the courts in the creation of the "prevention of significant deterioration" program, in the prevention of dispersion of pollutants, and in the requirement of regulation of risk-creating substances is chronicled and criticized in Melnick, *Regulation and the Courts.*

57. 867 F.2d 654 (D.C. Cir. 1989). See also *Meredith Corp. v. FCC,* 809 F.2d 863 (D.C. Cir. 1987). In *Red Lion Broadcasting Co. v. FCC,* 395 U.S. 367 (1969), the Supreme Court had upheld the fairness doctrine against constitutional attack, saying that "It is the right of the viewers and listeners, not the right

of the broadcasters, which is paramount. . . . There is no sanctuary in the First Amendment for unlimited private censorship operating in a medium not open to all."

58. 450 U.S. 582 (1981).

59. See Chapter 2, above.

60. See L. Scott Powe, *American Broadcasting and the First Amendment* (1988).

61. See, e.g., *Securities Indus. Assn v. Board of Governors of the Fed. Reserve Sys.*, 807 F.2d 1052 (D.C. Cir. 1986); *Investment Co. Inst. v. FDIC*, 815 F.2d 1540 (D.C. Cir. 1987); *Securities Indus. Assn v. Board of Governors of the Fed. Reserve Sys.*, 821 F.2d 810 (D.C. Cir. 1987); *Investment Co. Inst. v. Conover*, 790 F.2d 925 (D.C. Cir. 1986); Langevoort, "Statutory Obsolescence."

62. See R. Bork, *The Antitrust Paradox: A Policy At War With Itself* 409–410 (1973).

63. 436 U.S. 49 (1978).

64. See Stanley Fish, *Is There a Text in This Class?* (1980).

65. See, e.g., Jacques Derrida, *Of Grammatology*, Gayatri Chakravorty Spivak, trans. (1976). The quotation marks in text are necessary because of the uncertain and attenuated connection between deconstruction in literature and philosophy and its distant cousin in law, which, though attempting to draw on the work of Derrida, usually amounts in practice to quite ordinary efforts at subverting or undermining a particular line of reasoning.

6. Applications

1. See Donald Horowitz, "Reasoning from the Regime," forthcoming.

2. 29 U.S.C. §655(b)(5), 651.

3. 448 U.S. 607 (1980).

4. Ibid. 630.

5. Ibid. 642.

6. 29 U.S.C. 655(b)(5) (emphasis added).

7. 448 U.S. at 645 (plurality opinion).

8. 448 U.S. at 670 (Powell, J., concurring).

9. A different result might be appropriate if the scientific evidence is uncertain. If a significant risk is impossible to show because the data are unclear, perhaps employers, rather than workers, should bear the burden of medical uncertainty. The plurality did not make clear how such considerations would bear on the problem of carcinogen regulation if they had been squarely confronted by OSHA.

10. 452 U.S. 490 (1981).

11. Ibid. 508–509.

12. See *Public Citizen v. Young*, 831 F.2d 1108 (D.C. Cir. 1987), cert. denied, 108 S.Ct. 1470 (1988).

13. 451 U.S. 1 (1981).

14. 42 U.S.C. §6010 (1982) (current version at 42 U.S.C. §6009 (Supp. IV 1986)).

15. Ibid.

16. See 451 U.S. at 42–47 (White, J., dissenting).

17. 451 U.S. at 17 (footnote and citations omitted).

18. See *City of Cleburne v. Cleburne Living Center*, 473 U.S. 432 (1985).

19. 443 U.S. 193 (1979).

20. 42 U.S.C. 2000e-2(d) (1976).

21. 42 U.S.C. 2000e-2(j) (1976).

22. 443 U.S. at 204.

23. 443 U.S. at 209 (Blackmun, J., concurring).

24. 443 U.S. at 219–222, 226–230 (Rehnquist, J., dissenting).

25. See Bernard Meltzer, "The Weber Case: Judicial Abrogation of the Anti-discrimination Standard," 47 *U. Chi. L. Rev.* 423 (1980).

26. See Richard Lempert, "The Force of Irony: On the Morality of Affirmative Action and *United Steelworkers v. Weber*," 95 *Ethics* 86 (1984); David A. Strauss, "The Myth of Colorblindness," 1986 *Supreme Court Review* 99.

27. 109 S. Ct. 2115 (1989).

28. 401 U.S. 424 (1971).

29. See David A. Strauss, "Discriminatory Intent and the Taming of Brown," 56 *U. Chi. L. Rev.* 935 (1989).

30. See Ronald Dworkin, *Law's Empire* (1986).

31. See, e.g., *Sventko v. Kroger Co.*, 69 Mich. App. 644, 646–647, 245 N.W.2d 151, 153 (1976).

32. See ibid. 652–653, 245 N.W.2d 155–156 (Danhof, C. J., dissenting).

33. See *Phelps Dodge Corp. v. NLRB*, 313 U.S. 177 (1941), discussed in Douglas L. Leslie, *Labor Law in a Nutshell* 98 (2d ed. 1986).

34. 109 S. Ct. 2732 (1989).

35. Richard B. Stewart, "The Reformation of American Administrative Law," 88 *Harv. L. Rev.* 1667 (1975).

36. See Cass R. Sunstein, "Standing and the Privatization of Public Law," 88 *Colum. L. Rev.* 1432 (1988).

37. 5 U.S.C. §702 (Supp. V 1987).

38. *The Chicago Junction Case*, 264 U.S. 258 (1924).

39. See *Norwalk CORE v. Norwalk Redev. Agency*, 395 F.2d 920 (2d Cir. 1968); *Scenic Hudson Preservation Conf. v. Federal Power Comm'n*, 354 F.2d 608 (2d Cir. 1965); *Office of Communication of the United Church of Christ v. FCC*, 359 F.2d 994 (D.C. Cir. 1966).

40. *Assoc. of Data Processing Serv. Orgs. v. Camp.*, 397 U.S. 150 (1970).

41. *Simon v. Eastern Kentucky Welfare Rights Org.*, 426 U.S. 26 (1976); *Allen v. Wright*, 468 U.S. 737 (1984); *Center for Auto Safety v. Thomas*, 847 F.2d 843 (D.C. Cir. 1988).

42. To say this is not to deny that legal controls may have harmful effects on administration, by increasing paperwork and delay, by creating odd incentives, and by transferring conceptions of compensatory justice to regulatory settings, where they do not belong. See below.

43. For an elaborate argument to this effect, see Jeremy Rabkin, *Judicial Compulsions: How Public Law Distorts Public Policy* (1989).

44. See Raoul Berger, "Standing to Sue in Public Actions: Is It a Constitu-

tional Requirement?" 78 *Yale L. J.* 816 (1969); Louis L. Jaffe, "The Citizen As Litigant in Public Actions," 116 *U. Pa. L. Rev.* 1033 (1968); Steven L. Winter, "The Metaphor of Standing and the Problem of Self-Governance," 40 *Stan. L. Rev.* 1371 (1988).

45. *Switchmen's Union v. National Mediation Bd.*, 320 U.S. 297 (1943).

46. See Jerry L. Mashaw and David Harfst, *The Struggle for Auto Safety* (1990).

47. 470 U.S. 821 (1985).

48. See, e.g., *Adams v. Richardson,* 480 F.2d 1159 (D.C. Cir. 1973); *Environmental Defense Fund v. Ruckelshaus,* 439 F.2d 584 (D.C. Cir. 1971).

49. 456 U.S. 305 (1982).

50. 480 U.S. 531 (1987).

51. See, e.g., *Save Our Ecosystems v. Clark,* 747 F.2d 1240, 1250 (9th Cir. 1984); *People of Gambell v. Hodel,* 774 F.2d 1414, 1422 (9th Cir. 1985).

52. See, e.g., *J. I. Case Co. v. Borak,* 377 U.S. 426 (1964).

53. See *Cannon v. University of Chicago* 441 U.S. 677, 730–749 (1977) (Powell, J., dissenting); *Thompson v. Thompson,* 108 S. Ct. 513, 520–523 (1988) (Scalia, J., concurring).

54. See Richard B. Stewart and Cass R. Sunstein, "Public Programs and Private Rights," 95 *Harv. L. Rev.* 1193 (1982).

55. Compare *Cannon v. University of Chicago* 441 U.S. 677 (1979) and *Allen v. State Bd of Elections* 393 U.S. 544 (1969) with *Transamerica Mortgage Advisers, Inc. v. Lewis,* 444 U.S. 11 (1979); *Touche Ross & Co. v. Redington,* 442 U.S. 560 (1979).

56. See Note, "Preemption in the Burger Court," 75 *Colum. L. R.* 493 (1975).

57. See generally Richard B. Stewart, "Federalism and Political Economy in the Great Republic" (unpublished).

Conclusion

1. The quotation marks are necessary for reasons discussed in Chapter 1.

Index

Accountability, 30, 74, 165–166, 187, 190; of courts, 31; promoting political accountability, 171–172, 173, 187

Acid rain, 79, 89, 97

Activist court, 19–20, 157–159, 163

Adaptive preferences. *See* Endogenous preferences

Addiction, 44, 65–66

Administrative Procedure Act, 212–214

Affirmative rights, 17, 21–22, 29

Age discrimination, 2, 26

Agency costs, 99–100

Agricultural Adjustment Act, 24

Agricultural regulations, 103

Agricultural subsidies, 56, 69, 70; redistributive impact of, 101

Aid to Families with Dependent Children, 55

Air pollution. *See* Environmental law; specific laws

Airline regulation, 83, 89

Aleinikoff, Alexander, 129

American Textile Manufacturers Inst. v. Donovan, 197

Amoco Production Co. v. Village of Gambel, 221

Animal protection, 68–69

Antidiscrimination law, 2, 3, 25, 26, 31, 35, 37, 44–45; freedom of association and, 32; aspirations, 57; social subordination, 61–64; endogenous preferences, 66–67; interest-group transfers, 70; ben-

efits of, 80–81; affirmative action, 81, 95–96, 101, 152, 201–205; race-neutral policies, 96; inadequate implementation of, 99, 104; delegation of lawmaking power to courts, 117–118; equal protection violations, 167; implied rights of action, 183; discriminatory effect cases, 205–207. *See also* Age discrimination; Disabled persons; Racial discrimination; Sex discrimination

Antipollution law. *See* Environmental law

Antipoverty law, 25–26, 32, 55, 214–215; collective action problem, 55–56, 102; aspirations, 59; diversion of resources, 103

Antislavery movement, 18

Antisubordination, 29, 61–64, 103–104

Antitrust laws, 48–49, 50, 89, 185; delegation of lawmaking power to courts, 117; statutory obsolescence and, 176

Appropriations statutes, 169

Army Corps of Engineers, 17

Articles of Confederation, 13–14

Arts, contributions to, 59, 70

Asbestos regulation, 80

Aspirations, 3, 38, 39, 42, 47, 57–60, 101, 140, 228; endogenous preferences, 67; interest-group transfers and, 72–73; democratic aspirations, 101–102, 104, 113–114; inadequate implementation, 104; statutory interpretation and, 185

Attorneys' fees award, 209

Automobile emissions, 76, 78; costs and
    benefits of regulation, 86–87, 100, 182;
    old risk-new risk distinction, 92; coordi-
    nation of laws, 105; standing, 215
Automobile safety regulation, 26, 81; ben-
    efits of, 79; costs of, 82; expenditures
    per life saved, 94; interest-group pres-
    sures, 97; inadequate implementation of,
    99
Autonomy, 29, 34–35, 40–42, 45, 74, 90,
    99, 107, 146, 225–229; unanimous con-
    sent and, 36; endogenous preferences,
    66; state autonomy, 154; interpretive
    principles promoting, 187, 200–201. See
    also Liberty

Banking regulation, 103; chartering of na-
    tional banks, 19; interest-group trans-
    fers, 69–70; changed circumstances, 95,
    177; purposive interpretation and, 125–
    126; collective action problem, 173
Best-available technology strategies, 87–
    88, 92, 97, 106
Blackmun, Harry, 202, 204
Bob Jones University v. United States,
    126–127, 129, 173–174, 177
Brandeis, Louis, 212
Broadcasting. See Communications and
    broadcasting
Buchanan, James, 36, 39
Bureau of Fisheries, 17
Bureaucratic self-interest, 99, 101, 103

Calabresi, Guido, 177
Canons of construction, 147–150
Carcinogens, 82; food additives, 88–89,
    95, 121, 134, 176, 197–199; inconsist-
    ency of laws, 93–94, 173; expenditures
    per life saved, 94; changing knowledge
    about, 95; safe thresholds, 95; interest-
    group pressures, 97–98; inadequate im-
    plementation of laws, 99; coordination
    of regulatory efforts, 105; regulations
    limiting, 162–163; changed circum-
    stances, 177
Categorization of regulatory law, 71–73
Causation issues, 76, 214–216
Changed circumstances, 94–95, 105; stat-
    utory interpretation and, 121–122, 126–
    127, 174–175; interpretive principles
    and, 161, 174–177; statutory obsoles-
    cence, 174–177
Checks and balances system, 15–16, 22–
    24, 30, 102, 107; lawmaking primacy of
    legislature, 133–134; judicial deference,
    139–140, 142–144, 145–146, 156, 163,
    166; promoting better lawmaking, 154–
    155, 162; constitutional invalidity and
    doubts, 164–165; accountability, 165–
    166, 171–172, 187, 190
Chevron USA, Inc. v. Natural Resources
    Defense Council, Inc., 142–143, 224
Children's advertising, 32, 100
China, attack on collectivism in, 11
Cigarette regulation, 44
Citizenship, 71
Civil Aeronautics Authority, 24
Civil Rights Act of 1964, 62, 95–96; bene-
    fits of, 80; Title VII, 80–81, 118, 201–
    207, 209
Civil rights law, 25, 28, 32, 75; social sub-
    ordination, 61–64; implied rights of ac-
    tion, 183; tribal rights, 188–189; dis-
    criminatory effect cases, 205–207
Civil Service, 23
Civil War, 18
Civil Works Administration, 23
Civilian Conservation Corps, 23
Class actions, 180–181
Clayton Antitrust Act, 48
Clean Air Act, 26–27, 98; diverse opportu-
    nities for preference formation, 61; ben-
    efits of, 76, 81; compliance with air
    quality goals, 76; interest-group trans-
    fers and, 85–86; reform of, 109–110;
    Prevention of Significant Deterioration
    program, 85–86, 178–179; cost-benefit
    analysis, 86–87, 182
Clean Water Act, 26–27, 78
Clothing flammability regulations, 81
Coal industry regulation, 85, 97, 179
Coercion, 18, 40, 43, 50, 52, 65; agency
    inaction as, 219–220
Cognitive dissonance, 53, 63, 66
Collective action problem, 3, 6, 38–40, 42,
    45, 49–52, 55–56, 58–60, 69, 102–103,
    137, 140; intrapersonal, 65–66; legisla-
    tive purpose and, 123; interpretive prin-
    ciples and, 172–174; standing and, 215
Collective rights, 29
Collective self-determination, 35, 42, 57–
    60. See also Aspirations
Collectivism, 2, 11, 38, 228
Command and control strategies, 82, 87–
    88, 89, 92, 97, 105, 109
Commerce Department, 13

Commodities Exchange Authority, 19
Common law principles, 17–18, 141, 209, 228; interpretive principles and, 5–6, 210–226; New Deal and, 19–22; constitutional common law, 155–156; judicial review of, 211; environmental remedies and, 220–221
Communications and broadcasting, 2–3, 31–32, 42, 44–45; children's advertising, 32, 100; violence on television, 32; monopolies, 48; aspirations, 57–60, 183–185; diverse opportunities for preference formation, 61, 183–185; fairness doctrine, 61, 99, 104, 183–185; public broadcasting, 65; interest-group transfers, 70; changed circumstances affecting, 94–95, 175, 177; collective action problem, 102; interest-group pressures, 104–105; statutory interpretation of, 116–117; standing, 212, 216
Complex systemic effects of interventions, 91–93, 105, 178–179, 187–188, 190
Comptroller of the Currency, 17
Congressional reform, 108
Constitutional common law, 155–156
Constitutional democracy, 1, 227–230
Constitutional law, 36, 39, 102; New Deal reformation, 12, 18–24, 42, 193; history of, 13–18; Bill of Rights, 14, 16–17; commerce clause, 15; contracts clause, 17; eminent domain clause, 17; privileges and immunities clause, 17; judicial deference, 142–144, 156, 166; avoiding constitutional invalidity, 153–154, 164–165; underenforced norms, 155–157, 161, 163–168; interpretive principles, 163–168, 187, 190; avoidance of constitutional doubts, 164–165; nondelegation doctrine, 165–166; penumbral Constitution, 165; equal protection clause, 166–167; contract rights, 167–168; property rights, 167–168; procedural matters, 168, 177–178; welfare rights, 168; free speech issues, 185; hierarchy of interpretive principles, 187, 190; state autonomy and, 200–201; standing, 216–217; of regulatory state, 227–233
Constitutive, law as, 18
Consumer behavior, 57–59
Consumer Product Safety Act, 26; disclosure remedies, 53
Consumer Product Safety Commission, 27; benefits of, 79–80; mandatory smoke detectors, 81; effectiveness of, 82; expenditures per life saved, 94
Consumer products, 2
Consumer protection law, 3, 32; interest-group transfers, 5; 1960s and 1970s, 25–27, 29; public good problem, 52; information provided consumers, 52–53; externalities, 54
Contract law, 17, 33, 150; New Deal era, 20, 22
Contract rights, 167–168
Contractarian thought, 34–35
Conventionalism, 145–146
Coordination problem, 2–3, 30, 39, 42, 45, 49–52, 74, 105, 173, 230; failures of coordination, 93–94; deal-making approach and, 140–141; presumptions in favor of coordination, 187
Costs and benefits of regulation, 75, 176; willingness to pay, 41, 59, 75–76; transactions costs, 49–52; disclosure remedies, 52–53; externalities, 54–55, 89, 93; assessment of, 76–84; least-cost solution, 81–82; need for balancing, 90–91; uniform standards and, 90; expenditures per life saved, 93–94, 239–241; political judgments concerning, 97; agency costs, 99–100; tradeoffs, 105; proportionality, 181–182, 187–188, 190, 196; de minimis risks or problems, 183
Courts. See Activist court; Interpretive court; Interpretive principles; Supreme Court
Crib safety regulations, 79
Criminal procedure, 25

Damages relief, 220–221
Debtor relief legislation, 14
Deconstruction, 191
Deep ecology, 69
Deference to agency interpretations, 142–144; 224
Delaney Clause, 88–89, 95, 121, 134, 176, 198–199, 203
Deliberation. See Political deliberation
Deliberative democracy, 14, 57, 139, 164
Democracy, 57–60, 101–102, 164
Democratic aspirations, 101–102, 104, 113–114
Deontological tradition, 35
Department of Energy, 26
Department of Justice, coordination with FTC, 94

Department of Labor, 91, 195, 196, 197
Depression, 29
Deregulation movement, 1, 11, 30–31, 38, 83, 99–100, 104
Developmental Disabilities Assistance and Bill of Rights Act, 62, 199–201
Direct transfer payments, 56
Disabled persons, 2, 26, 28; social subordination, 62, 64, 201; benefits of antidiscrimination laws, 81; inconsistency of laws protecting, 93; diversion of resources, 103; coordination of laws, 105; equal protection violations, 167; implied rights of action, 183; bill of rights for, 199–201; constitutional law protecting, 201
Disadvantaged groups, 61–64, 166–167, 183
Disclosure remedies, 52–53, 109
Discrimination. See Civil rights laws; Disabled persons; Racial discrimination
Diverse experiences, preference formation and, 60–61
Drugs. See Food and drug regulation
Dworkin, Ronald, 131–132

Eastern Europe, attack on collectivism in, 11
Ecology, 69
Economic productivity, 21, 32, 38
Education: New Deal era, 21–22; 1960s and 1970s, 26; Civil Rights Act of 1964 and, 80; developmentally disabled persons, 199–201; standing, 215
Efficiency of regulation, 48–55, 75–87, 86–89, 100
Eisen v. Carlisle & Jacquelin, 180–181
Employment issues: New Deal era, 21–23; 1960s and 1970s, 27; minimum wage legislation and, 56; occupational health legislation and, 56; Civil Rights Act of 1964 and, 80–81
Employment Standards Adminstration, 28
"End of ideology" thesis, 131
Endangered species, 2, 26, 31–32; protection of aspirations, 58–59; irreversibility, 68; protection of nature, 68–69; environmental controls protecting, 78; collective action problem, 102
Endangered Species Act: externalities, 54; diverse opportunities for preference formation, 61; loss to future generations,

68; inadequate implementation of, 105; statutory interpretation of, 116
Endogenous preferences, 44–45, 60–61, 63, 64–67
Energy, 2; monopolies, 49; conservation programs, 59, 80; costs and benefits of regulation, 83; inconsistency of laws, 93
Enumerated federal powers, 15
Environmental law, 2–3, 25–28, 31–32, 35, 44, 45, 50; endogenous preferences, 40, 60–61; costs and benefits of, 49, 76, 78, 81–82, 87–88, 100; externalities, 54–55; protection of aspirations, 57–59, 185; diversity, 61; irreversibility, 68; loss to future generations, 68; protection of nature, 68–69; interest-group transfers, 70, 85–86; reduction of pollution, 77–78; industrial pollution, 77–79; unsolved problems, 79; best available technology strategies, 87–88, 89, 92, 97, 106; incentive-based strategies, 88, 109; rights vs. risk management, 89–91; health-based laws, 90, 106; right of clean air and water, 90; uniform standards, 90; methodology in data monitoring, 91; complex systemic effects, 91–92; underregulation, 91–92; old risk-new risk distinction, 92, 106, 110; multimedia pollutants, 94; dispersion of pollutants, 96–97; political tradeoffs in, 97; relocation of polluters, 97; overregulation, 100–103, 106; collective action problem, 102; coordination of regulatory efforts, 105; regional variations, 109; reform of, 109–110; statutory interpretation of, 115–116; political accountability, 171–172, 173; statutory obsolescence and, 177; standing, 212, 216; common law principles and, 220–221; injunctive relief, 220–221. See also names of specific laws
Environmental Protection Agency, 26, 28, 92; expenditures per life saved, 94; inconsistency of regulations, 94; implementation of laws by, 98–99
Equal Employment Opportunity Commission, 27, 81; inadequate implementation by, 99; deregulation movement, 104
Equal Pay Act, 62
Equitable balancing, 90–91, 221
Executive Order 11246, 81
Expedition policy, 30

Expertise in regulation, 30–31
Externalities, 54–55, 68, 89, 93

Factional power, 74
Factionalism, 14–16, 22, 29, 36, 99, 101, 107, 155, 169, 171, 178
Failure of regulation, 74–110. *See also* Implementation failure; Statutory failure
Fair Labor Standards Act, 24, 55
Fairness doctrine, 61, 99, 104, 183–185
Farm Credit Administration, 23
Farm Security Administration, 23
Federal Communications Act, 48–49, 185
Federal Communications Commission, 24, 58; fairness doctrine, 61, 99, 104; deregulation movement in, 99; interest-group pressures, 99–100; protection of aspirations, 185
Federal Communications Commission v. WNCN Listeners Guild, 185
Federal Deposit Insurance Corporation, 23
Federal Highway Traffic Safety Administration, 27–28
Federal Power Act, 24
Federal Power Commission, 19
Federal Radio Commission, 19
Federal Register, 28
Federal Reserve Act, 19
Federal Trade Commission, 19; coordination with Justice Department, 94; interest-group pressures, 98; collective action problem, 103
Federal Trade Commission Act, 24
Federalism, 14–16, 102, 164, 200, 225; antifederalists, 14; New Deal era, 22–24
Fish, Stanley, 144
Food and Drug Act, 24: disclosure remedies, 53
Food and Drug Administration, 162, 163, 176; effectiveness of, 82; Delaney Clause, 88–89, 95, 121, 134, 198–199; inconsistency of, 94
Food and drug regulation, 3; information provided, 53; drug packaging rules, 79; food additives, 88–89, 95, 121, 134, 176, 198–199; expenditures per life saved, 94; inefficiencies of, 100; pre-screening and monitoring, 110
Food Stamp Act, 26, 55
Frankfurter, Felix, 212
Fraud and deception, 2
Free market principles, 1–2, 18, 35–38; interpretation and, 141–142. *See also* Private markets
Free speech rights, 25
Free trade, 15
Freedom. *See* Autonomy; Liberty
Freedom of association, antidiscrimination law and, 32
Freedom of choice, interference with, 32, 38–46
Freedom of contract, 1, 3, 11, 12, 18, 33, 34, 37, 42; minimal state and, 35–36; prices and wages pursuant to, 39
Freund, Ernst, 130, 132
Fuel economy standards, 82
Functions of regulatory statutes, 47–73
Future generations, loss to, 68–69, 104

Government contractors, Executive Order 11246 and, 81
Government failure, 38, 45, 83, 84–107
Governmental neutrality, 20, 32, 41, 42
Great Lakes, 77–78
Great Society, 3, 24–31
Greenhouse effect, 79
Griggs v. Duke Power Co., 205–207

Hamilton, Alexander, 13, 22; *The Federalist*, 136
Hampton v. Mow Sun Wong, 166
Hand, Learned, 120
Handicapped persons. *See* Disabled persons
Hart, Henry: *The Legal Process*, 130
Hazardous waste. *See* Toxic and hazardous substances
Head Start, 26
Hearing, rights to, 168, 177–178
Heckler v. Chaney, 219
Helvering v. Gregory, 120
History of regulatory initiatives, 12–31
Holmes, Oliver Wendell, Jr., 113, 121, 126
Home Owners Loan Corporation, 23–24
Homosexuals, 175; social subordination, 62; equal protection violations, 167
Housing law, 21, 37, 56; redistributive impact of, 106; standing, 212

Immigration and Nationality Act, 129
Implementation failure, 97–102, 103–104, 106–107
Implied causes of action, 221–224

Implied repeals, presumption against, 169, 187
Incentive-based strategies, 88, 109
Independent Federation of Flight Attendants v. Zipes, 209
Indeterminacy, 7, 138–139, 144–145
Indian Civil Rights Act, 189
Indian tribes, 156, 157
Individual rights, 14, 16–17, 20, 22, 24, 29, 227. *See also* Rights revolution of 1960s and 1970s
Industrial Union Department, AFL-CIO v. American Petroleum Institute, 194–195
Inflation, 32
Information provided to public, 52–53
Injunctive relief, 220–221
Injustice, avoidance of, 179–181, 196, 198
Interest representation, 101–102
Interest-group pressures, 38, 98, 99–100, 102, 106, 136, 229; implementation failure and, 97–98; inadequate implementation and, 104–105; statutory content and, 130, 137–141; appropriations process and, 169
Interest-group transfers, 5, 12, 32, 47, 69–71, 139–140; aspirations and, 72–73; regulatory failure and, 84–86; skewed redistribution, 103; construction of statutes embodying, 185–186
International competitiveness, 32
Interpretive instructions, 135, 153–154, 162
Interpretive norms, 7, 114–115, 136, 146–147, 161; political character of, 7; value-laden, 7; extratextual norms, 137–144, 146, 157–158, 160, 189–191, 231–232; syntactic norms, 151–153, 162; substantive norms, 155–157, 162; underenforced constitutional norms, 155–157, 161, 163–168; institutional norms, 162–163, 169–170; regulatory failure, 170–186
Interpretive principles, 2, 4–6, 111–112, 116, 134, 147–159, 232, 233, 235, 235–238; will of the legislature, 4; common law principles and, 5–6, 210–226; deal-making approach, 6, 137–141, 146–147, 208, 231; private law principles, 6; unprincipled interventions, 6–7, 112; making sense of statutes, 7; nature of administrative state and, 7–8; objective interpretation, 7; courts as agents, 112–

137; textualism, 113–123, 125, 128, 138, 196; context in, 114–116, 118, 128, 145, 149, 157; culture in, 114, 116, 145; ambiguous language, 115, 116–117, 124, 128, 133, 140, 142, 144, 174, 176, 231; judicial equity, 116; delegation of lawmaking powers, 117–118; overinclusiveness, 118–119, 122, 124–125; underinclusiveness, 119–121, 122, 125; changed circumstances and, 121–122, 126–127, 161, 174–177; structural approaches to, 122–123; purposive interpretation, 123–127, 130; backward-looking interpretation, 126–127, 133; forward-looking interpretation, 126–127; legislative intent and history, 127–130, 133, 170; legal process approaches, 130–133, 138; judicial deference, 139–140, 142–144, 145–146, 156, 163, 166, 224; private ordering presumption, 141–142; conventionalism, 145–147; canons of construction, 147–157; judicial policy preferences, 148; particularism in, 149; plain meaning approach, 152–153, 154; clear statement principles, 154; promoting better lawmaking, 154–155, 162; constitutional norms, 163–168; rule of law, 166; postenactment history, 170; precedent, 170; statutory failure and, 170–186; procedural matters, 177–178; understanding systemic effects of, 178–179, 187–188; avoiding irrationality and injustice, 179–181, 196, 198; cost-benefit analysis, 181–182, 195–198; de minimis exceptions, 182–183, 187–188, 190; disadvantaged groups, 183–185, 187; interest-group transfers, 185–186; protection of aspirations, 185; hierarchy of, 186–188; institutional concerns, 187–188, 230; proportionality, 187–188, 190, 196; harmonization, 188–189; New Deal reformation and, 204–205, 207–226
Interstate Commerce Act, 75
Interstate Commerce Commission, 19, 103
Irrational outcomes, 118–119, 179–181, 196, 198
Irreversibility, 67–68

Jackson, Andrew, 17
Jefferson, Thomas, 22
Johnson, Lyndon B., 3, 26

Journal of Law and Economics, 47–48
Judicial discretion, 135–136, 157–158
Judicial policy preferences, 148
Judicial review, 15, 16, 218–220; New
   Deal era, 19–20, 23–24; accountability
   of courts, 31; right to, 168, 178; presumption in favor of, 169; standing,
   210–217; dependent on common law
   rights, 211; Administrative Procedure
   Act, 212–214; of agency inaction, 219–
   220. *See also* Interpretive principles; Supreme Court
Justice, 33–35, 39; unanimous consent
   and, 36

Kantian theory of individual liberty, 12
Kent v. Dulles, 166
Keynesian economics, 21
King v. Smith, 176

Labor organization, 41, 43, 208–209
Laissez-faire, 5, 6, 18–19, 42, 142, 228
Legal process, 130–133
Legal realism, 123, 148–149
Legislative history, 127–130, 133, 169–170
Legislative intent, 127–130, 133, 170
Liberty, 36–37, 38, 39, 40, 44. *See also*
   Autonomy
Llewellyn, Karl, 130, 132, 148–149
Lochner v. New York, 147, 156, 211–212
Low probability events, 53

Madison, James, 14–16, 22, 35, 57, 139
Majoritarian processes, 38, 60
Maritime Administration, 24
Market failure, 39, 45, 47, 48–55
Market ordering, 83, 101
Market outcomes, government interference
   with, 39–46
Market pressures, social subordination
   and, 62–63
Materials Transportation Board, 27
Medicaid, 26
Medicare, 26
Methodology, 91
Mine Safety and Health Administration,
   28
Minimal state, 34–46
Minimum wage law. *See* Wage and hour
   legislation
Monopolistic behavior, 48–49

Narcotics regulation, 44; externalities, 54;
   endogenous preferences, 64, 65, 67
National defense system, 49
National Environmental Policy Act, 26
National Highway Traffic Safety Adminis-
   tration, 81
National Labor Relations Act, 24, 208–
   209
*National Resources Defense Council v.
   Morton,* 171–172, 173
*National Resources Defense Council v.
   Thomas,* 182
National Traffic Safety Administration, 97
National Transportation Safety Board, 28
Natural Gas Act, 49, 83
Natural gas regulation, 89
Nature, protection of, 68–69
Negative rights, 17
Neutral principles of law, 18–19, 204
New Deal, 3, 30, 31, 90, 98, 99, 101, 108,
   141, 157, 227, 231; constitutional refor-
   mation, 12, 18–24, 42, 193; common
   law principles and, 19–22; "Second Bill
   of Rights," 21–22, 28; affirmative action
   programs and, 204–205; statutory inter-
   pretation and, 204–205, 207–226
Nixon, Richard, 29
Noise control law, 26
Noncommodity values, 59, 104, 185
Nuclear power, 2, 32; disclosure remedies,
   53; externalities, 54
Nuclear Power Act: disclosure remedies,
   53

Obsolescence problem, 94–95, 105; interpretive principles and, 174–177, 187
Occupational Safety and Health Act, 72;
   disclosure remedies, 53; externalities,
   54; costs vs. benefits, 75, 86; overregulation, 82, 196; redistributive impact of,
   91; underregulation, 91–92; reform of,
   109; legal process approach, 131; significant risk requirement, 181, 194–198;
   statutory interpretation of, 194–198
Occupational Safety and Health Administration, 27–28; cost-benefit analysis, 79–
   80, 181–182, 195–198; effectiveness of,
   82; expenditures per life saved, 94;
   interest-group pressures, 98
Occupational safety and health regulation,
   2–3, 26, 28–29, 31, 43; interest-group
   transfers, 5; information provided, 53;

Occupational safety and health regulation
  (*continued*)
  externalities, 54, 93; effect on employment, 56; redistributive rationales for,
  56; cognitive dissonance and, 66; overregulation, 82, 91–92, 196; costs of, 86;
  uniform design standards, 88, 90, 109;
  right to a safe workplace, 90; underregulation, 99, 106, 179, 196; redistributive
  impact of, 101; disclosure remedies,
  109; incentive-based strategies, 109; reform of, 109; collective action problem,
  173
Ocean Dumping Act, 26
Office of Management and Budget, 30, 108
Office of Surface Mining Reclamation and
  Enforcement, 27
Oil spills, 79
Old risk-new risk distinction, 92, 106,
  107, 109–110
Ombudsman function, 108
Overregulation, 100–103, 106, 194–199
Ozone layer, destruction of, 76, 79

Paradoxes of regulatory state, 74, 106–110
Pareto criterion, 34, 36–37, 39, 44, 65
Patent and Trademark Office, 17
Paternalism, 3, 20, 36, 43, 51
Pennhurst State School and Hospital v.
  Halderman, 199–201
Pension plan law: externalities, 54
Perestroika, 110
Pesticides, 26, 78, 82
Plain meaning, 113–122, 198–199
Planning function, 108
Pluralism, 140
Political behavior, 57–59, 69–71, 84–86
Political deliberation, 15, 74, 96–97, 105,
  164, 187, 230
Pollution. *See* Environmental law and spe-
  cific statutes
Pollution Standard Index, 76
Pornography, 32, 55
Posner, Richard, 132–133, 165
Pound, Roscoe, 23
Powell, Lewis, Jr., 195
Precommitment strategy, 58–60
Preemption issues, 225–226
Preference formation, 34, 38–42, 44–47,
  51, 57; meta-preferences, 58–59; diverse
  experiences and, 60–61; endogenous
  preferences, 64–67; aggregation of pri-
  vate preferences, 140

Presidency, 227, 232; New Deal era, 22;
  powers delegated to, 23, 154; 1960s and
  1970s, 25; coordination in executive
  branch, 74; authority over administrative process, 102; supervisory function
  of, 30, 107–108; powers delegated to,
  154; statutory construction and, 172
Prices: market prices, 19–20; freedom of
  contract and, 39
Prisoner's dilemma, 42–44, 49–51, 55
Private choice, facilitation of, 3
Private law model, 6, 20, 211–212, 214–
  217, 222, 233
Private markets, 1, 4, 6, 11, 12, 31, 141–
  142, 228. *See also* Free market principles
Private ordering, 1, 3, 11, 12, 32–45, 228,
  231; presumption in favor of, 6, 141–
  142; constitutional history and, 15–17
Private property, 1, 11–12; constitutional
  history and, 16–17
Private right principles, 1, 46
Private rights of action, 221–224
Procedural matters, 168, 177–178, 210–
  217
Property law, 17, 33; New Deal era, 20–22
Property rights, 167–168, 211
Proportionality, 181–182, 194–198
Public choice theory, 6, 36–37, 39, 46, 69–
  71, 137–141
Public-interest groups, 103
Public ordering, 32–45
Public Utility Holding Company Act, 24
Public Works Administration, 23
Purposive interpretation, 123–127

Racial discrimination, 2, 25–26; cooperative solutions to, 50–51; externalities,
  55; social subordination, 62–63; endogenous preferences, 67; benefits of antidiscrimination laws, 80–81; affirmative
  action, 81, 95–96, 101, 152, 201–205;
  inadequate regulatory controls and, 82–
  83; race-neutral policies, 96; redistributive impact of, 101; collective action
  problem, 102–103; inadequate implementation of laws, 104; statutory interpretation of laws, 116–117, 183; equal
  protection violations, 167; implied rights
  of action, 183; discriminatory effect
  cases, 205–207
Racial quotas, 75
Radin, Max, 130
Railroad regulation, 103

Ratemaking: cost-of-service, 89

Rawls, John: *A Theory of Justice,* 33

Reagan, Ronald: deregulation movement, 1, 30–31

Recession of 1970s and 1980s, 30–31

Recycling programs, 59

Redistribution of resources, 17, 20, 37, 39, 55–57, 61, 91–93, 106; nullified by market, 37, 56; skewed redistribution, 100–101, 103; state's police power, 167–168; statutory interpretation, 186

Regional and industrial variations, 90, 108–109

Regulated entities and regulatory beneficiaries, 213–214

Regulatory agencies: history of, 19, 24, 26–29; expenditures for, 28; autonomy of, 29–30, 155, 169–170, 218–219; control over, 29–30, 31, 212–213; failure of, 133–137; judicial deference to, 142–144, 145–146, 163, 166, 224, 231; delegation of policymaking authority to, 165–166, 187–188; inaction, 219–220

Regulatory failure, 74–110

Regulatory harms, 214–215

Regulatory initiatives, 2–3; history of, 12–31

Regulatory process, 101–102

Regulatory reform, 106–110, 230

Regulatory state: statutory interpretation and, 7–8; coherence and integrity of, 12, 227–229; goals of, 12–13, 47–71; as post-New Deal republicanism, 12; New Deal era, 18–24; 1960s and 1970s, 24–31; problems of, 74–75, 84–106; reform of, 106–110; constitution of, 227–233

Rehnquist, William, 202–203

Rent control, 56; redistributive impact of, 106

Rent-seeking, 48, 70–72

Republicanism, 12, 35: Madison's concept of, 14–16, 22, 35, 139

Resource Recovery and Conservation Act, 27

Retroactive controls, 92

Reviewability, 218–220

Rights, regulatory interests as, 29, 90–91, 105, 110

Rights revolution of 1960s and 1970s, 1, 12–13, 24–31, 102, 141, 225, 231

Risk management, 29, 89–91

Robinson-Patman Act, 98, 185

Roosevelt, Franklin Delano, 3, 23; defense of Social Security, 20; "Second Bill of Rights," 21–22, 28

Rule of law, 166

Sacks, Albert: *The Legal Process,* 130

Safe Water Drinking Act, 26

Santa Clara Pueblo v. Martinez, 188–189

Scalia, Antonin, 128

Scientific uncertainty, 76, 100

Seatbelt laws, 51, 65–66, 79

Section 1983, 117–118

Securities and Exchange Act, 24

Self-determination, 14, 22

Self-government, 14

Self-interested representation, 16, 29, 74, 99, 107, 155, 169, 171, 178

Separation of powers principles, 143. *See also* Checks and balances system

Sex discrimination, 2, 25–26, 67; social subordination, 62–63; benefits of anti-discrimination laws, 81; inadequate regulatory controls and, 82–83; affirmative action, 96; inadequate implementation of laws, 104; equal protection violations, 167; implied rights of action, 183

Sexual harassment, 41, 44

Sherman Antitrust Act, 48, 117, 176, 185

Side-effects of regulation, 88–89

Sierra Club v. Ruckelshaus, 178–179

Smog, 79

Smoke detectors, mandatory, 81

Smoking, restrictions on, 51, 52, 65–66

Social choice theory, 38, 46

Social contract theory, 17

Social Security, Roosevelt's defense of, 20

Social Security Act, 55

Social Security Administration, 23

Social subordination, 61–64, 67, 96, 103–104, 201

Solid waste disposal, 78–79

Standing to sue, 210–217

State government, 17, 154; free trade barriers, 15; police power, 20; New Deal era, 22–23

States' rights, 17–18

Statutory design, failures in, 84–97

Statutory failure, 2, 4, 190; statutory functions and, 102–106; interpretive principles and, 170–186

Statutory interpretation. *See* Interpretive norms; Interpretive principles; Legal process; Legislative history; Legislative

Statutory interpretation (*continued*)
    intent; Purposive interpretation; Textual-
    ism
Statutory obsolescence, 174–177, 187
Steelworkers v. Weber, 152, 201–205
Structural approaches, 122–123
Structural reform, 107–109, 230
Supreme Court: New Deal era, 20, 23;
    Burger Court, 157; Warren Court, 157.
    See also names of specific cases
Surrogate motherhood, 53
Syracuse Peace Council v. FCC, 185

Taxation exemptions, 169; and standing,
    215
Technocratic and engineering judgments,
    96–97
Technology-based strategies, 87–88
Tennessee Valley Authority, 23
Textualism, 113–122
Thatcher, Margaret, 1
Third parties, harm to, 39
Tort law, 17, 20
Toxic and hazardous substances, 2, 26, 79,
    82; transportation of, 26–27; disclosure
    remedies, 53; costs of regulation, 86; un-
    derregulation of, 91–92, 106; inade-
    quate implementation of laws, 99; signif-
    icant risk requirement, 181, 194–198;
    statutory interpretion pertaining to,
    194–198
Toxic Substances Control Act, 26–27
Toxic waste dumps, 79
Transactions costs, 49–52
Transportation industry regulation, 69, 82,
    173
Treasury Department, 13

Underregulation, 98–100, 106
Unemployment, 32
Uniform design standards, 88
Utilitarianism, 12, 34–37, 43

Victimization, 66–67
Voting rights, 25
Voting Rights Act of 1965, 80

Wage and hour legislation, 18, 20–21, 32,
    37; collective action problem, 55–56; ef-
    fect on employment, 56; redistributive
    impact of, 91, 101, 106; statutory inter-
    pretation of, 116
Wages, 20, 39. *See also* Wage and hour leg-
    islation
Wards Cove Packing Co. v. Atonio, 205–
    207
Water pollution. *See* Environmental law;
    specific laws
Wealth transfers, 6, 15
Weinberger v. Romero-Barcelo, 221
Welfare, 34–39, 42–45, 74, 228–229;
    New Deal era, 21; unanimous consent
    and, 36; endogenous preferences, 66
Welfare economics, 46
Welfare programs, 26; redistributive im-
    pact of, 101; "man in the house" rule,
    176
Welfare rights, 168
Willingness to pay, 41, 59, 75–76
Wittgenstein, Ludwig, 119, 196, 203
Workers' compensation, 207–208
Works Progress Administration, 23

Yaari, Menahem, 65
Young v. Community Nutrition Institute,
    162–163